NORTH CAROLINA
STATE BOARD OF COMMUNITY COLLEGES
LIBRARIES
FORSYTH TECHNICAL COMMUNITY COLLEGE

D0081714

Interpreting
Wittgenstein

Interpreting
Wittgenstein

A Cloud of Philosophy,
a Drop of Grammar

Ronald Suter

Temple University Press
Philadelphia

LIBRARY
FORSYTH TECHNICAL COMMUNITY COLLEGE
2100 SILAS CREEK PARKWAY
WINSTON-SALEM, NC 27103-5197

Temple University Press, Philadelphia 19122
Copyright © 1989 by Temple University. All rights reserved
Published 1989
Printed in the United States of America

The paper used in this publication meets the minimum requirements of American National Standard for Information Sciences—Permanence of Paper for Printed Library Materials, ANSI z39.48-1984

Library of Congress Cataloging-in-Publication Data

Suter, Ronald, 1930–
    Interpreting Wittgenstein : a cloud of philosophy, a drop of
grammar / Ronald Suter.
        p.   cm.
    Bibliography: p.
    Includes index.
    ISBN 0-87722-664-4
    1. Wittgenstein, Ludwig, 1889–1951.   I. Title.
B3376.w564s88   1989
192—dc20   89-33537

192
Wit
1989

$13.00

1.5.96

For Carmen, my all-the-world

I can know what someone else is thinking, not what I am thinking. It is correct to say "I know what you are thinking," and wrong to say "I know what I am thinking." (A whole cloud of philosophy condensed into a drop of grammar.)

Ludwig Wittgenstein

Contents

Acknowledgments

I am indebted to many people for help with this book. Over the years I have used portions of it in courses and colloquia and have benefited from the questions and comments of colleagues and students—those of Chuck Bruce, Jim Hanink, Allan Hart, Larry Hauser, Stanley Heckman, Betina Henig, Steve Holtzman, Robert Jaksa, Michael Jankoviak, George Kerner, Donald Koch, Ronald Miller, Larry Ort, David Robinson, Carol Slater, Timothy Sommers, Gary Supanich, and Christopher Weiss. Larry Hauser also helped with the index. My daughter Sonia read the entire manuscript— some parts more than once—correcting errors and giving me many valuable suggestions. In addition, I profited greatly from comments on several chapters of my manuscript by Jorg Baumgartner, Martin Benjamin, George Ferree, Richard Hall, Charles McCracken, Julius Moravcsik, and Winston Wilkinson. As ever I am grateful to Katherine McCracken for her splendid editing. I also thank Jane Cullen and Richard Gilbertie of Temple University Press and Steve Wallace for their many helpful and intelligent suggestions. Finally, particular appreciation is given to Michigan State University for a 1988–1989 AURIG research grant and to Dean Eadie of the College of Arts and Letters for instituting the enlightened policy of releasing faculty from teaching and other duties to do research. I was the beneficiary of this new policy during the fall term of 1988, which helped me to complete this work.

Preface

This book is mainly for teachers, graduate students, and advanced under-graduates in philosophy, sociology, anthropology, psychology, history of ideas, and literature, as well as for general readers new to Wittgenstein's philosophy and hoping to make sense of it. Given the difficulty of Witt-genstein's philosophy, a book like this should give those outside of philos-ophy proper entrée to it. Although it is not mainly directed to Wittgenstein scholars, I think it will also be of interest to them, as it includes a number of substantive analyses.

While there are many books available on Wittgenstein that examine the development of his philosophy—Norman Malcolm's *Nothing Is Hidden: Wittgenstein's Criticism of his Early Thought,* P. M. S. Hacker's revised edition *Insight and Illusion: Themes in the Philosophy of Wittgenstein,* Merrill and Jaakko Hintikka's book *Investigating Wittgenstein,* the first volumes of Hacker and Baker's *Wittgenstein: Understanding and Meaning,* and of David Pears's *The False Prison*—the emphasis in this book, by contrast, is on Wittgenstein's mature conception of philosophy and the application of his philosophical methods to traditional and contemporary problems in their historical and philosophical context. The book shows how Wittgenstein's philosophy can be applied in quite powerful ways to many philosophical problems.

Various views are challenged in this work. One is that Wittgenstein must no longer be seen as an analytic philosopher because he repudiates one kind of philosophy—the kind exemplified by Russell's theory of descrip-tions. K. T. Fann gives such an argument in *Wittgenstein's Conception of Philosophy* (p. 62). I try to show that this inference depends on not fully understanding Wittgenstein's doctrine of family resemblance. An even more extreme view is that Wittgenstein repudiates philosophy altogether. In *Ethics without Philosophy: Wittgenstein and the Moral Life* (pp. 148, 153), James C. Edwards, following Richard Rorty, contends that Wittgen-stein rejects philosophy itself—and not just analytic philosophy—because Wittgenstein repudiates certain kinds of philosophy or philosophical theo-rizing.

Finally, it has been alleged by Russell Nieli in *Wittgenstein: From Mys-ticism to Ordinary Language* (pp. 238, 244) that Wittgenstein defends tribal conformism and that he actually recommends that we guide ourselves in life by "the customs and conventions of the ordinary man," no matter what they are. Nieli may have been led astray here by Nicholas F. Gier's *Wittgenstein and Phenomenology* (p. 214). Gier thinks a consistent Wittgensteinian cannot criticize racists or Nazis, since Wittgenstein argues that language-games and forms of life have to be accepted. It is time—in 1989, the hundredth anniversary of Wittgenstein's birth—that such serious charges be dealt with and set straight.

This book is divided into three parts. Part I examines Wittgenstein's radically new conception of philosophy and contrasts it with more traditional views. Parts II and III have as their theme the practice of Wittgensteinian philosophy in its historical and philosophical context. They show how Wittgenstein's approach to philosophy dissolves many traditional problems in metaphysics, epistemology, and the philosophy of language, thereby confirming—even though they do not prove—his mainly negative but therapeutic conception of philosophy.

In Chapter 1, the focus is on his new conception of philosophy. Wittgenstein of the *Investigations* seems to look upon philosophy merely, or at least primarily, as eliminating philosophical muddles, as destroying "houses of cards" (PI, §118), for example, by breaking the hold that certain incorrect pictures and misleading analogies in the grammar of our language have on us (PI, §115). In Chapter 2, I give an account of the doctrine of family resemblance, explaining the assumption Wittgenstein is combating, what the doctrine amounts to, and why it is not an answer to the problem of universals. I show also how this doctrine entails a rejection of philosophical analysis based on the model of Russell's theory of descriptions. In Chapter 3, I look at the similarities and differences Wittgenstein recognizes or is responding to in Freud and what Wittgenstein finds right and wrong in Freud's approach. This illuminates Wittgenstein's way of philosophizing. It also shows some of his concepts in action. For example, when he attacks Freud's account of dreams, we see the doctrine of family resemblance at work: dreams, he says, do not have the common essence that Freud attributes to them of being hallucinated wish fulfillments. The discussion also clarifies why Wittgenstein makes the startling remark that he considers himself a disciple and follower of Freud.

In Part II, in Chapters 4 through 8, three traditional philosophical views of the mind and the body—philosophical behaviorism, mind-brain identity theory, and Cartesian dualism—are given a Wittgensteinian shredding. The focus is now on the other-minds problem, the acquisition of psychological concepts, and the mind-body problem. The last chapter of Part II, Chapter 8, clarifies Wittgenstein's crucial notion of criteria and how this applies to his view of the mental.

Part III shows how Wittgenstein would deal with various puzzles and philosophical problems: traditional and contemporary problems about time, dreaming, proper names, and rules. In particular, Chapter 9 shows how Augustine is led astray by certain pictures and the surface grammar of the language, culminating in an erroneous account of time. Next, Descartes's skeptical dream argument is explained and dissolved (Chapter 10). Wittgensteinian criticisms of Russell's theory of proper names (Chapter 11) and of Saul Wittgenstein's[1] discussion of rule-following (Chapter 12) are made explicit in the last two chapters of Part III. Finally, an Appendix explains, for those not familiar with Russell's theory of descriptions, some puzzles it resolves and other problems and puzzles it gives rise to.

List of Abbreviations

The following abbreviations, listed alphabetically, are used to refer to Wittgenstein's works:

BB   *The Blue and Brown Books,* with preface by Rush Rhees (New York: Harper, 1958). Followed by page number.

CV   *Culture and Value,* ed. G. H. von Wright, trans. Peter Winch (Chicago: University of Chicago Press, 1980). Followed by year of entry and page number.

L1   *Wittgenstein's Lectures, Cambridge 1930–1932,* from the notes of John King and Desmond Lee, ed. Desmond Lee (Totowa, N.J.: Roman & Littlefield, 1980). Followed by date and page number.

L2   "Wittgenstein's Lectures in 1930–33," recorded by G. E. Moore, *Mind* 63 (1954); 64 (1955). Page references are to its reprinting in Moore's *Philosophical Papers* (New York: Collier Books, 1966), pp. 247–318.

LC   *Lectures and Conversations on Aesthetics, Psychology and Religious Belief,* ed. Cyril Barrett (Berkeley: University of California Press, 1966). Followed by page number.

LE   "Wittgenstein's Lecture on Ethics," *Philosophical Review* 74 (Jan. 1965). Followed by page number.

LLW   *Letters from Ludwig Wittgenstein,* with a memoir by Paul Engelman, trans. L. Furtmueller (Oxford: Basil Blackwell, 1967). Followed by date.

NB   *Notebooks 1914–16,* ed. G. H. von Wright and G. E. M. Anscombe, trans. G. E. M. Anscombe (Oxford: Basil Blackwell, 1961). Followed by date of entry and page number.

OC   *On Certainty,* ed. G. E. M. Anscombe and G. H. von Wright, trans. D. Paul and G. E. M. Anscombe (New York: Harper, 1969). Followed by section number.

PG   *Philosophical Grammar,* ed. Rush Rhees, trans. Anthony Kenny (Berkeley: University of California Press, 1974). Followed by page number.

PI   *Philosophical Investigations,* 3d ed., ed. G. E. M. Anscombe and Rush Rhees, trans. G. E. M. Anscombe (New York: Macmillan, 1958). Followed by section number for part 1, page number for part 2.

PR   *Philosophical Remarks,* trans. Raymond Hargreaves and Roger White (New York: Harper & Row, 1975). Followed by part and section number.

RFM *Remarks on the Foundations of Mathematics,* ed. G. H. von Wright, R. Rhees, and G. E. M. Anscombe; trans. G. E. M. Anscombe (Oxford: Basil Blackwell, 1956). Followed by part, section, and/or page number.

TLP *Tractatus Logico-Philosophicus,* trans. D. F. Pears and B. F. McGuinness, with introduction by Bertrand Russell (London: Routledge & Kegan Paul, 1961). Followed by proposition number.

Z   *Zettel,* ed. G. E. M. Anscombe and G. H. von Wright, trans. G. E. M. Anscombe (Oxford: Basil Blackwell, 1967). Followed by section number.

Part I
Wittgenstein's Conception of Philosophy

Chapter 1

Wittgenstein's Conception of Philosophy

1.1 Wittgenstein's Conception Differs from the Traditional Conceptions

The philosophers, Plato says, "are those who are able to grasp the eternal and immutable"—the beautiful itself, justice itself—things that have true being (*Republic* 480). On the first page of his *Principia,* Descartes defines philosophy as "the study of wisdom" or the "perfect knowledge of all things that man can know"; it seeks to provide a secure foundation for all knowledge. Since Hume takes the science of man to be "the only solid foundation for the other sciences," his philosophical aim is to ground "this science . . . on experience and observation."[1] Kant, Aristotle, Aquinas, Hegel, and most of the other major philosophers in the history of Western philosophy agree that, whatever else it may do, philosophy aims at giving a true account of things, its purpose being to arrive at important knowledge about reality and the universe that can be formulated or at least shown.[2] As Spinoza says, "Philosophy has no end in view save truth."[3] We shall see that G. E. Moore and Bertrand Russell[4] are very much part of this tradition, while Wittgenstein's mature conception of philosophy is radically opposed to it.

The early Wittgenstein, Russell of the *Philosophy of Logical Atomism,* Moore, and before them Frege[5] all conceive of philosophy as having this traditional function and purpose. It is true that in "On Denoting" Russell also stresses something else, which becomes the focus of philosophy for Wittgenstein—how well your philosophical approach can dissolve various puzzles. However, while Russell says puzzles are to logical theories as experiments are to theories in the physical sciences, he also attempts, in his philosophy of logical atomism, to ground metaphysics on logical doctrine.[6] In "What Is Philosophy?" Moore maintains that "the first and most important problem of philosophy is: To give a general description of the *whole* Universe,"[7] mentioning all the most important kinds of things that are in it and how they are related to each other. The early Wittgenstein thinks that, strictly speaking, such truths can only be shown, not said.[8] The later Wittgenstein completely rejects this conception of philosophy and no longer appeals to his earlier technical distinction between what can be said and what can be shown.

Frege, Russell, and Whitehead (though perhaps not Moore), think it is the job of philosophers to provide a foundation for arithmetic and possibly for other things as well. The later Wittgenstein—and maybe also the early one—denies that this is the job of philosophy. He asks: "What does mathematics need a foundation for?" His reply: "It no more needs one, I believe, than propositions about physical objects—or about sense impressions, need *analysis*. What mathematical propositions do stand in need of is a clarification of their grammar, just as do those other propositions" (RFM, pt. 5, §13, p. 171; see also pt. 2, §§43, 53; pt. 4, §§46, 48, 52; pt. 5, §§8, 16). In the *Philosophical Investigations* he makes a closely related point: "Philosophy may in no way interfere with the actual use of language; it can in the end only describe it. For it cannot give it any foundation either. It leaves everything as it is" (PI, §124). Well, if we know that something cannot be done—it's in principle impossible to do it—it is foolish to continue demanding that we do it.

Frege, Russell, and the early Wittgenstein are all suspicious of our ordinary language; they see it as grammatically misleading, a source of philosophical trouble. Philosophy must take care, therefore, not to be misled by grammar, but to look to the deeper logic of language that is to be found in the formalized artificial language of the logician. That is why part of the philosopher's task is to discover or construct a perfect language with the help of logic, this perfect language reflecting the underlying reality. The later Wittgenstein agrees that ordinary language is misleading, a source of philosophical trouble. "Our grammar is lacking," he says, "in [the] sort of perspicuity" that gives us "*a clear view* of the use of our words" (PI, §122). In this respect his *Philosophical Investigations* is continuous with his *Tractatus*. But the later Wittgenstein denies Frege's and Russell's contention that ordinary language is imperfect, or that the philosopher should discover or construct a perfect language. Ordinary language is in order as it is. There seems to be no better language to be discovered or constructed. Even its vagueness and ambiguity are not imperfections; they may be just what we need. Think of political rhetoric and poetry.

The moral the later Wittgenstein draws from these warnings about the misleading nature of everyday language is that we must pay attention to its grammar, where "grammar" means something more than just the grammar we all have had taught us in grade school—that verbs must agree with their subjects in person and number, and so on. That we are not allowed to say, "The boys *is* here," Wittgenstein notes, does not give rise to "philosophical discussion," unlike the grammatical rules he focuses on (L1, 1931–32, p. 98). We must try to understand the deeper grammar of our language, that is, the grammar that ordinary grammarians are not interested in and do not even notice. Surface—or ordinary—as well as depth grammar together provide the rules for correct use of an expression, while depth grammar by itself points out subtle violations of these rules. For example, the sentence "I know I am in pain" seems to be in order as far as ordinary grammar goes (unlike "The boys is here"), but Wittgenstein would contend it violates a deeper grammar, making it nonsensical (PI, §246). Finally, it is not his view that we need a special artificial language in which to do philosophy. The formal systems of Russell and Frege are themselves misleading and at best irrelevant, since the rules of our language are, for the most part, different and more complex. We find out what the rules of our language are by consulting the ways in which words are ordinarily used in the contexts in which they are at home.

1.2 Philosophy Is to Be Conceived in Mainly Negative Terms

Wittgenstein of the *Investigations* seems to look upon philosophy merely, or at least primarily, as removing blocks to the understanding, as eliminating philosophical muddles, as destroying "houses of cards" (PI, §118), for example, by breaking the hold that certain pictures and misleading analogies in the grammar of our language have on us (PI, §115). "All that philosophy can do is destroy idols. And that means not making any new ones—say out of 'the absence of idols.'"[9] He conceives of philosophy as beneficially destructive, rejecting the traditional view that it should aim at giving a true account of things. Its purpose is not to arrive at important truths about reality and the universe. Generally, we shall need to reject the philosophical question rather than answer it, for instance, "the *philosophical* question: 'Is the visual image of this tree composite, and what are its component parts?'" (PI, §47). Instead of providing solutions to philosophical problems—the mind-body problem, the problem of other minds, the problem of skepticism, of the external world, the problem of universals, and the like—Wittgenstein tries to show that such problems are nonsensical. This would also hold for present or future philosophical problems. Wittgensteinian philosophy attempts to dissolve such philosophical problems by passing "from a piece of disguised nonsense to something that is patent nonsense" (PI, §464). Wittgenstein says his aim in philosophy is "to show the fly the way out of the fly-bottle" (PI, §309).[10] The piece of disguised nonsense will be at the basis of the problem and will be something the confused philosopher very much wants to say. When it is shown to be nonsense, the philosopher in the fly-bottle will no longer want to assert it, and the so-called problem will be dissolved or vanish. That, roughly, is the way in which this sort of philosophy tries to achieve its aim.

You may be puzzled and wonder how it can plausibly be maintained that there are no real philosophical problems. What about the moral problem of allocating scarce resources, such as organs for transplant? Or the problem of abortion? Or Raskolnikov's struggle whether he should give himself up to Christ? Or whether he ought even to believe in God? Surely these are genuine problems that philosophers sometimes discuss. Yes, but Wittgenstein would view these as religious or moral problems, not philosophical ones. Philosophy may occasionally illuminate such questions—for example, by inquiring into the nature of justice, the concept of person, the fetus, Christ, and God—but it is not going to solve or dissolve them. So the examples given are not counterexamples to the view that all philosophical problems are simply muddles that need dissolving, not solving. As for traditional philosophical problems—the mind-body problem, the problem of other minds, the problem of skepticism, of the external world, the problem of universals, and the like—Wittgensteinian philosophy tries to show that these problems are nonsensical, as we shall see.

We dissolve philosophical problems by pointing out that certain phrases or sentences are nonsensical—for example, "whether the good is more or less identical than [sic] the beautiful" (TLP, 4.003). No doubt Wittgenstein would agree that whenever we do this, we have learned something, and not just about words but about the world. We have learned that a particular questioner was confused, or perhaps that we were, if we were the ones who were tempted to formulate such a "question." This is to learn a psychological or sociological fact. To this extent philosophy remains a source of truth. The philosopher also uncovers philosophical truths or true philosophical theses, according to Wittgenstein. But he says these are hardly worth formulating for their own sake, since they are indisputable, hence trivial. So the point of Wittgensteinian philosophy cannot be the formulation and defense of philosophical theses.

He writes: "If one tried to advance *theses* in philosophy, it would never be possible to debate them, because everyone would agree [with] them" (PI, §128). "In philosophy [done the right way] we do not draw conclusions. 'But it must be like this!' is not a philosophical proposition. Philosophy only states what everyone admits" (PI, §599). He is talking here about philosophy done his way. He is aware that there are other views of philosophy.

This largely negative conception of philosophy, with its primary focus on language, is his view already in the *Tractatus*, except that there he still holds that there are important things that can be shown though they cannot be said. However, already in that work he says:

> Most of the propositions and questions to be found in philosophical works are not false but nonsensical. Consequently we cannot give any answer to questions of this kind, but can only point out that they are nonsensical. Most of the propositions and questions of philosophers arise from our failure to understand the logic of our language. (TLP, 4.003)

That is why the philosopher must pay attention to the logic of our language. Not surprisingly, the *Tractatus* contends that "all philosophy is a 'critique of language.'" According to Wittgenstein, the philosopher shows —as Russell does, for example, in his theory of descriptions—that "the apparent logical form of a proposition need not be its real one" (TLP 4.0031). (See also TLP 4.11–4.112 and 6.5–6.521.) Wittgenstein thus asserts:

> The correct method in philosophy would really be the following: to say nothing except what can be said, i.e. propositions of natural science—i.e. something that has nothing to do with philosophy—and then, whenever someone else wanted to say something metaphysical, to demonstrate to him that he had failed to give a meaning to certain signs in his propositions. Although it would not be satisfying to the other person—he would not have the feeling that we were teaching him philosophy—*this* method would be the only strictly correct one. (TLP 6.53)

In both his earlier and later views Wittgenstein regards philosophical problems as results of misunderstanding the language. It is a precondition of philosophy that there be some misunderstanding to which you address yourself. This need not be the misunderstanding of a previous philosopher. It could be your own, or some other philosopher's or nonphilosopher's confusion. A corollary is that if there were no misunderstanding of the language, there would be no philosophical problem. Without such a misunderstanding, the utterance of the philosopher would lack significance, for by itself, he insists, it is trivial. Moreover, the presupposed misunderstanding seems always, or at least for the most part, to reflect a failure to understand our language. It is this misconception that results in the philosophical problem. Since, on his view, "philosophy isn't anything except . . . the particular individual worries that we call 'philosophical problems'"

(PG, p. 193), it is conceivable that philosophy might come to an end. If philosophers ceased to misunderstand the language, they would have nothing more to do.

Not that Wittgenstein was attempting, or expected, to eliminate philosophy, ushering in the possibility of a post-philosophical culture, as Rorty suggests.[11] He was not envisioning the end of philosophy. Thinking this means the end of philosophy would be like thinking medicine will come to an end when we cure everyone who is sick at this moment or every disease we know about right now. Wittgenstein was well aware that our language, given our tendencies to generalize and to oversimplify, continually gives rise to new philosophical problems and to old ones in new forms. The last two thousand years of philosophy give us ample reason to think that human beings will continue to be bewitched by language. He says himself:

> We are still occupied with the same philosophical problems as were the Greeks . . . because our language . . . keeps seducing us into asking the same questions. As long as there continues to be a verb "to be" that looks as if it functions in the same way as "to eat" and "to drink," as long as we still have the adjectives "identical," "true," "false," "possible," as long as we continue to talk of the river of time, of an expanse of space, etc., etc., people will keep stumbling over the same puzzling difficulties and find themselves staring at something which no explanation seems capable of clearing up. (CV, 1931, p. 15)

I doubt, then, that he thinks that we shall ever completely eliminate philosophy. We clear up some philosophical muddles, but new ones crop up. So there is no reason to think that philosophy will ever really get finished.

Nevertheless, in both the earlier and later periods, Wittgenstein holds that the philosophical problem, if dealt with properly, will disappear completely. "The clarity that we are aiming at is indeed *complete* clarity. But this simply means that the philosophical problems should *completely* disappear" (PI, §133). This passage does not mean, as Kenny suggests, that Wittgenstein regards it as the job of philosophy "to achieve an order, an order which gives complete clarity." If we think it does mean this we make his conception of philosophy appear more like certain traditional views than it really is. Kenny creates this misleading impression by omitting the last sentence from the above quotation (from section 133) and then prefacing the whole passage with the first sentence of section 132. This gives us the new quotation: "We want to establish an order in our knowledge of the use of language: an order with a particular end in view; one out of many possible orders; not *the* order" (this is the first sentence of §132). "The clarity that we are aiming at is indeed *complete* clarity" (from section 133).[12] Omitting the important next sentence from the original passage—"But this simply means that the philosophical problems should *completely* disappear"—Kenny obscures the sort of "complete clarity" Wittgenstein is after, distorting his position. He does this in an attempt to present evidence for saying that Wittgenstein has a positive as well as a negative conception of philosophy. As Wittgenstein expressly says, however, the *complete* clarity he is aiming at is to make the philosophical problems *completely* disappear. So Kenny's selective quotation of the text fails to provide any evidence for thinking that Wittgenstein has a positive as well as a negative conception of philosophy.

Some of Wittgenstein's own comments about grammar and essences, however, may suggest that he actually does have a positive and not just a negative conception of philosophy. I have in mind: "Grammar tells what kind of object anything is"; and "Essence is expressed by grammar" (PI, §§373, 371). These remarks may make it appear that philosophy is a search for essences that we discover by a study of grammar. Saying this could be misleading. Nevertheless, there is a sense in which Wittgensteinian philosophy does indeed reveal essences and it discovers them by a grammatical inquiry. Because essence is expressed by grammar, we get clear about God's essence, or the essence of the mental—to take two examples—by inquiring into the use and grammar of God talk or by considering how we apply mentalistic terms. But revealing essences is not the purpose of philosophy. According to Wittgenstein, the "aim [of philosophy] is to remove particular misunderstandings; not to produce a real understanding for the first time" (PG, p. 115) or to lay out the essence of things—not even for the first time. Earlier philosophers presumably also display some of the essences of things, but in a different way. For some it is their main aim. While rejecting this as the purpose of philosophy, Wittgenstein offers a new technique for discovering essences through a grammatical inquiry. He wants philosophy to remove our misunderstandings by clarifying the use of our language—that is, by means of a grammatical inquiry, or "by looking into the working of our language" (PI, §109), reminding us what they are (PI, §127). In so doing, essences are uncovered. The aim of philosophy, however, is not to state these essences, since he thinks that would be to say something trivial. We state the essences of things by describing the use of words and sentences in the language or by pursuing a grammatical inquiry only if it helps us get rid of our misunderstanding or if it helps us to dissolve the problem—that is, if it helps us to attain our goal of making the philosophical problem disappear completely. Wittgenstein has no independent interest in describing the uses of language or stating the essence of things.

by a genuine problem. We have seen that he denies that philosophy has any theoretical aim. These points come out in the following passage:

> We may not advance any kind of theory. There must not be anything hypothetical in our considerations. We must do away with all *explanation,* and description alone must take its place. And this description gets its light, that is to say its purpose, from the philosophical problems. (PI, §109)

To repeat, the point of giving the description is to eliminate the philosophical muddle. We describe our uses of language only to uncover nonsense. As he says, "the results of philosophy are the uncovering of one or another piece of plain nonsense and of bumps that the understanding has got by running its head up against the limits of language. These bumps make us see the value of the discovery" (PI, §119).

When he talks about philosophy eliminating muddles that philosophy creates, we, of course, have to distinguish two sorts of philosophy: the kind he recommends and the kind he is combating. It is the latter philosophy that is supposed to get us into the muddles, while the former—Wittgenstein's kind—gets us out of them. That is one reason why he likes to compare his way of doing philosophy with therapy and talks of it "as in certain ways like psychoanalysis." Saying it is *like* psychoanalysis is not, of course, to say that it *is* psychoanalysis. This is only an analogy. He says it is also "like a hundred other things."[17] We shall look more closely at this analogy in Chapter 3, which examines Wittgenstein's view of Freud (see Section 3.2).

1.3 Philosophy Must Avoid Subliming the Logic of Our Language

In sections 89–135, and especially in sections 89–93, of his *Investigations,* Wittgenstein talks about the sense in which language and logic have been taken to be something sublime. Subliming language is the attempt to find a justification, explanation, or foundation for our linguistic practices. We sublime our language when we give in to our tendency to look for hidden essences, not the straightforward essences that grammatical inquiry reveals. For example, we would be subliming some of our uses of language if we tried to provide a cognitive foundation for our moral or mathematical discourse. This is something Russell and Whitehead (*Principia Mathematica*) and Frege (*The Basic Laws of Arithmetic*) are guilty of in the case of math. But philosophy, Wittgenstein says, "cannot give [the actual use of language] any foundation." "It can in the end only describe it," since, as he says, "it leaves everything as it is" (PI, §124).

Wittgenstein wants philosophers to point out what we do, in particular, the activity that is involved in our use of language. He is recommending that they engage in something like philosophical anthropology. "What we are supplying are really remarks on the natural history of man: not curiosities however, but rather observations on facts which no one has doubted[18] and which have only gone unremarked because they are always before our eyes" (RFM, pt. 1, §141, p. 43). It is what we do that plays the role of the given for him. That is what he sees as fundamental. This is why he quotes with approval the saying from Goethe's *Faust* (I, iii, 60), "Im Anfang war die Tat" ["In the beginning was the deed"] (OC, §402), where it is understood that "words are also deeds" (PI, §546). The contrast here is not with "In the beginning was the Word . . ." (John 1:1), for God's word was itself a deed. Rather, Wittgenstein contrasts what he calls the "language-game," which is "language and the actions into which it is woven" (PI, §7) with language when it "is like an engine idling," that is, not working (see PI, §132). "Our language-game is an extension of primitive behavior. . . . [It] is behavior" (Z, §545). He urges us to "look on the language-game as the *primary* thing" (PI, §656). "Our mistake is to look for an explanation where we ought to look at what happens as a 'proto-phenomenon.' That is, where we ought to have said: *this language-game is played*" (PI, §654).

Hume's account of language and of how it is learned would be an example of the sort of thing he is objecting to. Hume seems to think we learn language through ostensive definitions. But Wittgenstein points out that such definitions already presuppose our having some knowledge of the language. Consider the case of the color word "red." How do we point to redness? We have to point to a particular object that is red. And how are we to know that it is the color rather than the shape or something else that is being pointed to? We must already have the concept of color to understand, or ask for, an ostensive definition of this word. More will be said about how we learn our language and acquire our concepts, especially psychological ones, in the discussion of Cartesianism, especially in Chapter 7.

Wittgenstein's notion of the given is also far richer than that of many other philosophers—for example, Russell, twentieth-century sense-data philosophers, or modern philosophers like Descartes and Hume: the given for the last two are thoughts and perceptions. These are their simples. The later Wittgenstein is also opposing attempts to reduce things to absolute simples, that is, to explain and/or to justify language in terms of such simples. Russell, in the *Philosophy of Logical Atomism,* tries to do this by using universals and sense-data as his simples; and in the *Tractatus* Wittgenstein himself tries to do something similar, except that he never gives any examples of his simples, which he calls "objects."

In the *Investigations,* Wittgenstein offers an interesting and important attack on attempts to draw this sort of distinction between absolute simples and what is complex. He sees that these are not absolutes. The distinction always depends on what sense of these words we have in mind. For " 'simple' means: not composite. And here the point is: in what sense 'composite'? It makes no sense at all to speak absolutely of the 'simple parts of a chair' " (PI, §47). That is, we cannot just say something is or is not complex.

> If I tell someone without any further explanation: "What I see before me now is composite," he will have the right to ask: "What do you mean by 'composite'?" For there are all sorts of things that that can mean! —The question "Is what you see composite?" makes good sense if it is already established what kind of complexity—that is, which particular use of the word—is in question. (PI, §47)

He illustrates by considering a chessboard. Even this is not "absolutely composite." You might be tempted to think it is, saying it's composed of thirty-two white and thirty-two black squares. But Wittgenstein points out that we could "also say, for instance, that it was composed of the colors black and white and the schema of squares. . . . Asking 'Is this object composite?' *outside* a particular language-game is like what a boy once did, who had to say whether the verbs in certain sentences were in the active or passive voice, and who racked his brains over the question whether the verb 'to sleep' meant something active or passive" (PI, §47). Even the simplicity of the color of a square on a chessboard is not absolute. "Does it consist of pure white and pure yellow? And is white simple, or does it consist of the colors of the rainbow? —Is this length of 2 cm. simple, or does it consist of two parts, each 1 cm. long? But why not one bit 3 cm. long, and one bit 1 cm. long measured in the opposite direction?" (PI, §47). A monochrome square can also be looked at in different ways. In one language-game it's simple. "But under other circumstances," Wittgenstein says, "I should call a monochrome square 'composite,' consisting perhaps of two rectangles, or of the elements color and shape. But the concept of complexity might also be so extended that a smaller area was said to be 'composed' of a greater area and another one subtracted from it. Compare the 'composition of forces,' the 'division' of a line by a point outside it" (PI, §48). Such confusions about absolute simples encourage us to sublime our language. They are examples of the language bewitching us.

But the language bewitches us in other ways as well. For example, it tempts us to see thought as

surrounded by a halo. —Its essence, logic, presents an order, in fact the a priori order of the world: that is, the order of *possibilities,* which must be common to both world and thought. But this order, it seems, must be *utterly simple.* It is *prior* to all experience, must run through all experience; no empirical cloudiness or uncertainty can be allowed to affect it. —It must rather be of the purest crystal. But this crystal does not appear as an abstraction; but as something concrete, indeed, as the most concrete, as it were the *hardest* thing there is (*Tractatus Logico-Philosophicus* 5.5563).

We are under the illusion that what is peculiar, profound, essential, in our investigation, resides in its trying to grasp the incomparable essence of language. That is, the order existing between the concepts of proposition, word, proof, truth, experience, and so on. This order is a *super*-order between—so to speak—*super*-concepts. Whereas, of course, if the words "language," "experience," "world," have a use, it must be as humble a one as that of the words "table," "lamp," "door." (PI, §97)

Someone may object: But what about terms like "electron," "atom"? Don't we have to look to science instead of examining our language to increase our understanding of such notions? Wittgenstein might answer that if we want to get clear about these words and concepts, we have to examine their use in the language. But that, of course, means seeing how they are used in the sciences, since that is where these terms are mainly used. So technical terms do not constitute a counterexample to his approach.

But if the linguistic practices of scientists count, why not also count the linguistic practices of philosophers to determine what words mean? They do count if the words are philosophical ones—for example, "a priori," "modus ponens," "language-games," "illocutionary act," "deontologist."[19] If we want to understand what such words mean, we have to see how they are used in the different branches of philosophy or by the different philosophers. Finally, if we want to know what a particular philosopher means by even an ordinary word—for example, Heidegger by "care" and "guilt"

—we must look closely at his use of these terms. Only then will we grasp what he means by them or what his technical notions of care and guilt are.

If we want to understand what nonphilosophical words actually mean, however—words like "guilt," "experience," "knowledge," "good" that have their life outside of philosophy—we have to attend to their actual use outside of philosophy. That is why Wittgenstein says, "When philosophers use a word [e.g. 'know'] . . . and try to grasp the *essence* of the thing, one must always ask oneself: is the word ever actually used in this way in the language-game which is its original home?" (PI, §116). If it is not used that way in the language-game—for example, the philosophers say that you can know what is not the case—they would be misusing the word "know." This is a linguistic fact. That is why Wittgenstein repeats, "Philosophy may in no way interfere with the actual use of language; it can in the end only describe it" (PI, §124). Philosophy is neither just another science nor a super-science.

A caveat needs to be added here about the expression "a word's original home." This may be misleading. It suggests that there is only one home for each word. In fact, a word can have several "original homes." Think of the terms "God" or "morality." Those who think like Jerry Falwell will not use these terms the way those do who are influenced by Paul Tillich or Saint Thomas Aquinas. They have different but related concepts of God and of morality corresponding to their different and overlapping uses of these terms. So Wittgenstein should be taken as urging us to look at how the word is actually used in each of its "homes," if there is more than one. That means we cannot be indifferent either to how words are used in different places or how their use has evolved over time. Wittgenstein recognizes that language-games can change with time (OC, §256; PI, §23). The ancient Hebrews used the term "God" differently from the early Christians, and we probably use the term still differently today. All of this is relevant to determining what the word "God" means and has meant.

So far I have considered two categories of words: first, scientific and philosophical words insofar as they are technical words that do not occur in everyday language. I concluded that Wittgenstein holds that we should look to science and philosophy, respectively, to see how such words function. But for a second category of words—terms from everyday language that philosophers use—we should only attend to how they are actually used outside of philosophy, unless we just want to understand what a particular philosopher means by them. It might be objected that, if this is correct, Wittgenstein has a double standard. Consider words from science whose original home is also natural language—for example, the following terms from physics: "force," "energy," "charge," "space," "time," "particle," "attraction," "motion," "spin," and so on. Despite the fact that these words are all drawn from everyday language, Wittgenstein does not criticize physicists for misusing them because their use of them diverges from the way these words are used outside of physics. Why then does he insist that "philosophy may in no way interfere with the actual use of language" (PI, §124) and that philosophers should attend only to the actual use of such words outside of philosophy?

Two replies may, I think, be made to this objection. First, there is no standard, agreed-upon philosophical use of words like "good," "know," "experience," "guilt," and so on. The situation is quite different for the corresponding terms in physics that are drawn from everyday language. Words like "force," "energy," "charge," and so on have agreed-upon technical uses; physicists don't argue with each other on how these terms function in physics. They also know that their technical uses of these terms differ from their ordinary uses outside of physics.

Even if this were not so, however—that is, if there were standard, agreed-upon philosophical uses of the everyday words philosophers deal with—these uses would be irrelevant to Wittgensteinians unless they helped them understand how *we* use these words, since that is what they are interested in and need to understand. An example may help clarify the point. Suppose that all non-Wittgensteinian philosophers used the word "know" in such a way that it becomes a contradiction to say you know a contingent matter of fact. Then, according to this use of the term, knowledge of other people would be logically impossible. If we accepted this use of the term, we would have to be skeptics about other minds, as well as about many other things. However, if this use of "know" is actually in conflict with our use of the word—as it in fact is—it has no relevance to *our* question, namely, whether *we* can have knowledge of other minds.

1.4 Philosophy Has the Same Kind of Depth as Grammatical Jokes

Wittgenstein implies that a philosophical muddle or problem is deep the same way a grammatical joke is:

> The problems arising through a misinterpretation of our forms of language have the character of *depth*. They are deep disquietudes; their roots are as deep in us as the forms of our language and their significance is as great as the importance of our language. —Let us

ask ourselves: why do we feel a grammatical joke to be deep? (And that is what the depth of philosophy is.) (PI, §111)

Let us look at some grammatical jokes to see what he has in mind. Anscombe and Rhees report that Wittgenstein himself gives as "a good grammatical joke, the Mock Turtle's remark 'We called him Tortoise because he taught us.' "[20] Puns play on the sound of words, in this case, the identity of sound of "Tortoise" and "taught us"—at least in such accents as the British or the New York. It would be ridiculous, however, to think that because these words are tied together in sound they must somehow be connected in meaning. The Mock Turtle's explanation of why Tortoise is called Tortoise is absurd because it involves such a conceptual twist.

Next take what is sometimes called a Dumb Dora joke, done by George Burns and Gracie Allen. "The phone rang and she says, 'Oh, you are!' and hung up and George says, 'Who was that?' and Gracie says, 'That was a man and he said he was brown from the sun.' "[21] Here the caller uses the expressions "brown" and "the sun" as proper names of himself and of a newspaper, while Gracie takes "brown" to be used as a predicate and "the sun" to refer to the sun in our solar system. She assimilates different uses of words. You could say Gracie was led astray by the surface grammar of the language. She is involved in a confusion similar to the confusions philosophers get into. For example, the Cartesian philosopher takes "I" and "a pain" to be proper names in "I have a pain," whereas "I" is really an indexical expression and "a pain" functions here as a predicate.

An excerpt from a Joey Bishop monologue gives us another nice example of a grammatical joke. He says: "I like working in Hollywood as opposed to New York. You get paid three hours earlier."[22] Bishop's non sequitur rests on a misconception of our temporal language. When it is 3 P.M. in California, it is true it is 6 P.M. in New York, but that does not mean you get paid three hours earlier in California than in New York. We shall see in Chapter 9 that Augustine's confusions about time are also conceptual.

Arthur Schopenhauer gives a fine example of a grammatical joke when he tells the story "of an actor, called Unzelmann, who was rebuked by his director and colleagues for too much improvising. One day Unzelmann appeared in a play that demanded his presence on stage with a horse. During the performance the horse dropped something natural to the horse but unbecoming and unusual in the midst of a scene. The audience roared with laughter. Unzelmann turned to the horse and said: 'Don't you know we are forbidden to improvise?' "[23] Unzelmann himself improvises at the same time as he absurdly reproaches the horse, who can't improvise, for doing so. The horse can no more improvise than it can expect a bonus in a week's time. The joke reminds us what it is to improvise and under what conditions it makes sense to reproach someone for improvising.

The following exchange between husband and wife does something similar. "Wife: To think that I trusted you all these years! Husband: Oh, darling, don't reproach yourself now."[24] Of course she is not reproaching herself, but him. There is an absurdity and outrageousness in his spurious misinterpretation of her complaint.

In all of these examples the jokes arise through misinterpretation of the forms of our language. We feel these jokes to have a kind of depth because they remind us what the forms of our language really are; they remind us about certain conceptual facts; they help us grasp the deeper grammar of the language. As we shall see, this is just what philosophy does, on Wittgenstein's view. So the depth of philosophy and of grammatical jokes are comparable. They are both deep and not deep in essentially the same way. That is no doubt why he tells Malcolm—"without being facetious"—that "a serious and good philosophical work could be written that would consist entirely of *jokes*."[25]

There is an impulse to misread these remarks as trivializing philosophy. After reading Wittgenstein, Steve Martin, who apparently was planning to become a professional philosopher, became a comedian. Rorty describes Wittgenstein's philosophical works as a "parody" and "a few volumes of satire."[26] He has even spoken of the *Investigations* as a "joke book,"[27] confusing what Wittgenstein says can be done with what he did. We must remember that Wittgenstein's comparison of philosophy with grammatical jokes, like his comparison of philosophy with therapy, is only an analogy. He does not mean they are the same and that whatever can be said of one can be said of the other. The comparison certainly does not imply that philosophy has no more weight or importance than a grammatical joke, but only that they both arise out of, and depend on, similar sorts of misperceptions or misunderstandings of the grammar of our language.

1.5 Why This Sort of Philosophy Is Hard

Wittgenstein says his aim in philosophy is, "To show the fly the way out of the fly-bottle" (PI, §309). Or, as we saw before in §109, to get rid of muddles, remove the misunderstandings. I have emphasized that he is aiming at a *complete* disappearance of the philosophical problems. We also have seen that we are supposed to make the philosophical problems completely disappear not by explaining or deducing anything or by looking for what is hidden. Rather, we dissolve the problems by "simply [putting] everything before us." "Everything lies open to view" (PI, §126).

Do these statements imply that philosophy should be easy? I do not think so. Notice, first, the formidable-sounding requirement: the Wittgensteinian philosopher is to put *"everything* before us" (my emphasis). Even if we qualify this to mean everything relevant to the dissolution of the philosophical problem, and that these will only be trivialities, not new facts, this still may not be an easy thing to do. Wittgenstein himself reports that it is a "difficult thing [to] to get a 'synopsis' of [the relevant] trivialities, and that our 'intellectual discomfort' can only be removed by a synopsis of *many* trivialities—that 'if we leave out any, we still have the feeling that something is wrong.' "[28] A Wittgensteinian philosopher can go wrong, then, by omitting some relevant trivialities, in which case the philosophical problem will not completely disappear. This may be one reason why he cautions that "getting hold of the difficulty *deep down* is what is hard. Because if it is grasped near the surface it simply remains the difficulty it was. It has to be pulled out by the roots" (CV, 1946, p. 48).

The difficulty of grasping the roots of the problem and of bringing in enough of the relevant reminders about how we use language also explains why Wittgenstein recommends a slow cure. He says the *"slow* cure is all important" (Z, §382). If we try to rush it, we may not completely dissolve the problem. We should not be misled, then, by Wittgenstein's remark that philosophy "neither explains nor deduces anything" and has "no interest [in what is hidden]" (PI, §126). That in no way implies it is easy. We know he never thought it was. To do philosophy well takes an open mind, imagination, skill, determination, and a talent for thinking.

The following passage suggests a second reason why philosophy is not easy:

> Compare *knowing* and *saying*:
>   how many feet high Mont Blanc is—
>   how the word "game" is used—
>   how a clarinet sounds.
> If you are surprised that one can know something and not be able to say it, you are perhaps thinking of a case like the first. Certainly not of one like the third. (PI, §78)

The second case is also different from both of the other two, since knowing how the word "game" is used leaves it open whether you are able to say how it is used. Most of us have no trouble using the word "game," but probably we would not do very well describing how it is used. Wittgenstein points out that the same problem arises with other words. "We know how to use the word 'not'; the trouble comes when we try to make the rules of its use explicit. Correct use does not imply the ability to make the rules explicit" (L1, 1931, p. 53). In short, even though it is possible to say how we use words—including those we know how to use—it is often hard to say how we use them. The point holds generally for knowing how to do something. "Knowing how to do A," where *A* is an action, does not imply knowing how to say how to do A. You may know how to dance the tango, for example, or how to use the word "game," yet not be able to give an accurate account of how you dance the tango or how you use the word "game." So, although the philosopher says only what we already know— for example, how we use certain everyday words—it may not be easy to articulate what it is we know in such cases.[29]

Recall that Wittgenstein says philosophical problems are dissolved "by looking into the workings of our language, and that in such a way as to make us recognize those workings: *in despite of* an urge to misunderstand them" (PI, §109). The words in italics in this passage reveal still a third reason why philosophy done Wittgenstein's way is hard. The initial diffi- culty of seeing how we use certain words in our language is compounded by our urge to misunderstand the workings of our language. That is, we are tempted not to recognize how we use words, even though we ourselves know perfectly well how to use them. We shall look at some of the reasons why Wittgenstein thinks we are tempted to fall into such errors in the next section. One reason is that we combine a fondness for generalization with "a taste for desert landscapes"[30]—a dislike of messy analyses. These ten- dencies easily lead to giving an oversimplified and incorrect account of our use of the language. For these and other reasons, Wittgenstein says phi- losophy is not just a matter of intellect but also of will. Philosophical prob- lems are not to be perceived as purely intellectual problems. To dissolve them we have to resist many of our natural tendencies. We need to work on our wills and not just on our intellects.

> What makes a subject hard to understand—if it's something signifi- cant and important—is not that before you can understand it you need to be specially trained in abstruse matters, but the contrast between understanding the subject and what most people *want* to see. Because of this the very things which are most obvious may become the hardest of all to understand. What has to be overcome is a diffi- culty having to do with the will, rather than the intellect. (CV, 1931, p. 17)

Maybe this helps explain why Wittgenstein's later writings so often sound like confessions of intellectual temptations encountered and overcome. More will be said on this when we turn in the next section to the question of what makes us go astray in philosophy and also in the chapter on Wittgenstein's view of Freud.

But let us look next at still a fourth reason why philosophy done his way is hard. The metaphor he gives here is beautifully fitting.

> Why is philosophy so complicated? It ought, after all, to be *completely* simple. —Philosophy unties the knots in our thinking, which we have tangled up in an absurd way; but to do that, it must make movements which are just as complicated as the knots. Although the *result* of philosophy is simple its methods for arriving there cannot be so.
>
> The complexity of philosophy is not in its matter, but in our tangled understanding. (PR, pt. 1, §2)

Wittgenstein implies here that philosophical problems are the result of our tangled thinking. To understand them you must follow the twists and turns of this thinking. You must follow the fly into the fly-bottle, see how it gets into it, follow all the moves it makes. Only then will you be in a position to show the fly—or the philosopher—the way out. For example, following their penchant for generalizing, philosophers "lay down rules" for how we use certain words, and then note that when they "follow the rules, things do not turn out as" they had assumed. The philosophers get entangled in their own rules. "This entanglement in our rules is what we want to understand (i.e. get a clear view of)" (PI, §125). We get this understanding by reminding ourselves of what you already know: that the words "know," "pain," etc., are used in this or that way. Philosophers in this manner will begin to see the way out of their predicaments. The whole inquiry will have been complex, even though the results won't be.

1.6 Some of the Reasons We Go Astray

What makes us go astray in philosophy? In the *Blue Book,* Wittgenstein answers that our craving for generality—our craving for unity—is one of the causes of our subliming the language. It is this craving that gives rise to our tendency to sublime the logic of our language. This in turn is due to certain other human tendencies, three of which are the following. (1) We are inclined to think that there is something common to things subsumed under general terms—terms like "game" or "leaf"—which justifies our calling them games or leaves. (2) We have a tendency to think we understand such a general term, say, the term "leaf," if we possess a general picture of a leaf. (Locke and Hume, for example, would think so.) (3) We are preoccupied with the methods of science (BB, pp. 17–18).

Perhaps there is a shift in the *Investigations*. In this later work he seems to see our tendency to sublime language as due primarily, if not solely, to a failure to understand our language. "A main source of our failure to understand is that we do not *command a clear view* of the use of our words. . . . A perspicuous representation produces just that understanding which consists in 'seeing connexions.' Hence the importance of finding and inventing *intermediate cases*" (PI, §122). Another way to put this is to say we are taken in by the surface grammar. Consider, for example, the expressions "exists," "is good," and "is red." They are all three classified as predicates. So we think they must function in much the same way. We assimilate different uses of words. A few confusions like this and we construct an ontological argument for the existence of God and for the nonexistence of the devil.[31] As Wittgenstein says, "we remain unconscious of the prodigious diversity of all the everyday language-games because the clothing of our language makes everything alike" (PI, p. 224).

Notice that the question "What makes us go wrong?" is a psychological or sociological question. A more important question for us may be whether we go wrong, or better, whether we always go wrong when we raise philosophical problems. Are they all muddles? No doubt we sometimes do go wrong in philosophy. This book will provide several examples of going wrong—Augustine's discussion of time, the dream argument, etc. But to find cases that confirm Wittgenstein's negative view of philosophy is not to establish it. Indeed, it is unclear how it could be established. To establish it, it seems that every possible philosophical position—past, present, and future—would have to be examined. We would also have to rebut all alternative views of what the task of philosophy is or ought to be.

Finally, another point to bear in mind is this: Wittgenstein's philosophical aim may be a bad one—his conception of philosophy may be inadequate—but it doesn't follow that he is a bad philosopher or that there is nothing important that we can learn from him. The issues of the "depth," the difficulty, and the therapeutic aim of Wittgensteinian philosophy begun in this chapter are continued in Chapter 3, on Wittgenstein and Freud.

1.7 His Conception Compared with Socratic Recollection

According to the Socratic theory of recollection, the knowledge we want in philosophy is innate in us in the sense of being inherited from a prior life; our task is to recollect it, to make this implicit knowledge explicit. The particular aim is to find a definition of a concept—of goodness, knowledge, piety, or the like. For Wittgenstein, too, philosophy reminds us of what we already know. "Philosophy simply puts everything before us, and neither explains nor deduces anything. —Since everything lies open to view there is nothing to explain. For what is hidden, for example, is of no interest to us" (PI, §126)

In a way we could say Socrates and Wittgenstein both think they have nothing positive to teach,[32] though they both closely examine ideas put forth by others, refute them, and exhort and persuade. The philosophical truths or true philosophical theses Wittgenstein uncovers he sees as indisputable and trivial; he thinks there is a sense in which he is not telling us anything we did not know all along. Wittgenstein also says he does not want his work "to spare other people the trouble of thinking. But, if possible, to stimulate someone to thoughts of his own" (PI, p. x). This seems to be Socrates' attitude too. They both try to get us critically to scrutinize our own ideas in the same careful way they do.

Wittgenstein disagrees with Socrates, however, that the knowledge we remind ourselves of is innate in us, that we have it in us already at birth, indeed even before birth. He thinks we acquire it only when we learn our language. Moreover, we remind ourselves of this knowledge, according to him, not in order to define words and concepts, but to dissolve our philosophical problems. Wittgenstein rejects philosophical analysis that seeks to give analytic definitions of things of a kind or the sort of analysis that defines or analyzes a sentence as Russell does with his theory of (definite and indefinite) descriptions (see the Appendix). The later Wittgenstein thinks it may neither always be possible to give such analyses, since many things are not susceptible to such analyses, nor even desirable, since they are often quite unilluminating, and because they rarely help dissolve our problems. This goes along with Wittgenstein's rejection of his earlier appeal to the notion of absolute simples mentioned above. The kind of analysis he recommends is one that appeals to the use of language, one that shows distinctions. We shall see how this approach to philosophical analysis is connected with his doctrine of family resemblance.

Chapter 2

The Doctrine of Family Resemblance

2.1 The Assumption Wittgenstein Is Combating

I mentioned in the last chapter that Socrates is fond of asking questions of the form: What makes a such and such a such and such? For example, what makes an instance of knowledge, a circle, or a pious act an instance of knowledge, a circle, or a pious act? His answers take the form: It has a particular property, essence, or some common and distinctive characteristic. This latter statement might be trivial, for example, if we say good things are good, beautiful things are beautiful, because they have the property of goodness or of beauty. But the aim is to find nontrivial answers, something like: Circles are circles because they are a locus of points equidistant from a center on a plane. Or: Bachelors are bachelors because they are unmarried men of marriageable age.

It is a widespread view that things called by the same general name uniquely share something in common. It may be a single universal, characteristic, or a conjunction of characteristics. Plato makes just this assumption when he asks "What is piety?" in his dialogue the *Euthyphro.* He hopes to find some essence or set of traits that all pious things uniquely share. He makes the same assumption when discussing justice in the *Republic,* knowledge in the *Theaetetus,* love in the *Symposium.* Many twentieth-century philosophers assume the same thing. For example, Santayana, discussing beauty, says he wishes "really" to define it. According to him, such a definition "must be nothing less than the exposition of the origin, place, and elements of beauty as an object of human experience." It would tell, among other things, "why, when, and how beauty appears, what conditions an object must fulfill to be beautiful," and "what is the common element in all beautiful things."[1] Set theorists likewise assume that members of a set, or class, share a common defining feature. We shall see in Chapter 12 that "Saul Wittgenstein"[2] presupposes this when he examines the notion of rule-following. It seems that even Ludwig Wittgenstein makes this assumption in the *Tractatus* when he considers the nature of language. He conceives of language in that work as "the totality of propositions" (TLP, 4.001) and believes propositions are either pictures of atomic facts or truth functions of propositions that picture atomic facts. He takes this to be the hidden essence of language, once again subliming the logic of our language. (Section 1.3 explains the notion of subliming the logic of our language.)

This view that things called by the same general name uniquely share something in common is sometimes called essentialism. It is the heart of much philosophy, from Plato to the present. The possibility of philosophical truth about what things are really like seems to be founded on it. As Rorty says, "The history of attempts to [isolate the True or the Good, or to define the word 'true' or 'good'], and of criticisms of such attempts, is roughly coextensive with the history of that literary genre we call 'philosophy'—a genre founded by Plato."[3] In the twentieth century, Russell, Moore, and many others have been engaged in philosophical analysis, conceived of as a form of definition. The idea was that the proposition analyzed—the *analysandum*—must be logically equivalent or synonymous with the proposition in terms of which it is analyzed—the *analysans*.

The later Wittgenstein rejects the underlying assumption of this sort of philosophical analysis when he reconsiders "the great question . . . what the essence of a language-game, and hence of language, is: what is common to all these activities, and what makes them into language or parts of language" (PI, §65). He says: "Instead of producing something common to all that we call language, I am saying that these phenomena have no one thing in common which makes us use the same word for all, but that they are *related* to one another in many different ways. And it is because of this relationship, or these relationships, that we call them all 'language'" (PI, §65). "We see that what we call 'sentence' and 'language' has not the formal unity that I imagined [in the *Tractatus*], but is the family of structures more or less related to one another" (PI, §108). In short, he now denies that language has an essence, in the sense of having a common and peculiar property, rejecting his earlier view that it consists of truth functions of elementary propositions that picture states of affairs.

The *Tractatus* view goes wrong in three ways, according to the later Wittgenstein. First, it sublimes the logic of our language. Second, it attributes to language an essence that it does not have. Third, it is mistaken in even assuming that language has an essence. Not that Wittgenstein is saying that there is no one characteristic common to all language. There are such characteristics and he knows there are. For example, he himself points out that language must have rules, or be governed by conventions, and have "enough regularity" (PI, §207). When criticizing Freud he seems to add a third requirement—namely, that they be translatable into other languages (see Section 3.1). But these are only necessary conditions of language, not necessary and sufficient conditions.

2.2 What the Doctrine Amounts To

What Wittgenstein says about language in his *Investigations* is related to what has come to be known as his doctrine of family resemblance. Calling it a "doctrine," however, could mislead us. He himself never refers to it as such, perhaps recognizing that that might suggest we are dealing here either with a theory or some sort of dogma or matter of faith.[4] It would be less misleading to call his remarks about family resemblance simply some observations about language from which certain methodological recommendations can be drawn, or to say that the doctrine should be taken as a noncontroversial philosophical principle. He develops this principle primarily in sections 65 through 77 of the *Investigations*.

What are the observations? First, that things that are all called by one name—things of a kind—do not always have one unique thing in common. It follows that they need not always have common and peculiar characteristics. That is, it is not a necessary truth that things subsumed under a general name—"unicorn," "chair," "game"—must have some essential property that makes them things subsumable under that name or that makes them things of that kind. They may just resemble one another the way members of a family resemble each other. "Some of them have the same nose, others the same eyebrows and others again the same way of walking; and these likenesses overlap" (BB, p. 17). Members of a family may have many family resemblances without every member sharing any one trait unique to that family. Wittgenstein wants to say that things of a kind may only have a family resemblance and not all have one unique thing in common. Actually, his family-resemblances analogy is not too apt for his purpose since family members do all have one thing in common in virtue of which they are members of a family—namely, common parents—and this is a unique fact about them. On the other hand, he might reply that having the same parents is not an observational characteristic or one that can be perceived straight off by the senses. Wittgenstein's other image of a chain or cord seems better. The point is, there may be a vast chain of characteristics—not necessarily one single one, or one conjunction of characteristics—some or all of which things of a kind alone possess.

2.3 The Doctrine Not an Answer to the Problem of Universals

Some think these observations about language are an answer or solution to the problem of universals.[5] This is the problem of explaining what makes things of a kind, such as furry things, things of that kind. It also might be described as the problem of explaining why we call things of a kind what we do. (The problem is sometimes called the *one-many* problem, since the one quality of furriness, or the general term "furry," can be applied to many furry things.) Wittgenstein's observations of family resemblances, however, are not proposed as a solution to this problem. Nor are they meant to be a general account of how we recognize and classify things. Wittgenstein is not saying we call things what they are on the same basis as we call members of a family family members—because they resemble each other in many different ways. If Wittgenstein were saying this sort of thing, he would merely be giving one of the traditional, nominalistic, answers to the problem of universals. He would then run into the objections, first, that his explanation explains nothing, since it is circular. Second, he could be accused of contradicting himself, since we have seen in the last chapter that he denies that there are any genuine philosophical problems. So he is committed to dissolving the problem of universals, not to solving it. But Wittgenstein's negative observations about general terms, by themselves, are no more meant to dissolve than to solve the problem of universals. They do not solve the problem of universals, for they do not explain why things are the sorts of things they are. I think Wittgenstein would try to dissolve the problem of universals—show it not to be a real problem—along the lines D. F. Pears suggests.[6]

2.4 Origin and Fruitfulness of the Doctrine

Let us turn now to his prime illustration of the doctrine of family resemblance: the case of games. "We are inclined to think that there must be something in common to all games . . . and that this common property is the justification for applying the general term "game" to the various games; whereas games form a *family* the members of which have family likenesses" (BB, p. 17). In some games the point is to win, but that is not true of all games. Some are played with many people; some are played alone. Some are board games; some are not. "Similarities crop up and disappear. . . . We see a complicated network of similarities overlapping and criss-crossing: sometimes overall similarities, sometimes similarities of detail" (PI, §66). We do not find a single defining characteristic or set of characteristics that things must have in order to be games and by virtue of which they are games. For this reason "one might say that the concept 'game' is a concept with blurred edges" (PI, §71). We can call such concepts "family-resemblance" concepts and also call things that do not have necessary and sufficient conditions family-resemblance kinds of things.

Fann observes that William James makes a similar point in his book the *Varieties of Religious Experience,* a work Wittgenstein was known to admire. James writes, "Let us . . . admit freely at the outset that we may very likely find no one essence, but many characters which may alternately be equally important to religion."[7] Von Wright thinks the idea of "family resemblance" may come from Spengler. He says,

> It appears to have its origin in Spengler's notion of the *Ursymbol* (archetype). This characterizes each one of the great cultures and constitutes what Wittgenstein, writing about this, in fact calls (CV, 1931, p. 14) a family resemblance between a culture's various manifestations—its mathematics, architecture, religion, social and political organization, and so forth.[8]

Kenny suggests the idea may have an even older origin, noting that "the medieval scholastics who developed the theory of analogy" also reject the view that there must be "a unique essence common to all uses of a word."[9]

2.5 Some Dos and Don'ts of the Doctrine

Let us consider some attendant methodological recommendations of this view. Whenever we ask a question of the form "What is X?" or "What makes a thing the kind of thing it is?" we should never simply assume that it must have something in common with other things of that kind, a single characteristic or essence, by virtue of which it is a thing of that kind, or that being X must consist in having a conjunction of unique characteristics. Wittgenstein stresses we must *"look and see"* in each case. He even says, "To repeat: don't think, but look!" (PI, §66). This is not a plea for thoughtlessness but rather for having an open mind. He wants us to look at the facts of the case rather than dogmatically to assume that there must always be such an essence to be discovered and that the philosopher's job is to discover it.

When we act on this advice and actually "look and see," we find that most, if not all, of the concepts in which philosophers have taken a special interest—concepts such as goodness, moral rightness, beauty, truth, existence, knowledge, belief, evidence, causes, reasons, emotions, pleasure, sensations, pain, and so on—are family-resemblance concepts. It follows that it is futile to endeavor to define or to analyze them in terms of necessary and sufficient conditions.

2.6 Some Misunderstandings of the Doctrine

Fogelin says Wittgenstein "goes badly wrong" when he includes evaluative concepts—for example, good and beauty—among family-resemblance concepts. He objects to his suggestion (in PI, §77) that the concepts of aesthetics or ethics are indefinable because they have blurred edges. This assumes—wrongly, Fogelin thinks—that these concepts function descriptively. Moreover, he observes, "if the *Oxford English Dictionary* is correct, [the meaning of the term 'good'] is relatively clear-cut" and not at all vague or hazy. The term "good" seems to be definable as "the most general adjective of commendation."[10]

What Fogelin overlooks is that treating "good" and "beautiful" as family-resemblance terms in no way implies that they are not also evaluative. Obviously they function evaluatively, and Wittgenstein himself acknowledges that we use them to commend and approve of things (LC, see pp. 1–5). Wittgenstein is merely pointing out that it is impossible to give nontrivial necessary and jointly sufficient conditions for something's being good or beautiful, which seems to be true enough. That is, there seems to be no common and peculiar set of characteristics shared by all things that are good or beautiful. Taking such a position, Wittgenstein allies himself with the antidefinists in philosophy: philosophers like Hume, Moore, Pritchard, Ayer, Stevenson, and Hare, who deny that evaluative terms can be defined solely in nonevaluative terms. This is, of course, not to deny the uninteresting truth that what is good is, by definition, what is commendable or desirable.

Wittgenstein's view of family resemblance can easily be misunderstood in other ways as well. He is not saying or implying that there won't—or cannot ever—be such a property, or essence, that things of a kind share uniquely, or even that we can never discover things to have such an essence. Nor is he committed to the weaker claim that we can never uncover necessary conditions for things. We have already seen he acknowledges some necessary conditions for language. He suggests the same thing about games—for example, that games must have a beginning: "Of course [the game of chess played by Adelheid and the Bishop] has [a beginning]; otherwise it would not be a game of chess" (PI, §365). I think he would also agree that they all must have rules. Nor is he even saying that if there is a common set of characteristics things of a kind share, this must be a most unusual happening. He nowhere implies that every concept is a family-resemblance concept. The concept of a circle, of a bachelor, of validity, of an alcoholic beverage, for example, clearly are not. We can define what it is to be a bachelor, a logically valid argument, or a circle by stating their common and peculiar characteristics. We have already done this for bachelor and circle. And as John Wisdom notes, "all alcoholic drinks possess something in common . . . alcohol," which is why we say they are alcoholic drinks.[11] So there are cases where we can find common and peculiar characteristics of things.

Wittgenstein is warning us *not* to assume that all cases are like this. Again, he is showing us differences between things—one of his themes. He advises us in each case simply to consider each instance without prejudice, with open minds—to open our eyes and to "*look and see*" (PI, §66). What he means is that we should look at instances of a kind of thing—for example, games—to see whether they do or do not have a set of unique characteristics in virtue of which they are called games. That is, we should examine the use of the general term with open minds and see whether we in fact apply it on the basis of a single feature or set of features shared uniquely by all things to which the term truly applies. This is surely sensible advice with which we ought to have no trouble agreeing.

But if Wittgenstein is telling us to look and see whether things of a kind have necessary and sufficient conditions or are merely family-resemblance things, isn't he urging us to engage in an empirical and theoretical undertaking? We form experimental hypotheses about whether characteristics A, B, and C constitute necessary and jointly sufficient conditions for kind X. Then we have to test the hypothesis against many different cases. If it stands up under the first *n* tests, it is confirmed to that degree. Our hypothesis now gives us a provisional explanation of the phenomena. Compare a scientist who hypothesizes that teeth emerge in children if and only if conditions A, B, and C obtain (the right sort of vascular pressure, mineral salts, blood vessels, nerves, and so on are present in the surrounding tissue). Experiments are then performed to test the hypothesis. If it is confirmed, the scientist has a provisional explanation of how teeth emerge in children.

There are several things wrong with this representation of Wittgenstein's position. First, he does not recommend that we formulate such generalizations. He is not trying to develop theories. Rather, he cautions us not to assume that generalizations of the kind described are either desirable or generally true. Second, in his philosophy, he neither employs hypotheses nor experiments. When he "looks" at things of a kind—for example, games—he merely considers what we would call a thing of that kind, and then points out how diverse and overlapping the characteristics of such things are. What we are left with, even if it were a true generalization— for example, "Bachelors are unmarried men of marriageable age"—would explain nothing. It would merely tell us something implicit in our language but which we hadn't attended to. That is why he says, "Philosophical analysis [unlike analysis in science] does not tell us anything new," even when it succeeds in replacing one statement with another that is synonymous with it (L1, 1930, p. 35). And when it substitutes one form of expression for another that has a more precise and unequivocal use—as is done in that form of philosophical analysis known as explication—we no longer are even given an analysis of our concept, but only of one that is akin to it (PI, §76). Contrast analysis in science. The scientists who discovered the chemical composition of water or the necessary and sufficient conditions for the emergence of teeth in children discovered something new.

2.7 The Case of Games

Well, let us make a start at carrying out Wittgenstein's advice in the case of games. For brevity, I shall use some symbols. Using them will also help emphasize the overlapping similarities and differences among games. The symbol " – " will be used for negation, to indicate that a game does not have a certain property.

Amus	It is played primarily for amusement.
Ball	It is a ball game.
Begi	It has a beginning.
Boar	It is a board game.
Capt	You win by capturing an opponent's pieces.
Card	It is a card game.
Chec	You win by checkmating the opponent's king or by forfeit.
Ches	It is played with chess pieces.
Cour	It is played on a court.
Hop	It is a hopping game.
Goal	It has goalposts.

Kick	It involves kicking.
King	There is a piece in the game called a king.
Lose	You can lose to your opponent(s).
Ment	It requires considerable mental effort.
More	You win by scoring more points than your opponent(s).
Net	There are nets in the game.
Oppo	You must have at least one opponent.
Rack	It is played with rackets.
Rule	It has rules.
Skil	It involves skill in balancing.
Stre	It requires physical strength.
Thro	It involves throwing.
Two	It requires two or more players.
Win	You can win in the sense of beating your opponent(s).

After briefly considering a few games, we might come up with the schematic summary that follows. The account is obviously not meant to be complete. In spite of that, it shows just how right Wittgenstein is in saying, "Similarities crop up and disappear. And the result of this examination is: we see a complicated network of similarities overlapping and criss-crossing: sometimes overall similarities, sometimes similarities of detail" (PI, §66). We do not find a single characteristic or set of characteristics that are common and peculiar to all games. Even the common property of having a beginning (Begi) and having rules (Rule) is not peculiar to games. The law and languages also have rules, and many things besides games have beginnings—marriages, life, friendship.

Chess	−Amus, −Ball, Begi, Boar, −Capt, −Card, Chec, Ches, −Cour, −Hop, −Goal, −Kick, King, Lose, Ment, −More, −Net, Oppo, −Rack, Rule, −Skil, −Stre, −Thro, Two, Win
Ring around the rosie	Amus, −Ball, Begi, −Boar, −Capt, −Card, −Chec, −Ches, −Cour, −Hop, −Goal, −Kick, −King, −Lose, −Ment, −More, −Net, −Oppo, −Rack, Rule, −Skil, −Stre, −Thro, Two, −Win
Tennis	−Amus, Ball, Begi, −Boar, −Capt, −Card, −Chec, −Ches, Cour, −Hop, −Goal, −Kick, −King, Lose, Ment, More, Net, Oppo, Rack, Rule, Skil, Stre, Thro, Two, Win

Patience (solitaire)	− Amus, − Ball, Begi, − Boar, − Capt, Card, − Chec, − Ches, − Cour, − Hop, − Goal, − Kick, − King, − Lose, − Ment, − More, − Net, − Oppo, − Rack, Rule, − Skil, − Stre, − Thro, − Two, − Win
Hopscotch	− Amus, − Ball, Begi, − Boar, − Capt, − Card, − Chec, − Ches, − Cour, Hop, − Goal, Kick, − King, Lose, − Ment, − More, − Net, Oppo, − Rack, Rule, Skil, Stre, Thro, Two, Win
Draughts (checkers)	− Amus, − Ball, Begi, Boar, Capt, − Card, − Chec, − Ches, − Cour, − Hop, − Goal, − Kick, King, Lose, − Ment, − More, − Net, Oppo, − Rack, Rule, − Skil, − Stre, − Thro, Two, Win
American football	− Amus, Ball, Begi, − Boar, − Capt, − Card, − Chec, − Ches, − Cour, − Hop, Goal, Kick, − King, Lose, − Ment, More, − Net, Oppo, − Rack, Rule, Skil, Stre, Thro, Two, Win

2.8 The Doctrine Rules Out One Paradigm of Philosophy

Let us return to the question of what this doctrine implies about how we are to do philosophy. Most important, we must always look and see how our words function, and not just assume that there will be a unifying essence uniting together things of a kind. That is, we should not assume that we must be dealing with words or concepts that can be analyzed in terms of necessary and sufficient conditions. Words can be meaningful and we can understand what they mean—know how to use them—even if they are not so analyzable. In short, we should be careful not to give in here, as in other cases, to our tendency to oversimplify.

Following this advice, we find that the concepts philosophers have traditionally been most interested in rarely have such essences. It therefore won't be possible to give definitions of them that express their essential nature in terms of necessary and sufficient conditions. Consequently, it won't be possible to give the sort of analysis of them Russell gives in his theory of descriptions. (See the Appendix for an account of this theory.) We therefore have good reason not to persist in trying to give such analyses of them. So we have at least one reason to stop modeling our philosophy on Russell's theory of descriptions or the Socratic pursuit of definitions.

Some think this must mean that the later Wittgenstein is repudiating philosophical analysis. Fann, for example, speaks of "his clear and forceful rejection of analysis. . . . Whatever he may be, the later Wittgenstein is no longer an *analytic* philosopher."[12] What Fann overlooks is that philosophers—as well as analytic philosophers—themselves form families in the same way games do. In the previous chapter (Section 1.2), we have seen that Wittgenstein recognizes that there is more than one way to philosophize, even though, in his view, there is only one right way to do it. Philosophers who get into fly-bottles may not be doing philosophy in the way he recommends, but they are no less philosophers, in Wittgenstein's estimation, than those who show them the way out. He recognizes that "philosophy" means different things to different people, especially at different times and places. This is confirmed by his indignant reaction to Drury's suggestion that he call his *Philosophical Investigations* "Philosophy." Drury reports his answering: "How could I take a word like that which has meant so much in the history of mankind; as if my writings were anything more than a small fragment of philosophy?"[13]

There is also more than one way to be an analytic philosopher. Wittgenstein, for example, is an analytic philosopher who points out ambiguities and distinctions in our language, drawing our attention to the implications of what we say. He does this with the aim of taking apart or shredding philosophical problems. Other analysts—those engaged in explication as Russell, Rudolf Carnap, and others often are (see the end of Section 2.6 on the notion of explication)—aim to give precise formal definitions of our less "exact" concept to make them suitable for formal logical use. To reject one paradigm of analytic philosophy—the one exemplified by Russell's theory of descriptions—is therefore not to reject analytic philosophy. We have seen that one of his reasons for opposing the attempt to analyze or to define words in terms of necessary and sufficient conditions is that he thinks it cannot generally be carried out with success, at least not for most of the concepts that have traditionally interested philosophers. The history of twentieth-century philosophy seems to support Wittgenstein's view. The various attempts to do this—behaviorism, phenomenalism, and the like—have turned out to be failures. The relevant concepts—for example, psychological concepts—are family-resemblance concepts; so they do not lend themselves to such analyses.

But Wittgenstein has another reason for opposing this traditional way of doing philosophy in which the philosopher tries to give necessary and sufficient conditions for concepts: he does not think such analyses help dissolve our philosophical problems. Dissolving such problems, however, is the aim of his investigations. (See the previous chapter.) In many passages he uses down-to-earth examples to ridicule definition-mongering analysts.

> When I say: "My broom is in the corner", —is this really a statement about the broomstick and the brush? Well [one sort of philosophical analyst might say], it could at any rate be replaced by a statement giving the position of the stick and the position of the brush. And this statement is surely a further analyzed form of the first one. — But why do I call it "further analyzed"? —Well, if the broom is there, that surely means that the stick and brush must be there, and in a particular relation to one another; and this was as it were hidden in the sense of the first sentence, and is *expressed* in the analyzed sentence. Then does someone who says that the broom is in the corner really mean: the broomstick is there, and so is the brush, and the broomstick is fixed in the brush? —If we were to ask anyone if he meant this he would probably say that he had not thought specially of the broomstick or specially of the brush at all. And that would be the *right* answer, for he meant to speak neither of the stick nor of the brush in particular. Suppose that, instead of saying "Bring me the broom," you said "Bring me the broomstick and the brush which is fitted on to it."! —Isn't the answer: "Do you want the broom? Why do you put it so oddly?" —Is he going to understand the further analyzed sentence better? (PI, §60)

Wittgenstein's answer to the last question is no. Analogous objections to the one he makes here might be made to Russell's theory of descriptions. (Some of these will be explored in the Appendix.) Wittgenstein compares analysts of the Russellian kind with people who try "to find the real artichoke [by stripping] it of its leaves" (PI, §164; cf. BB, p. 125).

We see, then, that in his later philosophy Wittgenstein has given up the attempt to discover a final analysis of our forms of language. He writes:

> But now it may come to look [wrongly] as if there were something like a final analysis of our forms of language, and so a *single* completely resolved form of every expression. That is, as if our usual forms of expression were, essentially, unanalyzed; as if there were something hidden in them that had to be brought to light. When this is done the expression is completely clarified and our problem solved.
> It can also be put like this: we eliminate misunderstandings by

making our expressions more exact; but now it may look as if we were moving towards a particular state, a state of complete exactness; and as if this were the real goal of our investigation. (PI, §91)

But moving towards a particular state of complete exactness is not the real goal of his investigation. He simply wants to eliminate the misunderstandings that underlie our philosophical problems and show us the way out of the fly-bottle. He offers philosophical therapy. Indeed, he believes, as we shall see in the next chapter, that his philosophical aims and methods resemble in some striking ways Freud's psychoanalytic goals and procedures, which are also therapeutic, despite their equally striking differences.

Chapter 3

Wittgenstein's Freud

3.1 Why It Is Important to Understand How He Views Freud

Freud (1856–1939) and Wittgenstein (1889–1951) are both revolutionary turn-of-the-century Viennese thinkers who have had a profound impact upon Western society, although Wittgenstein never stirred the popular imagination the way Freud did. In spite of offering a powerful critique of Freud, surprisingly Wittgenstein speaks of himself as "a follower" and even as "a disciple of Freud" (LC, p. 41). Hallett remarks, "with such 'followers,' one may ask, who has need of critics?"[1] Wittgenstein might well reply that you can learn from Freud, but only if you are critical, which psychoanalysis usually prevents (LC, p. 41). So you have to try to sort out what is valuable in Freud from what is not. I shall begin by looking at his criticisms. This should illuminate and develop the thoughts in Chapters 1 and 2. Understanding how Wittgenstein views Freud—the similarities and differences he recognizes or is responding to and what he finds right and wrong in his approach—will clarify Wittgenstein's own way of thinking.[2]

I shall not address the historical question of how alike and different from each other they really are or whether the criticisms are justified. I shall try to show, however, that Wittgenstein's criticisms shed light on his conception of philosophy or what he understands the philosopher's job to be. They also show some of his concepts in action. For example, when he attacks Freud's account of dreams, we see the doctrine of family resemblance at work: dreams, he says, do not share the common essence of being hallucinated wish fulfillments that Freud attributes to them. Nor does Wittgenstein think that there is a single line of explanation for all of the many different sorts of dreams (LC, p. 46).

The similarities Wittgenstein perceives between his thought and Freud's also represent some important features of Wittgenstein's way of doing philosophy. For example, he thinks that neither he nor Freud is doing science; that they both are engaged in a kind of therapy; that they try to persuade us to think in a certain manner, a manner contrary to the commonly accepted Cartesian view; that they both are concerned with the will as well as the understanding, with providing an accurate account of mental or psychological phenomena; that they stress the importance of seeing things in a larger context more than most thinkers do; and that they both offer ways to increase our self-knowledge. The discussion should also help to demystify Wittgenstein's remark that he considers himself to be a disciple or follower of Freud.[3]

3.2 Some of His Criticisms of Freud

Wittgenstein finds Freud's writings—for example, his book on the nature of jokes—a good source of philosophical mistakes. He accuses Freud of confusing the *cause* of laughter, which may be a desire to give vent to repressed sexual energy or to express hostility, with the *reason* for laughing. Moreover, it is often not clear whether Freud is offering a hypothesis or merely a way of representing or describing a fact. "What he says sounds as if it were science, when in fact it is only a 'wonderful representation'. . . . 'It is all excellent similes, e.g., the comparison of a dream to a rebus'," or to a riddle made up in part of pictures of objects or symbols whose names resemble the intended words or syllables in sound (L2, pp. 309–10). Wittgenstein seems to be saying that if what Freud says were a hypothesis, and not merely a way of representing or describing a fact, it would have empirical consequences. But then it would be testable, and often it is not clear to him how it could be. We shall see that the question whether Freud's views are testable is highly debatable.

Wittgenstein also objects to Freud's account of dreams. He disagrees that a dream's manifest content, what the dreamer reports the dream to be about—for example, a top hat and a wooden table—always has an underlying meaning, or a latent content, which is an unconscious wish or motive—say, the wish to sleep with your mother. Indeed, Wittgenstein gives the following reductio ad absurdum of the Freudian view that a dream is a kind of language. Suppose we take it to be a kind of language, to be a way of saying something. We should then find a way of translating its symbolism into the language of ordinary speech, ordinary thoughts, which is what dream analysts claim to be able to do. If something is a language it must be translatable into another language and that does not mean there can be an endless number of correct translations. Wittgenstein seems to hold translatability to be a necessary condition for something to be a language. But then, he notes, the translation ought to be possible both ways. It should be possible, employing the same technique, to translate ordinary thoughts into dream language. Yet Freud acknowledges that this never is done and cannot be done. The suppressed thought or wish, "I'd like to sleep with my mother," doesn't give rise to only one or two dreams—it could give rise to endless different dreams. So we should "question whether dreaming is a way of thinking something, whether it is a language at all" (LC, p. 48).

He agrees with Freud, however, that dreams are puzzling, "so that we want an interpretation of them." He even says, "There seems to be something in dream images that has a certain resemblance to the signs of a language." He likens dream imagery to a series of marks on paper or on sand or to "a cathedral in Moscow with five spires. On each of these there is a different sort of curving configuration. One gets the strong impression that these different shapes and arrangements must mean something" (LC, p. 45). So Wittgenstein does not deny that dreams resemble language in certain respects, even though they lack some of the essential features of language (see also LC, p. 48).

As mentioned, Freud wants to explain once and for all what dreaming consists of. He wants to find the *essence* of dreaming. "He would have rejected any suggestion that he might be partly right but not altogether so. If he was partly wrong, that would have meant for him that he was wrong altogether—that he had not really found the essence of dreaming" (LC, p. 48). The essence of dreams, according to Freud, is that they are hallucinated wish fulfillments. He calls the fulfillment of the wish the latent content of the dream, which exists in a hidden or repressed form that is capable of being brought to light through analysis. The manifest content— what is remembered of the dream upon awakening—is a distortion produced by an unconscious desire not to reveal the latent content.[4] Wittgenstein does not deny that some dreams are wish fulfillments (LC, p. 47). Indeed, he gives several examples: "A man is hungry and dreams of feasting, is thirsty and dreams of drinking, feels the need of passing water and he dreams of passing water. Some dreams are like this. This comes like a flash, a great light—an *aperçu*."[5] But, he charges, it is a muddle to think that *all* dreams are hallucinated wish fulfillments. He gives two arguments. First, this conflicts with the fact that there are dreams that spring from fear rather than from longing. That is, anxiety dreams seem to be counterexamples to the theory. Second, he notes that, according to Freud, most of dreams he considers have to be regarded as *camouflaged* wish fulfillments. Wittgenstein argues, "in this case they simply don't fulfill the wish. Ex hypothesi the wish is not allowed to be fulfilled" (LC, p. 47). Freud himself explains that the real wish is often not allowed to be fulfilled because the unconscious may repress it, forcing you to hallucinate something else instead. For example, when your real wish is to sleep with your mother, your censor has you dream of top hats and wooden tables instead. "If the wish is cheated in this way," Wittgenstein observes, "then the dream can hardly be called a fulfillment of it" (LC, p. 47).

Wittgenstein thinks it is likely that there are many different kinds of dreams, just as there are many different kinds of jokes, or many different kinds of language. It may not be possible to give one line of explanation for all of these things (LC, pp. 47–48; compare Wittgenstein PI, §65 on language). Like many other thinkers, Freud gives in here to what Wittgenstein calls a "craving for generality," or to what comes to the same thing, a "contemptuous attitude towards the particular case" (BB, p. 18). Freud looks for *the* underlying meaning of dreams, of verbal slips, of forgetting, and the like.[6] The resulting accounts he gives, however erroneous, have the appeal of simplicity.

Wittgenstein also questions Freud's technique of free association and his reliance on it in his interpretation of dreams. Free association is the process in which patients undergoing psychoanalysis report to their analysts their thoughts and feelings as they come, no matter how embarrassing or unimportant they may seem to them. Freudian analysts use the technique to understand their patients' unconscious drives and dreams by seeing connections between the ideas presented. Wittgenstein says Freud actually uses two different criteria for the right interpretation of a dream. One criterion is the judgment of the analysts, what they say or predict on the basis of their previous experience. Another, is the judgment of the patients or dreamers, what conclusions they are led to by free association (LC, p. 46). Wittgenstein observes: "It would be interesting and important if these two [judgments] generally coincided. But it would be queer to claim (as Freud seems to) that they *must always* coincide." That is, the judgment of the analyst may differ from that of the patient.

Another problem Wittgenstein sees in free association is that it can be affected by many different things. It is not affected only by the unconscious wish of the patient (LC, pp. 46–47). He gives the analogy of completing what seems to be a fragment of a picture. You might try hard to figure out what is the most likely way the picture went and come up with many different responses. Alternatively, you might instead simply "stare at the picture and make whatever dash first comes into your mind, without thinking." The second approach, which is like free association, might in many cases get better results. "But it would be astonishing," Wittgenstein thinks, "if it *always* produced the best results. [For] what dashes you make is likely to be conditioned by everything that is going on about you and within you" (LC, p. 47).

Using the method of free association Freud tries to show that a beautiful dream is really bawdy. How does he do this? By showing that the dream images—a flower, a tree—are related by a chain of associations to certain sexual objects. "Does this prove," Wittgenstein asks, "that the dream is what is called bawdy? Obviously not" (LC, pp. 23–24). The beautiful dream Freud is analyzing—the dream with flowers and trees—would not be the sort you would be looking for if you wanted to collect dream for a book entitled *Bawdy Dreams*. We can see that such a dream is not what is called bawdy by considering a case in which it is correct to speak of someone as talking bawdy—for example, the person tells a dirty joke. A bawdy dream would be something like that. Now contrast that case with the beautiful dream.

Still another problem with free association, according to Wittgenstein, is that we are not shown where to stop. Freud assumes whatever happens in a dream can be found to be connected with some wish that analysis can discover. But he gives conflicting criteria where to stop, where the right solution is. Sometimes it seems that the right solution, or the right analysis, is the one the patient and the doctor agree on. Sometimes it seems that the doctor alone determines what the right solution or analysis of the dream is: the patient's judgment can be rejected as mistaken (LC, p. 42). According to the second criterion, the doctor's analysis is correct or gives the right solution even if the patient is not satisfied by it or does not agree with it. According to the first, the right analysis satisfies the patient as well. But, as we have seen, these are two criteria that do not necessarily lead to the same conclusion.

Finally, Wittgenstein adds that free association will arrive at the same results as those Freud reaches no matter what you start with, even if you start with someone else's dream instead of your own. But this is simply because, as Wittgenstein says:

> The fact is that whenever you are preoccupied with something, with some trouble or with some problem which is a big thing in your life—as sex is, for instance—then no matter what you start from, the association will lead finally and inevitably back to that same theme. . . . You could start with any of the objects on this table—which certainly are not put there through your dream activity—and you could find that they all could be connected in a pattern like that. . . . [So] this sort of free association does not explain why the dream occurred. (LC, pp. 50–51)

These criticisms of free association are connected with the further charge that Freud is not really doing science, contrary to his own claims. Commentators note that it was Freud's belief that he introduced the scientific method to the study of the unconscious and that psychoanalysis has the status of a natural science.[7] Wittgenstein questions whether it has this status. He finds that many of the claims—for example, that one analysis is the right one—do not seem to rest on evidence (LC, p. 42). Nor does Freud establish his view that anxiety is always a repetition in some way of the anxiety we felt at birth. Wittgenstein even doubts that Freud could establish the latter claim by reference to evidence (LC, p. 43). Perhaps Wittgenstein thinks Freud could not do this because there is no clear way of determining what anxiety we felt at birth, much less whether it is the same anxiety that we felt at a later time. However, even if we think Freud could have provided evidence in support of his view, Wittgenstein stresses that he did not. Freud cites no psychological experiments in confirmation of it.

The empirical testability of Freud's account of correct explanations of jokes is also questionable, according to Wittgenstein. Freud contends that "jokes . . . are in fact never non-tendentious," that is, they are never innocent. They are always prompted either by a hostile or by an obscene purpose. Suppose, for example, that you lust after someone. In most situations propriety will require you to inhibit your desire. This takes psychical energy. You cannot satisfy your lustful feelings in a straightforward manner, so you do it indirectly by telling a joke. The release of the energy you were using to inhibit your libido gives you "new pleasure."[8] Maybe Wittgenstein wonders how we are to detect whether the joke releases any inhibitory energy. For he says that Freud gives us "an entirely new account of a correct explanation. Not one agreeing with experience [or supported by evidence], but one accepted [by the patient]" (LC, p. 18).

Wittgenstein asserts that Freud gives us "*speculation*—something prior even to the formation of an hypothesis." For example, speaking of overcoming resistance, Freud uses a legal metaphor. He says: "One 'instance' [jurisdiction or proceedings] is deluded by another 'instance'. (In the sense in which we [may] speak of 'a court of higher instance' with authority to overrule the judgment of the lower court)" (LC, p. 44).[9] That is, the analyst is supposed to be stronger than the delusion of the patient, able to combat and overcome it. But, Wittgenstein charges, "there is no way of showing that the whole result of [such an] analysis may not be 'delusion'" (LC, p. 44). In other words, maybe the analysts—who are seen here as making up a higher tribunal—never free the patient (the lower court) from delusion or, worse, they actually bring the patient to another level of delusion. There seems to be no way of establishing that it is not so, but there would be if Freud's claim about the analyst were a genuine hypothesis. What we have here is not a hypothesis but rather

> something which people are inclined to accept and which makes it easier for them to go certain ways: it makes certain ways of behaving and thinking natural for them. They have given up one way of thinking and adopted another. . . . [Freud] claims that his researches have now explained how it came about that anybody should think or propound a myth of [the ancient] sort [Oedipus, Electra, etc.]. Whereas in fact Freud has done something different. He has not given a scientific explanation of the ancient myth. What he has done is to propound a new myth. The attractiveness of the suggestion, for instance, that all anxiety is a repetition of the anxiety of the birth trauma is just the attractiveness of a mythology. (LC, pp. 44–45, 51)

What Freud propounds is a myth in the sense of being a story that ostensibly relates historical events to explain something and whose actuality appears not to be verifiable. An old example of a myth would be the creation story "according to which Earth, Erebus, and Love were the first of beings. Love (Eros) issued from the egg of Night, which floated on Chaos. By his arrows and torch he pierced and vivified all things, producing life and joy."[10]

Contrast with such myths the explanations given in physics. Wittgenstein says that an important characteristic of an explanation in physics is that "it should work"—that is, it should enable us to make successful predictions. Physics and engineering are connected: engineers don't want the bridges they make to fall down. As we have seen, Freud speaks of there being several instances [tribunals] in the mind [in consciousness]. But Wittgenstein notes that many of these psychoanalytic explanations are not confirmed by experience, as explanations in physics are. Instead, they express an *attitude* and "give us a picture which has a peculiar attraction for us" (LC, pp. 25–26).

Erik Erikson, who trained under Sigmund and Anna Freud, says, "Freud . . . had to have the courage to accept and to work with what he himself called his 'mythology'."[11] But it seems that Freud does not mean by a "mythology" quite what Wittgenstein does, since he thinks he is a scientist, giving a correct causal account of psychological phenomena.

Some philosophers maintain that Freudian theory can be tested and does have the kind of status required for scientific validity.[12] But whether it is testable, and how far it is, remain highly debatable.

Finally, Wittgenstein criticizes Freud for sometimes misusing our language and sometimes using words in technical ways without being aware that that is what he is doing. Freud's talk of unconscious intention—he assumes it makes sense to speak of such things—serves as a nice illustration. For example, Freud says you may have the intention not to return books you have been lent, but know nothing about it: "[The intention] reveals its presence by producing the forgetting. . . . There are purposes in people which can become operative without their knowing about them."[13]

Compare such talk with what Wittgenstein says about "unconscious toothache." He asks whether we should call a certain state of tooth decay, without what we commonly call a toothache, an "unconscious toothache." Then we could say we have a toothache but do not know it. That would parallel the psychoanalyst's talk of unconscious thought, acts of volition, etc. Wittgenstein says there would be nothing wrong in talking this way, since it would be just a new terminology that can easily retranslate into our more usual way of talking. Yet he points out that adopting this new terminology might mislead us into thinking that an important new discovery has been made or it might puzzle us in the way philosophers get puzzled. We might start wondering how can we possibly have an unconscious toothache and maybe be tempted to deny that it is possible. Whereupon the scientist will reply that it is an established fact. And Wittgenstein says the scientist will say this

like a man who is destroying a common prejudice. . . . You won't be satisfied, but you won't know what to answer. This situation constantly [regularly] arises between the scientist and the philosopher. In such a case we may clear the matter up by saying: "Let's see how the word 'unconscious,' 'to know,' etc. etc., is used in *this* case, and how it's used in others". (BB, p. 23)

As Wittgenstein says: "When philosophers use a word . . . and try to grasp the *essence* of the thing, one must always ask oneself: is the word ever actually used in this way in the language-game which is its original home? —What *we* do is to bring words back from their metaphysical to their everyday use" (PI, §116). He does not want philosophy to interfere in the slightest with the way we actually use language. Philosophy describes language, and leaves everything as it is (PI, §124).

3.3 Some Ways in Which Wittgenstein Thinks He Resembles Freud

We have seen that Wittgenstein speaks of himself as a follower and as a disciple of Freud (LC, p. 41). This implies that his views do not simply resemble the latter's, but that he learned from him and accepts many of his doctrines. The etymological sense of "disciple" is the Latin *discipulus,* which in English means "pupil." This does not, of course, imply that he accepts everything Freud believes. You may follow someone and still think many of his or her beliefs are confused and should be rejected. Rush Rhees asserts that Wittgenstein shows just how much there is in Freud's notion of "dream symbolism," for instance, or in the suggestion that in dreaming I am—in some sense—"saying something." Wittgenstein thus separates what is valuable in Freud from that "way of thinking" that he thinks needs to be combatted. It is common for philosophers to sort out the good and the bad thoughts in the thinking of those who have influenced them: Aristotle tries to do this with Plato and Marx with Hegel. Wittgenstein admires Freud for the observations and suggestions in his writings (LC, p. 41). He sees him as someone to learn from—even from his mistakes—since the mistakes also contain truth.

I shall not attempt to answer the question whether Wittgenstein's relation to Freud is comparable to that of Aristotle's to Plato, or whether it is like the relation of Marx to Hegel. Nor shall I try to determine to what extent Wittgenstein's thought is Freudian, that is, to what extent he was really a follower of him. I shall merely try to bring out some ways in which Wittgenstein thinks he resembles Freud, since I have already discussed some of the perceived differences. This may help clarify the sense in which he conceives of himself as a follower and disciple of Freud.

One similarity Wittgenstein finds is that neither of them is doing science. We have seen that, even though Freud wants to do science, Wittgenstein does not believe Freud actually does it. Wittgenstein does not think he himself is doing science either, but with the difference that he does not intend to when he is doing philosophy. Speaking of his own philosophical investigations, Wittgenstein says he is not engaged in empirical research: the considerations he appeals to "could not be scientific ones," there could not be "anything hypothetical" in his considerations, and he could not "advance any kind of theory." He wants instead to "do away with all *explanation*" in philosophy and to replace it with description. This description is to get its light, that is to say its purpose, from the philosophical problems. These are, of course, not empirical problems; they are solved, rather, by looking into the workings of our language, and that in such a way as to make us recognize those workings . . . *despite* . . . an urge to misunderstand them. The problems are solved, not by giving new information, but by arranging what we have always known. Philosophy is a battle against the bewitchment of our intelligence by means of language. (PI, §109)

Here we seem to be given a partial account of what is required for something to be a science: sciences have theories, propose hypotheses, offer explanations, and solve empirical problems by discovering new information. Wittgenstein thinks neither his investigations nor Freud's have these characteristics. That is, neither Freud nor Wittgenstein really theorize, hypothesize, nor explain, in a scientific sense; neither do they discover new information. Finally, because Wittgenstein's aim is to dissolve the problems he is concerned with by bringing together relevant things that we have always known, he says, "The work of the philosopher consists in assembling reminders for a particular purpose" (PI, §127). Wittgenstein would add that we do not assemble these reminders, or analyze concepts, for their own sake. He would say something analogous of what Freud does.

Second, Wittgenstein sees both of them as doing therapy. Wittgenstein says his aim is "to show the fly the way out of the fly-bottle" (PI, §309), to help us out of our philosophical puzzlement, to liberate us from our conceptual confusions. "A man will be *imprisoned* in a room with a door that's unlocked and opens inwards; as long as it does not occur to him to *pull* rather than push it" (CV, 1942, p. 42). Again, he says: "A *picture* held us captive. And we could not get outside it, for it lay in our language and language seemed to repeat it to us inexorably" (PI, §115). Notice that in all three of these illustrations the aim is to free yourself—either from a fly-bottle, a room, or from a picture—and it is possible to do this. If you cannot, it must be because you have not adequately understood the situation you are in. That is why Wittgenstein says, "A philosophical problem has the form: 'I don't know my way about'" (PI, §123). He gives two more metaphors: it's like a "mental cramp" that needs to be loosened or relieved (BB, p. 59) as well as like a knot in our thinking that needs to be untied. The latter metaphor fits in well with his view that, even though the results of philosophy are simple, "philosophizing has to be as complicated as the knots it unties" (Z, §452).

Fann also employs a metaphor to describe Wittgenstein's philosophical questions. He says they are like "'vexations' or 'intellectual discomfort' comparable to some kind of mental disease."[14] That again brings the latter's view close to Freud's. As we have seen, Wittgenstein himself compares the philosopher's treatment of a question to the treatment of an illness (PI, §255). He says for such "a disease of thought . . . [a] *slow* cure is all important" (Z, §382). Rush Rhees warns us of some of the ways in which Wittgenstein's analogy with illness and disease may be misleading.

> Philosophy as therapy: as though the philosopher's interest were in the personal disabilities of the perplexed: and as though he were not perplexed himself—as though philosophy were not discussion. Some remarks which Wittgenstein himself made are partly responsible for this. But he was suggesting an analogy with therapy; and he was doing this in an attempt to bring out certain features in the method of philosophy: to show the difference between what you have to do here and what you would do in solving a problem in mathematics or in science. It was not a suggestion about what it is that philosophy is interested in. If Wittgenstein spoke of 'treatment,' it is the problem, or the question, that is treated—not the person raising it. It is not the personal malaise of the 'patient' which makes the perplexity or question important. What has led me to this perplexity is not my personal stupidity. Rather it is a tendency in the language which could lead *anyone* there, and keeps leading people there.[15]

There are several good points Rhees is making here. He reminds us that Wittgenstein's philosophical therapy treats problems—philosophical ones —and that these do not spring from a neurotic mode of thought.[16] Nor do they arise because of personal stupidity. Rather, there is something in the language that keeps tempting people to raise them. The problems are not to be solved the way we solve problems in mathematics or in science. Finally, successful philosophical therapy requires discussion.

I think Wittgenstein would agree that much of this is also true of Freud: he also treats problems, but psychological ones; these problems do not arise because of personal stupidity—rather, there is alleged to be something in us and in society that leads people into these troubles and that keeps leading people to the same sort of trouble. Nor are these problems to be solved the way we solve problems in mathematics or in science. Finally, successful psychological therapy also requires a lot of talk. Indeed, psychotherapy is often spoken of as the "talking cure."

There is one way, however, in which Rhees's own statement might mislead us. He says Wittgenstein treats the problem, or the question, "not the person raising it." This may suggest that the problem exists on its own. But of course it does not. Philosophical problems, like psychological, moral, and all other problems, are always somebody's. Through discussion and persuasion Wittgenstein is trying to show the trapped philosopher how to get out of the fly-bottle.

Freud, too, wants to show the patient what he won't let himself know, to help him overcome his complex. So both Freud and Wittgenstein purport to do therapy, though they use different methods. While Freud uses the methods of psychoanalysis, Wittgenstein uses various philosophical methods. He says: "There is not *a* philosophical method, though there are indeed methods, like different therapies" (PI, §133). For both the *Tractatus* and the *Investigations,* philosophy is an activity rather than a body of doctrine. It is a matter of pursuing investigations that compel us, he says in his later work, "to travel over a wide field of thought criss-cross in every direction" (PI, p. ix). In the process we remind ourselves of trivialities that enable us to see conceptual connections and the deeper grammar of our language, dissolving our philosophical problem, which always turns out to be a misunderstanding. When successful, in some cases Freud too dissolves the patient's psychological problems. By following out the patient's recollections—"the threads of associations [connected with seemingly indifferent trivialities in a dream] . . . [that] cross and interweave with each other many times over in the course of their journey"—Freud seeks to uncover the patient's repressed dream-thoughts.[17] Similarly, by resuscitating the source of the patient's guilt in suppressed memories by the method of free association, Freudian analysis allows him to see that he did not really do anything terrible, but merely wished to; the guilt is thus undermined and vanishes.

Third, both speak to the will, not just the understanding, trying to persuade us to look at things in a certain way. Ilham Dilman writes: "One could say that psycho-analytic interpretations are meant to speak not only to the patient's understanding, but also to his will. They bring insight as much by defeating the patient's strategies of defense, or enabling him to dispense with them, as by bringing to his attention features of his character, thoughts and actions, and connecting them in new ways, presenting them under a new aspect."[18] Freud wants to show his patients what they won't let themselves know. Wittgenstein, too, tries to speak to both our will and our understanding, pointing out the need to resist our tendency to think in certain ways—for example, the Cartesian way—or to assume that our concepts must be in accord with some preconceived logical or epistemological ideals. We must overcome our contemptuous attitude towards the particular case, our excessive desire to generalize like a scientist, and our assumption

DISCARD LIBRARY
FORSYTH TECHNICAL COMMUNITY COLLEGE
2100 SILAS CREEK PARKWAY
WINSTON-SALEM, NC 27103-5197

that things of a kind must always have one thing in common that makes us call them things of that kind. We have to fight our deep temptation to overintellectualize things. Philosophy is in some ways like conversion. He says, "[it] demands a renunciation . . . a renunciation of feeling, not of understanding. Perhaps that is what makes it so hard for many people. It can be as hard to refrain from using an expression as it is to hold back tears or hold in anger."[19]

The previous point connects with Wittgenstein's claim that, in spite of appearances, neither Freud nor he discovers things. Wittgenstein observes:

> One thinks of certain results of psychoanalysis as a discovery Freud made, as apart from something you are persuaded of by a psychoanalyst, and I wish to say this is not the case. Those sentences have the form of persuasion, in particular [those] which say 'This is *really* this.' [This means] there are certain differences which you have been persuaded to neglect. (LC, p. 27)

Consider the example of a psychoanalyst trying to persuade you that really you thought so-and-so or that really your motive was so-and-so. Wittgenstein says this is not a matter of discovery, but just persuasion, since there is more than one way of looking at it. He acknowledges that what he is doing is also persuasion, except that he usually wants to persuade you of differences.

> If someone says: "There is not a difference," and I say: "There is a difference" I am persuading, I am saying "I don't want you to look at it like that." . . . I am in a sense making propaganda for one style of thinking as opposed to another. I am honestly disgusted with the other. Also I'm trying to state what I think. Nevertheless I'm saying: "For God's sake don't do this." (LC, pp. 27–28)

Wittgenstein wants to cure the sickness of philosophical problems by changing our mode of thought (RFM, pt. 2, §4, p. 57).

So both Wittgenstein and Freud are trying to change people's way of looking at things, trying to persuade, though not in the same way. Freud, because of his reductionist tendencies, de-emphasizes differences—for example, viewing dreams and hallucinated wish fulfillments as the same thing or ascribing one meaning to all verbal slips or cases of forgetting. Wittgenstein, by contrast, "often draw[s] your attention to certain differences" (LC, p. 27). This is so much one of his themes that Drury reports Wittgenstein's telling him "that he thought of using as a motto for the *Philosophical Investigations* a quotation from King Lear: 'I'll teach you differences.'"[20] In his classes at Cambridge, Wittgenstein said to his students, "I tried to show you that infinity is not so mysterious as it looks" (LC, p. 27). Finally, Wittgenstein thinks both his and Freud's persuasiveness rests not on giving new information, but rather on a rearrangement of what we already know. Therefore, the persuasiveness of both men is different in this respect from its counterpart in science, which is supposed to rest on nothing but evidence consisting of new information.

Another similarity Wittgenstein finds with Freud is that both of them seem to give us self-knowledge and, more than most, they stress the importance of seeing things in context. Speaking of Freud, Wittgenstein says: "One may be able to discover certain things about oneself by this sort of free association" (LC, p. 51). He also writes: "One may discover in the course of [analysis] various things about oneself" (LC, pp. 51–52). He even maintains that "in a way having oneself psychoanalyzed is like eating from the tree of knowledge. The knowledge acquired sets us (new) ethical problems; but contributes nothing to their solution" (CV, 1939, p. 34). These passages raise the question whether it is consistent for Wittgenstein to say such things about Freud. He certainly is conceding here that free association and psychoanalysis may be sources of self-knowledge. How can this be, given his previously mentioned criticisms of psychoanalysis and free association?

Wittgenstein may reply that free association and psychoanalysis can help us become aware of our preoccupations and concerns. He says himself, "whenever you are preoccupied with something, with some trouble or with some problem which is a big thing in your life . . . the association will lead finally and inevitably back to that same theme" (LC, pp. 50–51). So free association and psychoanalysis may help us discover what is bothering us, by helping us to see what we tend to dwell on, furthering self-knowledge. This may of course present us with new ethical problems. That does not mean that free association and psychoanalysis are able to solve these new problems or to explain our dreams. Wittgenstein in turn helps us attain self-knowledge by showing us how to get clear about our concepts and how to clear up our conceptual muddles.

Both thinkers in carrying out their investigations emphasize the organic and functional relation between parts and wholes rather than an atomistic approach. Freud, for example, thinks you cannot understand a joke, a slip of the tongue, a dream, and many other things by themselves: you have to relate them to other things to grasp their significance. Similarly, Wittgenstein says:

> An intention is embedded in its situation, in human customs and institutions. If the technique of the game of chess did not exist, I could not intend to play a game of chess. In so far as I do intend the construction of a sentence in advance, that is made possible by the fact that I can speak the language in question. (PI, §337)

So you cannot understand an intention by itself as Cartesians or identity theorists suppose.[21]

Both also reject the Cartesian view that every current psychological state is incorrigible and indubitable to you—that is, that you cannot make any mistakes about any of your present emotional and cognitive states. Consider, for example, a psychological state like being in love. Wittgenstein reminds us that "love is put to the test" (Z, §504). It may be meaningless to ask, "Am I really in pain?" but it is certainly not meaningless to ask, "Am I really in love?" You may find out that you are or are not. Talking about another emotion—fear—Dilman rightly observes: "Now if fear were a sensation, if it were a mental state constituted by the here and now of consciousness, in the way that Descartes imagined, then indeed a person could not be afraid and not know that he was, nor could he think he was afraid when he was not."[22] Dilman thinks that Freud, like Wittgenstein, also wants "to emphasize that there is more to a person than his conscious personality, that there are aspects of him that he does not recognize. His activities and intentions have dimensions of which he is not aware."[23] That is why both Freud and Wittgenstein allow for the possibility of self-deception, unlike Descartes, who thinks that every one of our present psychological states is incorrigible and indubitable to us. Indeed, Wittgenstein says, "nothing is so difficult as not deceiving oneself" (CV, 1938, p. 34).

There is a difference, however, in the methods Freud and Wittgenstein employ. Freud wants to reveal what is hidden—for example, childhood experiences that in no way "lie before" us—by uncovering what we already know but have buried in our minds or memory. Wittgenstein, in contrast, examines what is before us, "what lies open to view." Since, in philosophizing, we need to make explicit what lies before us, he says, "God grant the philosopher insight into what lies in front of everyone's eyes" (CV, 1947, p. 63). What is hidden does not interest Wittgenstein (see PI, §126), unless, paradoxically, its being hidden is a result of its being in plain sight like the document in Edgar Allan Poe's "The Purloined Letter." The letter in that story is right where it should be, but the Prefect of the Parisian police does not think to look in such an excessively obvious place. Instead, he searches every nook and corner in which it might have been concealed. Here simplicity and openness result in concealment. We have an analogous situation in philosophy. As Wittgenstein says, "The aspects of things that are most important for us are hidden because of their simplicity and familiarity. (One is unable to notice something—because it is always before one's eyes.)" (PI, §129)

These may seem to be puzzling remarks. Why should we need insight to see what lies in front of our eyes? Talk of seeing what lies right in front of our eyes, however, is a metaphor. Wittgenstein is speaking of ideas we are familiar with that easily muddle us; so it is not incorrect to speak of insight for "seeing" the way out of our muddled views. C. Auguste Dupin, the detective in Poe's story, had insight that enabled him to "uncover" the letter, but not because he had better eyesight or more information than the Prefect. Wittgenstein seems to be saying we face much the same situation in philosophy. "The problems are solved [read *dissolved*], not by giving new information, but by arranging [bringing together] what we have always known" (PI, §109). Freud says something similar: "Analytic therapy does not seek to add or introduce anything new, but to take away something [that obscures or hides], to bring out something [to make it visible]."[24] Both Freud and Wittgenstein emphasize achieving insight and coming to see things differently.

Finally, both are trying to give us an account of mental and psychological phenomena, though in different ways. Freud tries to give an *explanation* of psychological phenomena by stating what he believes are the laws of the psyche, by giving their essence. Wittgenstein does not think this can be done. But he believes we can give a *description* of psychological phenomena by examining the ways we use mentalistic and psychological terms. There is nevertheless a similarity in their approaches: "When a dream is interpreted [by Freud] we might say that it is fitted into a context in which it ceases to be puzzling" (LC, p. 45). Wittgenstein also tries to understand things by fitting them into a context, though in a different way. That is, both thinkers look beyond the immediately given. Freud wants to get beyond the manifest content, to get to the latent content. What Wittgenstein finds most striking about Freud, he says, is "the enormous field of psychical facts that he arranges" (L2, p. 310). Wittgenstein tries to do something comparable: he wants to get beyond the surface grammar—"what immediately impresses itself upon us about the use of a word . . . the way it is used in the construction of the sentence, the part of it—one might say—that can be taken in by the ear" (PI, §664). For example, the surface grammar tells us that "see" and "run" are both verbs, which obscures the deeper grammatical difference that seeing is a state, not an action, unlike running (Z, §208). Similarly, while we talk both about hearing God as well as presidential candidates, this covers up the deeper grammatical difference that you can only hear God if you are addressed by him, whereas presidential candidates can be heard even if they do not address you (Z, §717).

For Wittgenstein there is a

> mythology implicit in our speech-forms [that we easily surrender to]. . . . [Wittgenstein] wants to see through the surface grammar of a word to its depth grammar. This . . . is what made it natural for him to call himself a pupil or follower of Freud, for he had in Freud an example of how a new and deeper but often less flattering interpretation [a "bawdy" dream] could be substituted for the apparent meaning [a "beautiful" dream] and at the same time of how a mythology could captivate. He accepted and rejected Freud in equal measure, perhaps healthily.[25]

Or, putting Wittgenstein's point another way, he wants to get beyond language as a form of words, and instead to understand the use made of the form of words (LC, pp. 1–2). As he says: "The meaning of a word is its use in the language" (PI, §43).

> A main source of our failure to understand is that we do not *command a clear view* of the use of our words. —Our grammar is lacking in this sort of perspicuity. A perspicuous representation produces just that understanding which consists in 'seeing connexions.' Hence the importance of finding and inventing *intermediate cases*. The concept of a perspicuous representation is of fundamental significance for us. It earmarks the form of account we give, the way we look at things. (Is this a 'Weltanschauung'?) (PI, §122)

The foregoing similarity may help explain why people are inclined to accept and to reject the views of both men. Speaking of Freud, Wittgenstein remarks that many people are inclined to accept the explanations Freud provides in his analysis. Freud, on the other hand, "emphasizes that people are *dis*-inclined to accept [his explanations]." To this Wittgenstein replies, "if the explanation is one which people are disinclined [or unwilling] to accept, it is highly probable that it is also one which they are *inclined* to accept." On the surface this sounds like a contradiction, but I do not believe it is. Wittgenstein seems to be pointing to the psychological truth that human beings tend to be ambivalent about mythological explanations and about things against which they react strongly. The person who rants and raves against God or homosexuals—who protests too much—may secretly be attracted to God or homosexuals. Similarly, people may be charmed as well as frightened by Freud's idea of the unconscious. This possibility is nicely brought out by the two children in Gottfried Keller's short story *Romeo und Julia auf dem Dorfe.* Apparently fascinated by the hidden and uncanny, they put a live fly in the head of a doll, bury it, and then run away (LC, p. 25).

Like Freud, Wittgenstein is also aware of the resistance to his ideas and his way of thinking. This came out in Chapter 1 (see Section 1.5) when I discussed the reasons why Wittgenstein's way of philosophizing is hard. But (he must reason, if he is to be consistent) if people are disinclined (or unwilling) to accept Wittgenstein's account of things, "it is highly probable that it is also one which they are *inclined* to accept." Wittgenstein must therefore assume that human beings will tend to be ambivalent about both of their views. Recent history bears out this claim.

There seem to be several reasons—some of them the same, some of them different—why people may be disinclined to accept the accounts of both Freud and Wittgenstein. One reason may be that they are both opposed to traditional and accepted ways of thinking. Both men develop methods and conclusions new for their times and in conflict with established theories and prevailing views. It took courage for Freud and Wittgenstein to adopt their radically new positions. It is true that Wittgenstein thinks that neither he nor Freud originated this new way of thinking. According to him, they both built on the ideas of others. Wittgenstein says of himself: My originality belongs to the "soil, not the seed." If you plant a seed in his soil, he is suggesting, it will grow differently from how it will in someone else's soil. And he says the same is true of Freud. He believes the real "seed" of psychoanalysis comes from Breuer (CV, 1939–1940, p. 36). Whether this is true is not our concern. But true or not, certainly both men develop those germinal ideas into something novel and striking. Wittgenstein is aware of this. Indeed, he sees what he is doing as

a "new subject," and not merely a stage in a "continuous development." . . . A "new method" [has] been discovered, as had happened when "chemistry was developed out of alchemy." . . . It [is] now possible for the first time that there should be "skillful" philosophers, though of course there [have] in the past been "great" philosophers. (L2, p. 315)

I think he says there can be skillful philosophers now, just as there are skillful chemists, because philosophy, like chemistry, now has techniques that are available to everyone. One of the key techniques involves "[replacing] wild conjectures and explanations by quiet weighing of linguistic facts" (Z, §447). Finally, he assumes that his new philosophical methods, like the techniques of chemists, can be applied with more or less proficiency.

A second and quite different reason people may have for opposing Wittgenstein's approach to philosophy is that it strikes them as too untidy, too complex, it lacks the appeal of simplicity, it does not satisfy some of their cravings. Some people long to find the essence of things. There is something aesthetically appealing in claims of the form "*a* is *really* nothing but *b*," as in "water is really nothing but H_2O." Freudian doctrines, Russell's theory of descriptions, phenomenalism, behaviorism, and mind-body identity theory all have this sort of appeal.[26] On the other hand, some people are obviously attracted to Wittgenstein's approach, perhaps just because of its recognition of the richness and multiplicity of things: this makes it ring true for them. There are thus important differences as well as similarities in the appeal these two thinkers have.

Having seen how Wittgenstein views Freud, what he perceives to be right and wrong in his approach, we are in a better position to understand Wittgenstein's own method of philosophizing. His conception of philosophy and way of thinking should be clearer to us. This will be helpful in what follows. For in the remaining chapters, his new method of philosophizing will be applied to various philosophical views and problems. We shall see how fruitful the new approach is. Ample evidence will be presented that he is indeed right that many philosophers—past and present—get into muddles, among other reasons, because they do not command a clear view of the use of our words. We shall see that Wittgenstein's techniques can also be used to show them the way out of their confusions.

Part II, which begins with the next chapter, shows Wittgenstein's methods at work applied to philosophy of mind, perhaps the area the later Wittgenstein spends the most time on. Chapter 4 dispels the common misconception that Wittgenstein is some sort of behaviorist. It also explains how Wittgenstein would refute behaviorism. In Chapter 5, a thorough Wittgensteinian critique of mind-brain identity theory is given. Next, Chapter 6, explains Descartes's dualist position and how he would deal with the mind-body and the other-minds problem. Here the discussion is broadened to include the question whether nonhuman animals can also be said to have thoughts and feelings or whether Descartes is right in maintaining that they are merely mindless machines. Chapter 7 completes the Wittgensteinian refutation of Cartesian dualism, begun in the previous chapter, by carefully examining many of Descartes's most fundamental assumptions, especially how we acquire psychological concepts and the sense in which he holds psychological phenomena to be private. Finally, Chapter 8 explains Wittgenstein's own positive view, which is often called a "criteriological" position by those who are not taken in by the myth that he is a behaviorist. It is shown that the other-minds problem—which behaviorism, identity theory, and Cartesian dualism all come to grief on—does not arise in Wittgenstein's view of the mental.

Part II
Wittgenstein and Mind

Chapter 4

Behaviorism: Logical, Philosophical, Metaphysical

Logical, philosophical, and metaphysical behaviorism are not three different types of behaviorism. The three terms are treated here as roughly synonymous. The American psychologist J. B. Watson (1878–1958) is considered to be the founder of behavioral psychology. B. F. Skinner (b. 1904), another practicing psychologist, continues in this tradition. The unit of analysis for most behaviorists is molar behavior—larger units of behavior, especially as relatable to a prior deprivation or motivational pattern of the organism—not molecular behavior, as in protein binding to DNA or an electrochemical process in the brain. Paul Ziff and B. A. Farrell are two present-day philosophical behaviorists. Many think that the philosophers Gilbert Ryle and Ludwig Wittgenstein are also behaviorists.[1] This has some plausibility in the case of Ryle, but is a mistake applied to Wittgenstein. He quite clearly rejects behaviorism, as we shall see.

The analyses of the logical, philosophical, or metaphysical behaviorists are alleged to be true solely on the basis of the meaning of the words of which the analyses are composed. For example, Watson tells us what it means to be "a deeply religious man." He says, "It means that the individual goes to church on Sunday, that he reads the Bible daily, that he says grace at the table."[2] Since this is what it means, people who do these things must be deeply religious, while those who do not cannot be deeply religious. The behaviorism we are discussing here is a reductionist view. It tries to account for mental or psychological phenomena in terms of physical phenomena, in particular, in terms of behavior or the disposition (tendency, propensity, or inclination) of an organism to behave in certain overt ways. According to the logical form of behaviorism, all psychological talk is about nothing but behavior or about the disposition to behave in certain overt ways. That is, it is analyzable into, or definable in terms of, the latter, just as we might analyze sugar's solubility in water in terms of what it would do when placed in water. Thus, a behaviorist might say, "I like Brahms" or "Brahms pleases me" is synonymous with "I listen to the radio when it plays Brahms rather than turn it off, I buy and play records of Brahms, and I go to concerts where Brahms is played."[3] Such an analysis purports to provide necessary and sufficient conditions for liking Brahms.

The criteriological—or Wittgensteinian—position is quasi-behaviorist. It is quasi-behaviorist because it also makes a claim about the meaning of psychological words, connecting them with behavioral terms. Yet it is not to be confused with logical, philosophical, or metaphysical behaviorism, since, as we shall see, it rightly asserts nothing so strong as an if-and-only-if statement. That is, it does not offer necessary and sufficient behavioral conditions for psychological notions. It is not a reductionist view. Strawson, Wittgenstein, and Malcolm are criteriologists and quasi-behaviorists. Perhaps Ryle is too. These philosophers insist that we have behavioral criteria for the application of psychological terms, where a criterion for something is stronger than merely a piece of evidence for it, but weaker than a sufficient or necessary condition for it.[4]

If the logical behaviorist's analysis is given in terms of a piece of actual overt behavior, we have behaviorism "in its crudest form," according to Chappell. "[This] is the view that mental phenomena, experiences, sensations, just *are* pieces of behavior, that having a pain, for example, *consists* in doing and saying things."[5] Such a position would equate (in meaning) the psychological expression with a description of some piece of behavior.

This crude form of behaviorism can be complicated by bringing in past and/or future actions. But an even more plausible account would give a dispositional analysis or try to analyze the psychological notion dispositionally. For example, "A believes it is snowing" will take the following form: "If A were going outside, and given such and such other conditions, A would be disposed to put on boots." Ziff, Farrell, and maybe Ryle are behaviorists of this last sort. These behaviorists are more sophisticated than the crude variety.

It is also possible to have a mixed position. For example, U. T. Place[6] accepts a logical dispositional sort of behaviorism for concepts like knowing, believing, understanding, remembering, wanting, and intending. This is largely due to Ryle's influence. His *Concept of Mind* had an enormous impact on the philosophical world when it was first published in 1949. Yet Place does not accept this sort of behavioristic account for experiences; sensations; mental imagery; pain; twinges; how things look, sound, and feel; things dreamed of and pictured in the mind's eye. Place thinks these things are not reducible to overt behavior. He argues that we need a different theory for them—an identity theory—which will be discussed in the next chapter.

Before beginning the discussion of philosophical behaviorism, I would like to distinguish it from one more view—scientific or methodological behaviorism.[7] Methodological behaviorism says how scientific psychology should and should not be conducted. In particular, it says it must confine itself to publicly observable behavior and may not deal with introspection, or self-observation and the contemplation of your own mental processes and experiences. Methodological behaviorism opposes introspective psychology, which uses reports of thought processes and sensations and experiences of subjects as the preferred method for obtaining data. Methodological behaviorism, however, makes no metaphysical, logical, or conceptual claims about what is mental or psychological. Nor does it say that it is nonexistent or reducible to something else. Philosophical and methodological behaviorism are different, yet compatible. You can be both a philosophical and a methodological behaviorist. And if you are the former, you definitely ought to be the latter, but not conversely. I take it that Skinner is both a philosophical and a methodological behaviorist. Only philosophical behaviorism will be discussed here, since it "is a theory about the *nature* of consciousness and the *analysis* of expressions referring to consciousness."[8]

At first glance it seems that philosophical behaviorism solves both the other-minds problem and the mind-body problem. But of course it can do this only if it is true. So let us examine the position to see whether it can withstand scrutiny, beginning with the crudest formulation of the view.

4.1 The Crudest Form of Behaviorism

The crudest behaviorism identifies the mental phenomenon with a piece of actual behavior. Such behaviorists are rare, but Skinner sometimes talks like one; he seems not to like disposition terms. For example, he writes, "When we say, 'I have an idea; let's try the rear door; it may be unlocked,' what is 'had' is the behavior of trying the rear door."[9] Analytically, "Joe loves Mary Lu," in this view, might be thought to be equivalent to "his knees go knockitty-knock" or "Joe necks with Mary Lu during prime viewing time." Or anger might be said to consist in banging your fist on the table, or to consist in a piece of verbal behavior, for example, the utterance of the words "I'm angry."

As mentioned, one apparent advantage of this position is that it seems to solve the other-minds problem. Certainly, if "Jones is in pain" means "Jones goes through a series of movements, for example, groans, cries," then the question whether Jones is in pain is testable. It becomes public. We just look to see whether Jones is groaning or crying.

It also seems to solve—or, better, dissolve—the mind-body problem. Emotions, sensations, beliefs, and desires—and everything else mental— are actions of organisms. We no longer have the problem of relating mental entities, or a thing called the mind, to another thing called the body.

We quickly see, however, that the sort of behaviorism we are considering will not survive even a cursory examination. For example, we might find out later that even though Jones said he was angry or in pain, he was faking it—he might tell us so himself. In which case he was not in pain or was not angry. So the behavior is not sufficient. Nor is it necessary: he may be angry or in pain, but not tell anybody about it.

Suppose we try to remedy this by bringing in future actions. We say "Leslie understands how to continue the series" means "Leslie continues the series now or she continues the series later." But somebody can understand how to continue the series without ever doing it. A brick might fall on her head, and so when she was about to continue, she could not. Again, Leslie may never attempt to do it, even though she could. Maybe Leslie does not care to, it does not interest her. In short, this condition is not necessary. Nor again is it sufficient, since Leslie may continue the series as a result of hypnosis, and not really know how to do it. Let us turn, then, to the most tempting form of behaviorism.

4.2 Why Dispositional Behaviorism Is Untenable

The dispositional form of behaviorism holds that A is angry if, and only if, A is an organism that *would* foam at the mouth, gnash his teeth, pound his fist on the table, etc., in such and such circumstances. Or, "I want to get warm," means "If I were able to move into a warm place, I would."[10] In both instances the individual is said to possess a disposition to behave or to act in a given manner. Will these analyses do?

Let us begin by considering two questionable criticisms of the sophisticated or the dispositional form of philosophical behaviorism. Then we shall examine three criticisms that point out fundamental flaws in the doctrine.

4.2.1 A Quinean Objection

As we have seen, behaviorism in both its crude and more sophisticated dispositional form appeals to the notions of words having meaning and of some statements being true by definition, or true due to the meanings of the words of which they are composed. Such statements are said to be analytically true. Quine argues that both these notions of meaning and of analyticity are obscure.[11] So he is committed to holding that logical or philosophical behaviorism is an unclear position. In his view, there can be no clear distinction between the behaviorist's statements' being true by virtue of the meaning of the terms used and the statements' simply being true as a matter of fact. Further, Quine believes that subjunctive conditionals and dispositional statements are also unclear. Dispositionals assert that certain things have a disposition (tendency, propensity, bent, inclination) to behave in a certain way. For example, "The window has a disposition to fracture," "Joe has a tendency to lose his temper." We might naturally explain what these statements mean in terms of subjunctive conditionals, which are special hypotheticals—things of the form "If . . . then . . ."—in which the hypotheses or antecedents are meant to be false. For example, "If the window were hit lightly, it would break into pieces," "If Joe had heard that Bob disagreed with him, he would be very angry." Quine thinks subjunctive conditionals and dispositional statements are unclear because we explain the latter in terms of the former and we cannot give a truth-functional account of subjunctive conditionals, unlike "ordinary" if-then statements.[12]

He is right on both of the last claims, but it doesn't follow that that makes subjunctive conditionals and dispositional talk, and hence the dispositional form of behaviorism, unclear. These notions are said to be unclear and problematic only because Quine insists that we be able to give truth conditions for clear concepts. Apparently this is an assumption many logicians, especially Quineans, make. It has the consequence that most of our everyday concepts must be judged to be unclear, which amounts to a reductio ad absurdum of the assumption. The Quinean objection seems to rest on a restrictive, stipulative, and dubious definition of clarity. Dispositional behaviorism is not by its nature obscure—if we use the words "clear" and "obscure" as they are normally used—just because it makes essential use of dispositions and subjunctive conditionals. Nor is the notion of "meaning" unclear. We grasp the meaning of "meaning," according to Wittgenstein, when we grasp how the word is used in our language. So the Quinean objection by itself does not refute dispositional behaviorism. Let us turn next to another dubious objection to behaviorism. This one seems to be directed towards both the crude and the dispositional versions of behaviorism, and it is made by a famous Wittgensteinian.

4.2.2 Malcolm's Grammatical Objection

Norman Malcolm maintains that philosophical behaviorism is incompatible with a fundamental grammatical fact, namely, the asymmetry between the first-person singular and the second- and third-person use of psychological verbs in the present tense.[13] He bases this criticism of behaviorism on the following observation by Wittgenstein: "Psychological verbs [are] characterized by the fact that the third person of the present is to be verified by observation, the first person not" (Z, §472). I think Wittgenstein means that, normally at least, you do not say things like "I am afraid" or "I am angry" on the basis of having observed your behavior or by discovering that you are disposed to behave in such and such a way. Malcolm thinks that this implies two things. First, that "fear" does not refer to behavior or even to a pattern of behavior or to a disposition to behave in certain ways. Second, if an emotion did consist in behavior and/or a disposition to behave in such and such a way, or in a pattern of behavior, then you ought to be able to observe your own grief or anger. But Malcolm thinks this would be absurd. I agree it would be absurd to say you observe your own grief or anger. As Wittgenstein asks, "Which senses do you use to observe it? A particular sense; one that *feels* grief? Then do you feel it *differently* when you are observing it? And what is the grief that you are observing— is it one which is there only while it is being observed?" (PI, p. 187).

I believe Wittgenstein also wants to make another point in section 472 of *Zettel*. Not only do you not say, "I'm feeling lousy today," on the basis of observation, but normally you do not verify these first-person singular present-tense psychological reports. He makes this point explicitly in his lectures entitled "Philosophical Psychology": "The third person is 'verified by observation'; the first person is not verified; you do not find out what you wish, remember, believe, etc., by observing yourself." He repeats: "A characteristic of first person singular verbs (psychological ones) is that they are not based on observation; third person singular verbs are."[14]

In lectures, G. E. M. Anscombe once put Wittgenstein's view this way: The first-person use of psychological verbs is nondiagnostic, nonhypothetical, whereas the second– and third-person use is diagnostic, or involves hypotheses.[15] She hastened to qualify that she does not mean by this that the third-person use must be the fruit of inquiry or the result of any kind of skilled inquiry. It does not take the skills of a Sherlock Holmes to infer that someone hit by a car, who is bleeding and writhing, is in pain. Nevertheless, you tell *by something*. In such cases we can ask: "How do you tell? How do you know?" These questions are not normally excluded, whereas they normally are in the first-person use. Here you do not (typically) tell— that is, in your own case—that you are angry, afraid, or believe something or other. You just answer straight off that you do, or are, or are not, and without deriving a conclusion based on an inference. Talking about the sensation of pain, Wittgenstein says you do not identify your own pain by criteria; rather, you "repeat an expression" (PI, §290), that is, you say you're in pain or that it hurts. Nor do you make this utterance on the basis of having heard your own screams and groans. The question how do you know is out of order. It is out of order to ask, By what do you notice your pain? Nothing tells you that you are in pain, unless you want to say it's the pain that does. But that would be like saying, "It hurts because it hurts"!

I think a better way of speaking of Wittgenstein's distinction is to say that the second– and third-person use is evidential or, even better, criteriological, in contrast to the first-person use. This is less misleading. For the first-person use is, in a sense, not governed by criteria, unlike the other. Alternatively, there is no rule for the first-person use. This does not mean, however, that you may never appeal to evidence in your own case. For example, after looking in the mirror and remembering your outburst, you may concede that you were indeed angry, and that you have rather mixed feelings about Harry. A self-observant wife may gradually come to see, on the basis of the evidence, that she finds her husband boring. Moreover, recognition of this grammatical distinction does not imply that you can never be mistaken when giving first-person psychological reports in the present tense. We have in no way vindicated Descartes's conception of cogito judgments—psychological judgments in the present tense—as incorrigible or beyond correction.

Let us return now to Malcolm's criticism of behaviorism. Is he right in supposing that this grammatical asymmetry in *psychological* statements can be used to refute the behaviorist? I think not. For there is also an asymmetry—as Wittgenstein, Ziff, and Anscombe all notice—between statements in the first-person present tense and those in third-person present tense *about behavior.* Take the case of moving your arm. You do not normally tell by anything or, in particular, by observation, that you are moving your arm; yet this is how you normally tell that someone else is moving his or her arm. It does not follow from the behaviorist position that you cannot know in your own case whether you're having a certain emotion unless you observe yourself or that you tell by something that you are. Normally I know that I am A-ing (doing whatever I'm doing)—for example, behaving in an angry way—nonobservationally, and, indeed, I do not tell that I am by anything at all.

But how you tell what you are doing or what something is—that you are moving your arm, that something is water—is one thing. What it means to do it or to be a particular sort of thing—to move your arm, for something to be water—is not necessarily the same. Malcolm's objection overlooks this distinction. The meaning of the predicate "is angry" is the same whether I apply it to myself or you apply it to me. So what you say when you say I am angry and what I say when I say of myself that I am angry are the same, in spite of the fact that how you tell that I am, and how I tell that I am, may be different. Meaning is not equal to method of verification.

The next three criticisms, which are essentially Wittgensteinian in character, point out fundamental flaws in the doctrine, unlike the first two objections. I do not see how the philosophical behaviorist can satisfactorily answer them.

4.2.3 Behaviorism Disregards Context, Intentions, Desires

We can see that behaviorism does not pay enough attention to context in the above account of anger, in which being angry was said to consist in people being disposed either to foam at the mouth, to gnash their teeth, to pound their fists on the table, to scream incoherently, to stamp their feet, or to say or to report that they are angry, trembling all over, hands clenched, eyes ablaze, in such and such circumstances. It seems that one, several, or even all of these disjunctions may be true, and yet the person may not be angry. The person may be acting in a play, may just have taken a powerful drug, may be cheering at a football game, having an epileptic fit, be in love, want attention, be writhing because in the throes of laughter, or merely be pretending to be angry. Again, people may gnash their teeth not in anger, but to exercise their gums, because they are filing their nails, or because they are in pain or afraid. These disjunctions are not therefore sufficient.

Nor are they necessary, since someone may be angry without any of these disjuncts being true. He may, for example, be just sitting in a chair looking thoughtfully at the ceiling as he thinks of that damn kid of his and how he wrecked the family car. The same points seem to hold for other psychological notions. Of pain, for example, Shaffer says, "one can imagine a pain so slight or paralyzingly great that there is no disposition to behave; and one can imagine stoics who have so trained themselves that they have exterminated any such dispositions."[16] The disposition to express pain may have been effectively exterminated or suppressed into nonexistence because of a more powerful contrary inclination not to express it.

No doubt it is because of considerations such as these that Wittgenstein says: " 'But you will surely admit that there is a difference between pain-behavior accompanied by pain and pain-behavior without any pain?' —Admit it? What greater difference could there be?" (PI, §304). He also says, "And of course joy is not joyful behavior" (Z, §487). In short, we should confuse neither joyful nor painful behavior with either joy or pain as the behaviorist does. Malcolm observes, "A young woman's joyous exclamations, movements, smile, would not be manifestations of joy if they occurred in quite different circumstances. Instead they could belong to a bitter parody of joy; or they could be symptoms of madness."[17]

A behaviorist may reply that it is indeed important to bring in such contextual considerations, but that this can be done. What the criticism shows is that the analysis must bring in multitracked dispositions that mention both positive and negative circumstances. For example, we say: X is angry if, and only if, X does the sort of things mentioned above when not acting in a play, cheering at a football game, having an epileptic fit, pretending to be angry, or doing it to get attention. Baring your teeth is only relevant to anger if you are not in the bathroom, preparing to clean your teeth. But can the behaviorist bring in all of the relevant contextual considerations?

4.2.4 Behaviorism Fails to Account for Psychological Notions

Behaviorist theory cannot provide us with necessary or sufficient conditions of pain, love, anger, joy, and so forth. We can get sufficient conditions of these things only if we make the account circular. For example, we say something like, "if Mary sincerely says she is in pain, then she is in pain." If you understand what you are saying and you sincerely (truthfully) say you are in pain, you certainly are in pain! Here truth is guaranteed by the special criterion of truthfulness, since a person can't be in error about being in pain (PI, §288). Similar difficulties arise for the behaviorist statement, "if people are not inhibited, restrained, and so forth, and if they would be inclined to jump or shout *for* joy—but not because they are pricked by an ice pick—then they would be joyful." Ziff gives still another example of a circular account of anger.[18] Thus his form of behaviorism, when true, lacks content because it is circular.[19] The position, in effect, seems to be: "People are angry if, and only if, they behave in certain ways." Suppose we ask, "In what ways?" The answer is, "In angry ways." But what ways are these? Again, we get the reply: "These are the ways people behave when they are angry." The doctrine is saved by draining it of any content. Yet when we give it content, it becomes false. It is all very well for the behaviorist to talk about bringing in contextual considerations, but it seems to be impossible to bring in all possible relevant positive and negative circumstances and conditions. It is wildly implausible to think that anyone can. Certainly no one ever has done it. The behaviorist may reply: "But couldn't we get a better and better account each time one formulation was refuted? All we would have to do would be to include in our modified formulation those relevant considerations we initially failed to mention."

Churchland observes: "The list of conditionals necessary for an adequate analysis of 'wants a Caribbean holiday,' for example, [seems] not just to be long, but to be indefinitely or even infinitely long, with no finite way of specifying the elements to be included. And no term can be well-defined whose *definiens* is open-ended and unspecific in this way."[20] Admittedly, this objection is not a knock-down argument. It is hardly a proof of the sort you get in geometry or logic. As Hume points out, a finite number of confirming instances does not establish (logically) a universal generalization. Still, it is undeniable that every attempted behavioristic reduction has been a failure. The burden of proof is thus on the behaviorists to establish their positive doctrine, and it seems unlikely that they ever will be able to do it. As Churchland concludes: "Behaviorists were unable to state the necessary and sufficient *behavioral* conditions for the application of even a single psychological term."[21] Until they do this for at least one psychological term, we can reject the position as wildly implausible.

4.2.5 The Necessity of Mentalistic and Psychological Terms

The previous criticisms—because of their reference to intentions, wants, beliefs, desires, etc.—already seem to acknowledge that we need mentalistic or psychological terms in the behavioristic reduction. For example, we have to say, "If Mary is interested in doing it and not restrained, if she understands what it is to do such an act, if she does not intend to deceive someone, and so on, then she would do it." Ryle's account of laziness also cannot dispense with the psychological notions of sensations and feelings. He says: "To be in a lazy mood is, among other things, to tend to have sensations of lassitude in the limbs when jobs have to be done, to have cozy feelings of relaxation when the deck-chair is resumed, not to have electric feelings when the game begins, and so forth."[22] Some of the mentalistic terms used by behaviorists here, among others, are: "intends," "is interested in," "understands," and "has cozy feelings." If these terms were left out of the behavioristic accounts, the analyses would have no plausibility whatsoever.

Most behaviorists acknowledge that actions themselves are not reducible to mere physical movements. Motionists think actions are nothing but physical movements.[23] Actions involve the notions of intentions, purposes, motives, etc. Hamlyn and Ziff admit that human behavior is not just a series of human movements. So we cannot let "behavior" here stand for just any movement of an organism. If we did, it could be a physiological process, for example, the heart's pulsation. So behaviorism interpreted as a form of motionism must be abandoned.

These two concessions should make us question, however, whether behaviorism really does solve the other-minds problem, since we already have to know how to ascribe psychological and mentalistic terms to find out whether the right hand side of the if, and only if, statement is true; that is, we have to be able to check whether the person was *interested* in doing A, whether he or she was *bored*, had such and such feelings and sensations, and so on. In short, the behaviorist's equation is not really reductionist, it only appears to be. The mental or psychological has not really been replaced by the purely behavioral or nonmental. We grant too much to behaviorism if we believe it either solves or dissolves the other-minds problem. It does neither. So it doesn't even have the one big advantage it at first seemed to have. Behaviorism simply assumes that there is no other-minds problem, for if there were, we couldn't make sense of the analyses it recommends.

It is also doubtful whether it solves, or dissolves, the mind-body problem. It attempts to dissolve the problem by showing that there really are not two different sorts of things to relate to one another—minds and bodies. It tries to establish this by explaining away the mental or psychological, by reducing it to something physical—namely, to the purely physical behavior of an organism or to the disposition of an organism to behave in certain overt ways. Since behaviorism fails to carry out this reduction, it fails to dissolve the problem.

To summarize, behaviorism seemed at first to have two advantages. It seemed to take care of both the problem of other minds and the mind-body problem. We have found this to be an illusion. It no more succeeds in solving or dissolving either of these problems than it succeeds in carrying out its reductionistic analyses.

Behaviorism is right about one thing, however: that it is on the basis of behavior and facial expressions that we ascribe psychological predicates to other people. How else could we know what they think and feel, intend or desire? Quasi-behaviorism, or the criteriological view—which is really Wittgenstein's position[24]—preserves this truth of philosophical behaviorism, but without proposing the oversimplified or empty account behaviorists give of psychological concepts.

The big mistake of behaviorism, Wittgenstein would probably say, is that it misunderstands the nature of language. It imagines it to be simpler and neater than it is. It overlooks the fact that many—perhaps even most—

empirical concepts are family-resemblance or, to use Waismann's expression "open textured" concepts.[25] What Waismann means by "open textured" is that we want the terms of our language to be applicable to new situations, yet we cannot foresee completely all possible conditions in which they will be used. Behaviorism assumes we can do this. It does not look to see how psychological words are actually used. Like so many philosophical views it prejudges the question, oversimplifying reality. The same is true of other philosophical positions, for example, phenomenalism, or the view that tries to reduce physical-object talk to sense-data talk. There is every reason to think that most—maybe even all—psychological concepts are family-resemblance concepts.[26] That is, they cannot be analyzed in terms of necessary and sufficient conditions. It should therefore come as no surprise that the behaviorist cannot define them in purely behavioral terms.

Russell's theory of descriptions[27] was the model of philosophy for phenomenalists, behaviorists, and nominalists (the last wanted to get rid of talk of properties and groups). But all these twentieth-century attempts at reductionism have been failures.

In the next chapter we shall examine another materialist theory—the mind-brain identity theory—to see whether it gives a more satisfactory account of these matters. The mind-brain identity view was developed in part because of certain dissatisfactions philosophers had with philosophical behaviorism.

Chapter 5

The Mind-Brain Identity Theory

The identity theory, already crudely formulated in the writings of Thomas Hobbes, a contemporary of Descartes, predates behaviorism by several centuries. Anticipations of it can even be found among the ancient Greeks, who located the heart as the center of the mind. In the twentieth century, Herbert Feigl, U. T. Place, J. J. C. Smart, D. M. Armstrong, and Anthony Quinton all propounded a specifically mind-brain identity theory.

5.1 Place, Early Smart, and Quinton

It is useful to draw a distinction between what might be called the *identity thesis* and the *identity theory*.[1] The identity thesis is that consciousness is identical with a process or state in the brain. In other words, the identity thesis makes an identity claim, it says that two things, *a* and *b*, are identical, that is, are really one thing. Claims of this sort are true only if *a* and *b* have all of the same properties. The mind-brain identity theory is that the identity thesis that consciousness is identical with a process or state in the brain is "a reasonable scientific hypothesis, not to be dismissed on logical grounds alone,"[2] that is, because it involves any inconsistency or incoherence. The philosophical issue is whether this last assertion is correct—that is, whether the identity thesis can or cannot be dismissed on merely logical or conceptual grounds, by examining and analyzing the meaning of the key terms involved.

At the beginning of his discussion, Place asserts "there can be little doubt . . . that an analysis [of cognitive concepts like knowing, believing, understanding, remembering, and of certain volitional concepts like wanting and intending] in terms of dispositions to behave is fundamentally sound." But we need, he thinks, "some sort of inner process story" for pains, for twinges, for how things look and sound and feel, for things dreamed of and pictured in the mind's eye, for experiences and sensations.[3]

In 1959, three years after Place's article, Smart defends a similarly mixed position.[4] While we may not agree with Place and Smart in their acceptance of a behavioral analysis of these cognitive and volitional concepts, it does seem there really is a distinction here between cognitive and volitional concepts, on the one hand, and the experiential sort of concepts mentioned, on the other hand. Ryle draws a similar distinction in his *Concept of Mind*.[5]

Quinton wants to identify all mental states—anger, pain, sensations and emotions, as well as thoughts—with states or processes in the brain.[6] But he does not advance this version of materialism as one that is logically necessary. On the contrary, he says it is "a very general *contingent* or *empirical theory* about the nature of mental entities."[7] The qualifier "contingent" says that the theory—or what I would call the identity thesis—is possibly but not necessarily true. "Empirical" adds that its truth value is founded on experience or observation.

Place, too, thinks the identity thesis is a contingent, scientific statement, one that may or may not be true. It is like the statement that a cloud is a mass of tiny particles and nothing else or that lightning is a motion of electric charges. Opponents as well as supporters of identity theory would agree that these last two statements are true even though "there is no logical connection in our language between a cloud and a mass of tiny particles [or between lightning and a motion of electric charges]." As Place says,

> there is nothing self-contradictory in talking about a cloud [or lightning] which is not composed of tiny particles in suspension [or that is not a motion of electric charges]. . . . It is clear from this that the terms 'cloud' [and 'lightning'] and [the expressions] 'mass of tiny particles in suspension' [and 'a motion of electric charges'] mean quite different things.[8]

Yet we do not conclude from this that there must be four things, the mass of particles in suspension, which is different from the cloud, and a motion of electric charges, which is different from the lightning. In other words, terms that differ in sense (intension, meaning) may nevertheless have the same reference (extension, denotation). For example, "The first Roman Catholic president of the USA" and "the thirty-fifth president of the USA" both refer to the same individual—John F. Kennedy—even though they are not synonymous terms.

That sensations are identical with brain processes, then, is not a linguistic or conceptual claim. Smart, like other identity theorists, emphasizes this. "It follows that the thesis does not claim that sensation statements can be *translated* into statements about brain processes."[9] Whether the thesis is true or not is to be settled empirically, according to him. Smart also follows

Place in using the lightning example as an instance of the type of identity that he is saying *might* exist between sensations and brain processes.

Place remarks that "lightning is a motion of electric charges" is more like "consciousness is a brain process" than it is like "a cloud is a mass of tiny particles and nothing else," because you can observe a mass of water droplets if you are close enough, but you cannot observe the electric charges, at least in any direct way, any more than you can directly observe the consciousness.[10] Nevertheless, we accept the statement about lightning; so the statement about consciousness being a brain process may also be true. We cannot dismiss it a priori, on purely logical grounds. Why do we think the statement about lightning is a true identity statement? Place answers: "We conclude that lightning is nothing more than a motion of electric charges, because we know that a motion of electric charges through the atmosphere, such as occurs when lightning is reported, gives rise to the type of visual stimulation which would lead an observer to report a flash of lightning."[11] In short, it has been established empirically.

Smart, Place, Quinton, and the other identity theorists adopt their view in part because they think that if they do not, sensations, pains, etc., will remain mysterious mental entities and they will not be able to solve the mind-body or the other-minds problem. Quinton tries to show that his form of materialism, unlike dualism and behaviorism, solves not only the epistemological problem of other minds and the problem of mind-body causation, but also the problem of explaining the unity of the mind. "If mental states are identified with brain states the problem of the mind's unity is solved, for this unity is traced to that of an ordinarily identifiable material thing, the brain." And it solves the causal difficulty, for a piece of behavior on this theory has only one cause—namely, a condition of the brain. Finally, since brain states are in principle accessible, we have no insurmountable difficulty with the other-minds problem.[12]

Let us summarize the identity theory in Quinton's pure form, that is, unmixed with behaviorism. The theory is that:

1. Mental entities are contingently or empirically identical with brain states or processes. So the claim that they are identical should be confirmable or disconfirmable by empirical investigation. (The next four propositions follow from the identity thesis.)
2. Mental entities are located contingently in the brain. For example, "the anger that makes me shake my fist is located in the brain."[13] (The location objection tries to refute this claim.)
3. Brains have thoughts, sensations, emotions, and the like.

4. Mental entities, being brain states or brain processes, are in principle capable of being observed by everyone.
5. Since mental entities are physical states or events, it is in principle possible to be mistaken about them, even when they are your own. (The privacy objection denies that this is true of all mental entities.)
6. Mental entities, or brain states or events, cause our behavior.
7. It follows that behavior and facial expressions have no criteriological, or conceptual, connection with such mental entities, for these "outer" things have merely a causal connection with the mental entities. For example, typical angry behavior is not connected in meaning with anger; it is just the effect of anger.

Most of these statements will be criticized in the discussion that follows. Five Wittgensteinian objections will be considered, beginning with a criticism of claim number 2.

5.2 The Location Objection

The location criticism of identity theory derives from Wittgenstein. He implies, for example, that an emotion cannot be identical with a physiological occurrence. For if it were, it would be correct to ask, "Where do you feel grief?" or "Where, in general, do people feel grief?" Or love or hate? Wittgenstein says:

"I feel great joy." —Where? —That sounds like nonsense. And yet one does say "I feel a joyful agitation in my breast." —But why is joy not localized? Is it because it is distributed over the whole body? Even where the feeling that arouses joy is localized, joy is not: if for example we rejoice in the smell of a flower. —Joy is manifested in facial expression, in behavior. (But we do not say that we are joyful in our faces.) (Z, §486)

The main point here is that it makes no sense to localize joy or grief, but not because they are distributed over the whole body, as some feelings of physical well-being are. Nor is it that they are spread over several places in the body, as we might say the United States is spread over parts of the northern hemisphere. Could joy or grief be five centimeters from the tip of your nose, or in part there and another part of it near the elbow? This sounds like nonsense. Even if you say, "I feel it in the bottom of my heart, or in my soul," this is not to give it a location. No one thinks because you say this that if your heart were opened—literally—we would find joy or grief there. Similarly, "My head is bursting with excitement!" is a metaphor. It implies nothing about something being literally in your head. When textbooks and the press speak about the frontal lobes being the locus of reasoning, they just are pointing out that reasoning depends causally on that portion of the brain. Thus if it were destroyed, you would no longer be capable of analytical thinking.

Characteristically, Wittgenstein is reminding us about the way we do and do not talk of joy, love, and grief. He is directing our attention to obvious facts about our language that the identity theorist seems to overlook or misinterpret. The same points hold for desires, thoughts, moods, and emotions generally. But then these things cannot be physiological processes or brain events, for they are not in principle localizable, unlike physical processes.

Compare this other passage:

"Where do you feel grief?" —In the mind. —What kind of consequences do we draw from this assignment of place? One is that we do *not* speak of a bodily place of grief. Yet we *do* point to our body, as if the grief were in it. Is that because we feel a bodily discomfort? I do not know the cause. But why should I assume it is a bodily discomfort? (Z, §497)

Again, Wittgenstein seems to be implying that because it makes no sense to localize the emotion of grief, whereas bodily discomfort, as well as physiological occurrences and neural processes do have bodily place, they cannot be the same. Moreover, the fact that we do point to our body, as if the grief were in it, does not imply that the grief is localizable. We may be able to explain this on the grounds that it is the person who has the grief, and persons have a spatial location.[14]

The Wittgensteinian argument might be put this way. Psychological and physical process terms have incompatible senses or intensions, like "Michael Dukakis's wife on election day" and "Iris Murdoch's husband on election day." Being a wife rules out (conceptually or logically) being a husband, and vice versa. So we know prior to doing any empirical research that Michael Dukakis's wife on election day, if he had one then, must have been a female, and Iris Murdoch's husband on election day, if she had one then, must have been a male. Assuming you cannot be a male and a female at one and the same time, the person who was then Iris Murdoch's husband could not have been the person who was then Michael Dukakis's wife. As Leibniz notes, if *a* has a property that *b* lacks, then *a* is not identical with *b*. Now if *a* is a physical event and *b* is an emotion, *a* will have the property of occurring somewhere, unlike *b*. Hence *a* will not be identical with *b* (by *modus ponens*). So the identity thesis involving emotions is not comparable to lightning = an electrical discharge, or water = H_2O, for the last two sets of terms are compatible, unlike the emotion and the physical event terms.

Notice that the main point here has to do with localizability. Physiological occurrences and neural processes have a bodily place, but it makes no sense to say this of joy, grief, sadness, or thoughts. Since physical processes have a property that these psychological entities lack—spatial location—they cannot be identical with each other. The claim here is not that different senses imply different referents, only that incompatible senses imply different referents. Thus the vice president of the United States and the officer presiding over the United States Senate may be, and in fact are, identical, even though Michael Dukakis's present wife and Iris Murdoch's present husband are not—and cannot be—identical. So considering the linguistic meaning of psychological and physical terms is definitely relevant to assessing identity theory. None of this is meant to deny that physical events, in this case neural or brain events, might be the *cause* or *source* of mental events. This is another issue entirely. My concern here is only with the purported identity of these two unlike entities.

Smart himself alludes to the location criticism. He objects that after-images, unlike brain processes, are not in physical space. The conclusion of this argument is that "the after-image is not a brain-process."[15] We shall consider his reply to the location objection later. For the time being let us see how Malcolm develops the argument.

5.2.1 Malcolm's Formulation of the Location Objection

Malcolm gives a nice, explicit formulation of Wittgenstein's location objection. He uses it to refute Smart's view that our "immediate" or "inner" experiences takes place "inside our skulls" on the basis of these considerations of location. The logic of his argument is simple. First, he lets *p* be Smart's identity thesis. Then he tries to show that *p* implies *q*. Finally, he attempts to convince us that *not-q*. Therefore, *not-p* (by *modus tollens*). Here is his reductio of Smart's identity thesis in outline.[16]

1. Smart maintains there is a strict contingent identity (comparable to lightning is a certain kind of electrical discharge) between sudden thoughts and/or sensations, on the one hand, and brain processes, on the other.
2. If you claim that an identity is contingent and empirical, it should be provable or disprovable by empirical investigation. (This is by definition of "contingent" and "empirical.")
3. It is a necessary condition that if x and y are identical, if x occurs in a certain place at a certain time, then y occurs in the same place at the same time. (This follows from Leibniz's law, sometimes called the principle of the indiscernibility of identicals.)
4. A brain process occurs at a certain time in a certain location (inside the skull). This is something that can be determined empirically. There is no logically independent method of determining that a thought is located inside the skull. Indeed, the notion of a bodily location of thinking does not have any meaning at present.[17] (The latter claim is alleged to be a linguistic fact.)
5. So the necessary condition for strict identity cannot be satisfied if x is a brain process and y is a sudden thought.
6. Bodily sensations are located where they are felt to be.
7. They are never felt to be in the brain; so they are never located in the brain. (This is a fact.)
8. Hence bodily sensations are not brain processes either (p. 69).
9. So Smart's thesis is either false or meaningless, at least as applied to sudden thoughts and bodily sensations.[18]

Malcolm might also have concluded that Smart's thesis is not an empirical thesis, at least applied to thoughts, beliefs, and emotions, since there is no empirical and independent method of verifying that a thought, belief, or emotion is located inside the skull. We can locate a process in the brain, but we have no idea how to find or locate in space, much less in the brain, someone's belief or sadness; so we cannot discover that it is located in the very same place some brain process is located. Thus the alleged identities cannot be established empirically. Contrast the case of lightning, which is empirically identifiable at a specific place. We can verify its presence by seeing or photographing it. But we cannot observe the electric charges with the naked eye. Their presence is detected in other ways. Benjamin Franklin, the first to prove the identity of lightning and electricity (1752), used a pointed iron rod and a kite during a thunderstorm to draw off its charges. He independently verified that the electric discharge occurs at the exact same place and time as the lightning.

Note that Malcolm's refutation of Smart's view that bodily sensations and sudden thoughts are contingently identical with brain processes depends on the premise that bodily location of thinking does not now have any meaning. Some may object that this is not true, others that it is irrelevant even if true. Essentially the same argument could be developed to show that afterimages and many other psychological things cannot be identical with brain processes.

Smart gives two replies to the location objection. First, he says that he is talking about the experience of a sensation, pain, afterimage, not the sensation, pain, afterimage as such. The experience of an afterimage, for example, is not an afterimage; so the argument does not refute identity theory in these cases. But this reply is an evasion. The same objection applies to experiences: they cannot be identical with brain processes either because they are not located where brain processes are.[19]

Smart's second answer is that ordinary language either ascribes no place to conscious states or leaves open what place they are in and whether they are in any place.[20] According to Smart, if ordinary language leaves it open what place conscious states are in or whether they are in any place, all we have to do is to change ordinary language to bring it in line with the identity thesis. Smart says that such a change in the language "would be a very simple and painless one, involving hardly any readjustments to the rest of language."[21] Presumably we would just add a convention giving location to conscious states. But "conventions" are not something that we can simply "add on" at will. They do not come into existence at our bidding.

Let us suppose, however, that this is not a problem and we succeed in adding a linguistic convention giving conscious states a location or locatability. Locatability does not imply that conscious states will be in the brain. Pins are always in a place but they are rarely found to be in brains. Suppose next that we used a brain event, or some physiological condition, as a criterion of the occurrence of a sudden thought. Then, Malcolm says, the identity of a sudden thought and a brain process would no longer be a contingent thesis. "In order to keep the alleged identity purely contingent, and its verification purely empirical, one would need to have a procedure of verifying the occurrence of a thought inside the skull which was *not* conceived of as consisting in the verification of the occurrence of *some* [my italics] physical process inside the skull."[22]

Malcolm's claim, as stated, does not seem to be correct. To see this, suppose that the identity thesis is that the occurrence of a sudden thought = the firing of C-fibers in the brain and that we use some other brain event, or some physiological condition P, as a criterion of the firing of the C-fibers. The identity thesis doesn't thereby cease to be a contingent and an empirical thesis. It still could be either true or false and the thesis would still presumably be based on empirical evidence. Probably what Malcolm means is that the identity theorist cannot make the firing of C-fibers in the brain the criterion of the identity thesis, because then the thesis would cease to be contingent. For then he would have made it a matter of convention that having a sudden thought = the firing of C-fibers. In short, if Smart devises a linguistic convention that makes sudden thoughts intensionally as well as extensionally equivalent to brain processes, he will avoid the location objection, but only by making the thesis a necessary truth, contradicting his original claim. Malcolm is right about this.

5.2.2 Quinton's Reply to the Location Objection

Quinton is well aware of the location problem. It is the first objection he considers to his theory that brain and mind are, as a matter of contingent fact, identical.[23] He is aware that the claim that some mental entities have no spatial location directly contradicts his view that mental entities are located contingently in the brain (see the second claim in the summary of his identity theory, Section 5.1).

Quinton's initial reply is that mental entities must be spatial at least in the weak sense of being "where the people who are their owners or bearers are, that is, where their owners' bodies are."[24] He seems to be thinking of mental entities as comparable to bodily organs. Thus you might say that your liver is, in a weak sense, where you are. But, of course, livers do have a location, and (normally) that will be some place inside your body; so to know where you are is already to know, roughly, where your liver is. One of the things at issue, however, is whether mental entities are always like livers in having some sort of location. We cannot assume that an angry man's anger, like his organs, must be where he is. We have already seen that it makes no sense to talk of where we feel grief, where our thoughts are, and so on, for many psychological things.

Second, Quinton's initial reply can be faulted for not really answering the question. The query was not whether we can locate people who have emotions, pains, thoughts, etc., but whether we can locate these mental entities, and if so, whether they are ever found to be in the brain. Saying where the grieving widow is gets us no closer to assigning her grief a spatial location. We must not confuse the everyday inquiry, "Where is the person who has such and such an emotion or thought?" with the purely philosophical one—one that is only pursued in philosophy classrooms and studies—"Where is such and such an emotion or thought?" Quinton says the second question may be given his answer: it is where the person is who has it; or, alternatively, the dualist answer of Descartes and Hume: nowhere.[25] But there is also a third response to the question Quinton overlooks. We could reject the question as senseless rather than try to answer it. That is the sort of reply the Wittgensteinian would give.

Quinton has two arguments for his view, however, that still need to be considered. First, he says they must have a spatial location, because otherwise we could not individuate them—could not, for example, distinguish my grief from yours:

> Suppose that two people, A and B, undergo qualitatively indistinguishable sensations that are strictly temporally coincident, beginning and leaving off at the very same moment. How are we to justify the belief, which we should certainly hold in these circumstances, that there are two sensations going on here and not just one?[26]

Wittgenstein could give at least two replies to this argument. First, he could point out that it is not necessary to assign spatial location to mental entities in order to individuate them. We have ways of individuating thoughts, emotions, sensations, and the like that make no appeal to their spatial location. The same is true of many other things. For example, colors, musical works, and shapes can be individuated even though none of these things have spatial location. It is as senseless to ask, "Where is the color very dark purplish red, Beethoven's Fifth Symphony, the shape of a diamond?" as it is to ask, "Where is your grief or thought?" Yet we do not confuse very dark purplish red with the color yellowish white, Beethoven's with Tchaikovsky's Fifth, or the shape of a diamond with the shape of a heart. We can also tell when people have the same or different thoughts about something. Usually it suffices to ask them what they think about it.

Second, I think Wittgenstein would say that if two people undergo qualitatively indistinguishable sensations, they are having one and the same sensation, not two numerically distinct sensations, as Quinton alleges. I wonder whether Quinton would hold, by parity of reasoning, that two vases cannot have one and the same shade of light blue, since each has its own color, even if the colors are indistinguishable. Wittgenstein shows in sections 253, 293, and 398 of the *Investigations* that we have criteria for determining sameness of feeling, and that these criteria do not involve spatial location. Going by them it would be natural and correct to say that Quinton's two people A and B are experiencing one and the same sensation, not two different sensations, though each is of course experiencing a sensation. While there is only one sensation, it is had by two people.[27] Quinton's idea that psychological phenomena must have a spatial location if they are to be individuated is merely an expression of his materialism. He reasons like Wittgenstein's materialistic interlocutor who says: " 'After all, you *feel* sadness—so you must feel it *somewhere*; otherwise it would be a chimera' " (Z, §510). This only follows assuming a materialistic position.

Quinton's second argument for saying that mental entities have spatial location is also unsuccessful. He maintains that we can locate smells by locating "odoriferous particles."[28] No doubt it is true that we can locate such particles. But this again misses the point, for the dispute is not over the question whether it is absurd to locate such particles. The question is rather whether it makes sense to locate all mental entities. Locating the "odiferous particles" does not locate the smell the particles have any more than locating the pin that sticks you locates the pain that you feel. Quinton's confusion is that he locates the cause of the mental event, not the mental event itself.

I conclude that both of these considerations fail to make his case, and that he confuses the real question, "Where is the man who feels sad?" with the unreal or senseless question, "Where is his sadness?" Assigning a spatial location to such things as thoughts, sadness, and the like, would be to distort the way we use these terms of cognition and emotion. The location objection undermines identity theory formulated in terms of brain events by showing that it is in conflict with these linguistic facts, and that even when this is not true (in the case of pains, itches, and sensations), the psychological occurrences still are not found to be in the brain.

However, there is one counter to the location objection that has a limited effectiveness. All it requires is a slight modification of the formulation of the theory. Instead of couching it in terms of brain events or brain states, the identity theorist should instead talk only of brain states, since it makes no sense to talk of the spatial location of a brain state either. It would only be such states that would be said to be contingently identical with the mental entities. Malcolm mentions this possible answer to the location problem in the preface of his book *Problems of Mind*.[29] Such a version of identity theory is discussed by Jaegwon Kim.[30] Since brain states are not located anywhere—for example, it makes no sense to ask, "Where is brain state B with molecular structure S?"—the location objection is ineffective against the identity thesis that contends that thoughts, beliefs, emotions, desires, moods, and experiences are identical with brain states. On the other hand, the move to talk about states will not save the identity claim that itches, pains, cramps, and sensations are identical with brain states, because these sorts of things are locatable. You can have a pain in your arm, an itch in your scalp, a cramp in your stomach. So these phenomena still cannot be identical with brain states. In short, the location objection succeeds in refuting all formulations of the theory in terms of brain processes and some formulations of the theory in terms of brain states when it concerns things that have a spatial location. We know a priori, then, that Quinton's sweeping claim that all mental entities are contingently or empirically identical with brain states or processes cannot be true.

I turn now to four additional reductio ad absurdum arguments against identity theory. Like the location objection they all begin by supposing the theory to be true, only to show that it couldn't be because its being true would have absurd consequences.

5.3 Mental Entities Observable by Everyone

The argument that mental entities will be literally observable by everyone can be seen as an extension of the Wittgensteinian location objection. If identity theory were true (the argument goes), we should be able, with the right equipment, to observe and record not only angry people and people in pain, but their anger and pains as well—saying, there they are! Ed McMahon on the Johnny Carson show could not only say, "Here's Johnny!" but also, "Here's Johnny's memory of his latest divorce trial!" as he points to some neurons firing in Johnny's brain; and he would want the two statements to be taken in the same sense. It should be possible in principle to observe and even to photograph everything psychological, for example, Jane's excitement at winning a scholarship and Joe's restlessness during a dull committee meeting. We might then exhibit pictures of these things. The photographs might look like abstract art, but they would be totally representational. Again, not only could we observe and photograph Tom Sawyer's sore toe, but we could also observe and photograph the soreness he feels in it. Curiously, we would do all of these things by focusing our eyes and cameras on neurological events, on what's going on inside people's brains. By doing this it would also be possible, at least in principle, to give children ostensive definitions of love, pain, sadness, irritation, and of other psychological notions by pointing to the relevant thing going on inside people's brains. Perhaps brain scans would be used to help us carry out these educational tasks.

It seems absurd, however, to say we can literally do any of these things. Identity theory is in conflict with the linguistic fact that we don't say such things as, "Look, there's Jane's belief that a Republican will be our next president," or, "There is her memory of her first kiss!" as we point to her C-fibers firing. Or if we do say something like this, we take it to be elliptical for, "There is the cause, source, or physical basis of her belief or memory." That is, we are only making a causal claim, saying that that belief or memory is causally dependent on that portion of the brain. Thus we empirically confirm our assertion by seeing what happens when we touch that part of the brain with a lightly charged electric wire. If it causes the patient to describe her belief or to recall her memory we are satisfied that our statement is true.

Wittgenstein suggests identity theorists are led astray here by their picture of the inner process as the psychological phenomenon. The identity theorist reasons like Wittgenstein's interlocutor who says, "But you surely cannot deny that, for example, in remembering, an inner process takes place." Wittgenstein counters:

> When one says "Still, an inner process does take place here"—one wants to go on: "After all, you *see* it." . . . —The impression that we wanted to deny something arises from our setting our faces against the picture of the 'inner process.' What we deny is that the picture of the inner process gives us the correct idea of the use of the word "to remember." We say that this picture with its ramifications stands in the way of our seeing the use of the word as it is. (PI, §305)

5.4 The Privacy Objection and Quinton's Reply

A third criticism Wittgenstein would make of identity theory concerns the question of corrigibility (Quinton's fifth claim). Since mental entities are said to be physical, it would in principle be possible, or at least it would always make sense, to be mistaken about your own mental states. Wittgenstein would agree that it is possible to be mistaken about some of your own mental states, for example, your emotions. But he denies that it makes sense to doubt or to be mistaken about your present pains.

> I can't be in error here; it means nothing to doubt whether I am in pain! —That means: if anyone said "I do not know if what I have got is a pain or something else," we should think something like, he does not know what the English word "pain" means. . . . If he now said . . . : "Oh, I know what 'pain' means; what I don't know is

whether *this,* that I have now, is pain"—we should merely shake our heads and be forced to regard his words as a queer reaction which we have no idea what to do with. . . . That expression of doubt has no place in the language-game. (PI, §288)

In short, if you claim to doubt or wonder whether you have a pain, you do not understand the word "pain." The contrapositive of this is: if you understand the word "pain," then you will not claim to doubt or to wonder whether you have a pain. So if you sincerely report you are in pain, you are. What is more, the pain will be the way you say it is. It will have the nature you sincerely ascribe to it. If you are insincere in your report of a sensation, what you say will of course not be true, but not because you made a mistake about it. Identity theory fails to recognize these linguistic facts. Some things can be said about some mental phenomena that cannot be said about brain events or brain states, and vice versa.

We might sum up the privacy objection with regard to pain and sensations this way:

1. First-person present-tense reports of pain and of sensations generally are incorrigible. (Notice this is not true of reports of emotions, beliefs, and thoughts. So the privacy objection would not work for emotions, beliefs, and thoughts.)
2. This is not true of brain processes or the usual cerebral correlate, for we could (logically) be mistaken about such a matter, for example, whether certain neurons fired. (The equipment used to determine what neurons fired in the brain might be faulty and give us an incorrect account. Or maybe we didn't attach the electrodes properly.)
3. Hence the presence of a pain is not the same thing as the usual brain process or cerebral correlate; so you might have one without the other.

Smart's initial reply is that if such a thing happened, the identity thesis would be false.[31] But he adds that the first premise of this argument is false. The first-person report and what is reported are two distinct occurrences; therefore, it is logically possible for one to occur without the other.[32] He is of course right that it is logically possible for one to occur—the pain or the report—without the other. But that does not show that first-person present-tense pain reports are corrigible—that is, that you can be mistaken about your own present pain.

Contrast the way the words "pain" and "car" function. You can doubt or wonder whether you are seeing a car, even if you fully understand the word "car." The light may be bad, so you may not be able to make out whether it is a car, a boat, or something else. Here it makes sense to make a mistake and to doubt. Sincerely reporting it is a car does not entail that it is; so you may doubt that it is a car. Similarly, you could say, I have a car, but I do not know whether it is mine or someone else's; perhaps it is Jones's, not mine. Yet you cannot say I have a pain, but I do not know whether it is mine. I wonder whether it is someone else's. These two examples show how differently the words "pain" and "car" function in our language.

Let us consider now how Quinton argues against the privacy objection. He counters it in two ways. One way is to give a general argument in support of the view that no statements of fact are incorrigible. He gives this argument in chapter 6, "Certainty." Second, he tries to give counterexamples, examples of cases in which we have a pain but make a mistake about it, and in which we imagine we are in acute pain when we are not. Let us consider these purported counterexamples first. Here is one of them.

> Suppose I am suffering from a toothache and someone tells me an extremely complicated and fascinating piece of gossip which entirely engrosses my attention for the duration of his narrative but at the end of which the pain once again secures my attention. Would it be natural to say here that his recital acted as an anaesthetic in the sense that it eliminated the pain for the period of its duration altogether?[33]

He thinks this would not be the natural thing to say. He prefers to say the pain is still there, but I am distracted from it, I am not aware of it.

Here we have an illustration of language going on a holiday (PI, §38). Quinton thinks you may have a severe toothache and it may not hurt. So you could say, "It hurt terribly but I didn't feel a thing." But this would be absurd. When we put his view in these blunt terms, the plain nonsense of his position is uncovered (PI, §119). If you don't feel a pain, you don't have it. *Esse est percipi*—to be is to be perceived—for pains. It does not matter what takes the pain away, whether it be a piece of hot gossip, hypnosis, or some more ordinary anesthetics. That is why some fundamentalists objected to the introduction of anesthetics for childbirth. They recognized that if you don't feel any pain, you don't have any pain, which seemed to go against God's proclamation to Eve, "In sorrow thou shalt bring forth children" (Genesis 3:16). Of course, it is true that something may take your mind off your pain, yet you may still feel pain. But if it is diminished, it's not the same pain, since it now hurts less.

Let us consider next his second sort of case. This is one in which a person imagines he or she is in acute pain, but is not. Quinton gives three examples.

There is a conjuring trick whose equipment is one ordinary nail and another contraption whose outer thirds are just like the head and point of the ordinary nail but which has a D-shaped piece of wire in the intervening gap which can be fitted around the back of the finger. At the points where the wire is joined to the outer thirds there is glistening red paint to simulate blood. Slipped on to the finger and presented to someone so that the wire is out of sight it looks as if a nail has been painfully driven through the finger. Now suppose I shake someone's hand with this appliance concealed in my palm and in doing so slip it on to his finger which I then hold sharply up in front of his face. He is very likely to imagine that he is in acute pain, let out a cry and grip the apparently injured hand. It is highly probable that he will feel some referred pain in the finger but it will be much milder than the pain that he thinks he is having. The same thing would occur if one were suddenly to run a concealed lipstick down someone's cheek in circumstances where he could see his face in a mirror. He would suppose that he had been slashed with a razor. A more familiar case is that in which one puts one's hand under the flowing bath tap and withdraws it believing it to be very hot when in fact it is very cold. Admittedly there is some pain present in all these cases and it is also true that there is a lively expectation of pain to come but can this really be distinguished from the belief that one is in pain now in this sort of circumstance?[34]

Quinton thinks these three examples show that you can imagine you have intense, severe, or acute pain when it is really quite mild or nonexistent.

What are we to make of these examples? Consider the last one. It is true that you can think water is very hot when it is really very cold, and this belief may make you withdraw your hand. In such a case you may have thought that you had been injured. But it does not follow that for a moment you thought you felt intense, severe, or acute pain. The same goes for the first two cases. These are cases in which people think they have been wounded and with that naturally comes fear plus the expectation of pain, and the people may of course be mistaken that they will feel it. But that is not the same thing as erroneously thinking that you *now* feel intense pain. So neither of Quinton's two kinds of counterexamples are actually counterexamples. They neither show that you can have a pain of a certain nature and not be aware of it nor that you can think you have a pain of a certain severity when you do not.

In order to appease his reader—and I suppose not to appear unreasonable or too extreme—Quinton says his view does not overlook the "distinction between the mental and what may be called the *merely* physical." For he thinks "people do have a non-inferential awareness, in the ordinary, non-logical sense, of acts about themselves which, in practice, other people discover only by inference from the way they behave and in particular what they say."[35] Indeed, he says if you think you are in pain, you have "the best reason [you] can ask for in the circumstances for saying that [you are] in pain."[36] But it does not follow that you are. A brain surgeon may have a better reason for saying you are not in pain. It is in principle possible that what you take to be a severe pain may really be something else—perhaps a delightful tickle or nothing but a slight itch.

Rorty agrees with Quinton and Smart that sincere first-person sensation reports can be overridden. The person just might be making a mistake. Well, suppose Jones denies that he is in pain, and a brain surgeon, using a fancy machine, asserts that Jones is in pain because the machine detects that a certain physiological process is taking place inside Jones. Alternatively, suppose Jones cries out that he is in excruciating pain, but the doctor says no, he is not, because the physiological process stopped. What would we say? We would believe Jones in both cases, unless we had reason to suspect that he was lying or did not understand what he was saying. As Baier says, echoing Wittgenstein, it would be nonsense to say Jones is making a mistake.[37] Borst nicely sums up the point:

> It seems extremely doubtful whether a sincere first-person report of an intense pain could ever become corrigible without a radical change in our concept of pain; as Baier remarks, it makes no sense to say "I have a pain unless I am mistaken": there are no pain hallucinations.[38]

Identity theorists, by failing to recognize such grammatical facts, provide us with new ways to misuse our language.

While this is true, it must be admitted that the privacy objection does not completely refute identity theory. It has only a limited effectiveness, applying decisively only against the claim that pains, itches, or sensations are identical with brain processes or brain states. It has no force against the thesis that emotions are identical with brain processes or brain states. You may think, for example, that you are in love when you are not—maybe it's only infatuation—or that you are not when you are (David Copperfield with Agnes). And you can doubt whether you are truly happy. Quinton is

right, too, that you may think you regret something, or that you are sorry
about something, when you really are not. You can deceive yourself about
such matters.[39] Quinton's error is to think that the possibility of self-
deception also extends to things like pains, itches, and sensations generally.

5.5 The Loss of Conceptual Connection with Psychological Phenomena

We have seen that identity theorists maintain that mental entities like pain
or love—which they think are really brain events or brain states—cause
our behavior (Quinton's sixth claim). Joyful, sad, and angry behavior are
therefore nothing but the effects of different cerebral processes or brain
states. This implies that such behavior is not conceptually tied to the mental
states, since, in the usual view of causation, cause and effect—here the
cerebral process or brain state and the behavior it produces—are held to
be only contingently connected. So there is no conceptual connection between people's mental states and their resulting behavior and facial expressions for identity theorists (Quinton's seventh claim). Loving expressions
and loving behavior may be symptoms of a person's love, external signs of,
or evidence for it, but they cannot be conceptually tied to the love. That
is, such behavior has nothing to do with what it means to love someone.
Similarly, unloving behavior—for example, Dorian Gray's toward Sybyl
Vane (he goes to the opera right after she dies, talks of other women being
charming, of Patti singing divinely)—should have nothing to do with what
it means to fail to love someone.[40]
  Wittgenstein would say identity theory has things wrong way round.
According to him, you know the meaning of a term if you know how to
use it in the language (see PI, §§43, 432, 139). And you only know how
to use psychological words when you know what sorts of facial expressions
and behavior are criteria for identifying a person as being in such a state.
The criteria for such states—for being in pain, angry, in love, and the like—
consist in what people do and say. So Wittgenstein connects behavioral
criteria with the meaning of the psychological terms (PI, §244). It is only
when you master the use of such terms that you can be said to have grasped
the related concept. "You learned the *concept* 'pain' when you learned the
language" (PI, §384). Not that Wittgenstein is here endorsing the behaviorist viewpoint refuted in the previous chapter. He is not a reductionist.
He is just pointing out that to grasp the concept of pain, say—or to understand the meaning of the word "pain"—you have to understand how a

pained expression, and natural pain behavior, are related to the feeling of being in pain. To understand how to use the words "sad" and "pain" you must know, among other things, that crying is one criterion of being sad or in pain, that it is one natural way to express these feelings (PI, §257). Identity theorists fail to appreciate the importance of behavior for ascribing mental and psychological predicates, the role it plays in our lives. They fail to understand that "an 'inner process' stands in need of outward criteria" (PI, §580). Without such outer behavioral criteria for the inner, we could not understand our psychological language. Speaking of a timid face, for example, he says:

> It is possible to say "I read timidity in this face" but at all events the timidity does not seem to be merely associated, outwardly connected, with the face; but fear is there, alive, in the features. If the features change slightly, we can speak of a corresponding change in the fear. (PI, §537)

So if identity theory were correct, we wouldn't have any psychological language or psychological concepts, or if we did, they would be quite different from the psychological language and psychological concepts we now have.

Quinton might reply that he is not concerned with the meaning of psychological terms or with giving cerebral processes or brain states any kind of conceptual connection with mental states. He might add that, in spite of this, his view continues to recognize the evidential importance of behavior and facial expressions. You don't, then, need to carry around CAT scan equipment to perform brain analyses on other human beings to infer their current psychological states. Being effects of brain states or brain processes, behavior and facial expressions provide us with evidence for the existence of the cerebral correlate. No doubt, but that would not be evidence for saying the person is in any kind of psychological state unless we retained the conceptual connection between behavior and the psychological states. That is, we can only say that brain state B is evidence for being in mental state M if earlier we have found them to be correlated. But that means we must first have independently identified that the person was in mental state M. And how did we do that? By using the usual behavioral criteria for being in mental state M that the identity theorist has implicitly rejected. Identity theorists thus surreptitiously employ the usual behavioral criteria that they are committed to rejecting.

Further, if identity theorists are right that the cerebral process actually *is* the pain or the anger, its presence should settle the question whether people are in pain, angry, or infatuated rather than in love more conclusively than anything else. Yet we know it does not. Their behavior is more to the point than what is going on in their brains. What settles the matter with finality, if anything does, will be what people do and say, and how, with what facial expressions, and in what situations.[41] So the identity theorist's view is dramatically opposed to Wittgenstein's, who takes behavior and facial expressions to be our criteria for the mental.

This criticism, of course, is connected with the question of whether the identity theorists really solve the other-minds problem. Remember, Quinton, for one, thinks this is one of the strengths of the position—that it has no problem of other minds, unlike dualism, for cerebral processes are, at least in principle, accessible. It is certainly true they are accessible. But this point by itself does not solve the other-minds problem. It would only solve it if the brain event or brain state actually were the mental state; but it isn't. The only reason we may think it is is that we have found it correlated with people being in such and such a mental state. But it has already been pointed out on several occasions that that does not make the brain event, or the brain state, identical with the mental state.

5.6 Our Brains—Not We—Have Thoughts, Sensations, and Emotions

Another reductio of identity theory goes as follows. If the theory were true, it would be the brain that has pains, feelings, opinions. Psychological characteristics would be ascribed to our brains, not to us. We should be able to say that it is in love, happy, knows such and such, had a bad day today, and so on. If the brain is in pain, it seems we should comfort it instead of the person. Human beings would be reduced to their brains, which seems absurd. How can a whole be reduced to one of its parts?[42] Wittgenstein would object that it only makes sense to ascribe psychological predicates to people or to beings who closely resemble people. "Only of a living human being and what resembles (behaves like) a living human being can one say: it has sensations; it sees; is blind; hears; is deaf; is conscious or unconscious" (PI, §281). That is why we don't say of a stone that it is in pain (PI, §283), of a stove that it feels remorse, or "of a table or a chair: 'Now they are thinking,' nor 'Now they are not thinking,' nor yet 'They never think'; nor do we say it of plants either, nor fishes, hardly of dogs; only of human beings." Indeed, he says, "I shouldn't know what it would be like if a table were to think" (Z, §129; see also PI, §361). Well, brains hardly behave like living human beings. They can't be said to behave at all! So you cannot say of brains any more than of tables, stones, or stoves that they have sensations, feelings, or opinions. It is people who have these things, or beings that closely resemble people.

Identity theorists might reply that we can still talk of people having sensations, feelings, opinions, and the like, derivatively. For if your brain has these things, then you have them too, just as you have a bruise if you have a knee that has a bruise. But having is not a transitive relation.[43] Because *a* has *b* and *b* has *c,* it does not follow that *a* has *c.* It may or may not. For example, if you have a son and he has AIDS, it doesn't follow that you also have AIDS.

I hope it is now apparent how Quinton, and the identity theorists generally, oversimplify and distort our use of mentalistic and other psychological terms. A thought, emotion, or sensation cannot be identical with an event in the brain. This has been shown to be impossible simply by logical or conceptual considerations alone. We may well ask, How did Quinton and the other identity theorists come to such a distorted view? Wittgenstein offers a possible answer when he writes: "Where our language suggests a body and there is none: there, we should like to say, is a *spirit*" (PI, §36). That has led philosophers to dualism and all the troubles that dualism gives rise to, insurmountable problems that Quinton and other identity theorists fully appreciate. These theorists may then have returned to the first alternative and temptation—to see if a body could not be the thing they were looking for. Realizing it couldn't plausibly be an "outer" bodily thing, for example, behavior—they were already aware of some of the drawbacks of behaviorism when they first formulated mind-brain identity theory—they opted for an "inner" body. As we know, their favorite bodily candidate became a brain event or brain state. We have seen, however, that this view is quite untenable: it can be refuted a priori on the grounds that brain events and brain states don't have the right characteristics to be identical with psychological and mental things.

There is another fundamental criticism that should be mentioned, even though it will only be developed a couple of chapters later. Identity theorists, like Cartesians, assume that mentalistic terms—"pain," "intending," "meaning," "expecting," "understanding," "sad," "happy," "joy," and the like—always function as referring expressions, as designators, which designate a single thing or event. Quinton, for example, takes it for granted that this is how such terms function; he never argues for the view. Hence his pursuit of the thing, event, or state that they refer to or designate. As mentioned, they don't seem to designate "spiritual" things or "outer" behavioral events, and so (he seems to reason) it is reasonable to think they refer to "inner" bodily nonspiritual things or events. Brain events seem to be Quinton's favorite candidates, though he sometimes uses the language of brain states as well. This has absurd consequences, as we have seen in the foregoing criticisms, confirming Wittgenstein's view that philosophers get entangled in their own (usually implicit) rules (PI, §125). Wittgenstein helps get us untangled by assembling reminders about how we, in fact, use psychological terms (PI, §127). Besides the absurd consequences already mentioned, another is that we cannot have the very same feeling or thought if the theory is formulated in terms of events, since your feeling will be a brain event in your brain and mine another event in my brain; so our feelings will be two distinct physical events occurring in different brains.[44] Quinton welcomes this conclusion, saying, "The one possibility that does not seriously occur to us is that what is going on here is a single, shared sensation."[45] I shall give Wittgensteinian arguments against this underlying assumption that psychological things are always specific events in Section 7.6.

Contrast Wittgenstein's expressed view in *Zettel*. Replying to the claim that " 'joy' surely designates an inward thing," he says: "No. 'Joy' designates nothing at all. Neither any inward nor any outward thing" (Z, §487). He is implying we should not think of it as a single thing or a specific event. It is a mistake to identify it with anything. He says something similar about sensations in the *Investigations,* when he remarks, paradoxically, that pain "is not a *something,* but not a *nothing* either!" (PI, §304). I think he means it is not a something like a cow or a pencil, something to which the numerical/qualitative distinction would apply. But as I said, these points will be developed more fully in Chapter 7.

In the next chapter another traditional philosophical view of the mind and the body—Cartesian dualism—will be examined, to see whether it has more success dealing with the other-minds and the mind-body problems. We shall find that Cartesian dualism deals with the distinction between human beings and other animals very differently from how materialistic theories like behaviorism and the mind-body identity theory do. For the latter theories, the distinction is quantitative, merely one of degree; so some psychological predicates apply to nonhuman subjects as well as to human beings. For Cartesian dualism, in contrast, human beings and other animals are radically different in kind. Consequently, a whole range of predicates that apply to human beings—psychological predicates—ceases to have any application to nonhuman animals, according to Descartes.

Chapter 6

Cartesian Dualism

Having seen Wittgenstein's rejection of any sort of materialism in the last two chapters, we might expect him to be some sort of dualist—someone who holds that there are basically two kinds of things or events in the world, material and spiritual. This and the next chapter will show why he is not. Cartesian dualism is a position that derives mainly from Descartes, the great seventeenth-century philosopher and mathematician, although a similar view already can be found in Plato's *Phaedo*. It is a subtly persuasive and natural view once the mind is accepted as problematic and as something distinct from the brain. For Descartes, a human being consists of two distinct things combined together: a mind, or soul, and a body. Less fashionable today, dualism continues to find defenders. James B. Pratt and Karl Popper are two of its twentieth-century advocates.[1]

6.1 Six Main Tenets of Descartes's View

Descartes's position can be summed up, at least roughly, in the following six main tenets.

1. Human bodies are in space and time. Minds are nonspatial but temporal. In other words, our thoughts and experiences occur in temporal order—one before or at the same time as another; but never in spatial order—at such and such a distance from, or literally next to, one another.
2. All bodies are subject to, and explainable in terms of, the laws of physics. Minds are not subject to such laws.
3. Bodies are public. Minds are private, in several senses. One sense in which minds are private is that we get our psychological notions directly from the psychological phenomena we are experiencing. For example, Descartes would say he knows what pain is from having it. "In the same way in order to know what doubt is, or thought, it is only requisite to doubt and think. That teaches us

all that we can know of it."[2] Two additional senses in which minds are private are mentioned in the next tenet, tenet number 4.

4. There is an outer perception of bodies. This sort of perception is corrigible, involving sense organs. There is also inner perception of what is mental, though only in a person's own case. This sort of perception is incorrigible, that is, beyond correction, hence indubitable. The mind has perfect and immediate knowledge of its own present mental states, but not of other minds. This is a second sense in which minds are private. A third sense is that two or more people can never have the very same feeling or thought.

5. A mind cannot doubt its own existence, but it can doubt the existence of bodies, even its own body. Hence Descartes takes the mind—the thing that thinks—and the body to be two distinct entities. Since minds and bodies are conceived of as distinct kinds of things, they are separable and in principle can exist independently of one another. That is, it is possible for one to exist without the other. Descartes thinks it is therefore possible that minds or souls are immortal. That they are actually immortal cannot be proved, only that it is possible. So belief and faith in immortality does not go against reason.

6. Minds and bodies causally interact. That is, a physical event—a blow to the head—may affect your mind: make you feel bad, feel pain. Similarly, a mental event or state—your being afraid—may cause the physical event of your running away from what you fear.

6.2 Descartes's Unsatisfactory Answer to the Mind-Body Problem

There have been three traditional dualistic answers to the mind-body problem. One is interactionism, which is Descartes's answer, as we can see from tenet number 6. Descartes thinks it is an undeniable fact that minds and bodies, or mental and physical events, causally interact with each other. James Pratt and Karl Popper also affirm mind-body interaction, though with some differences.

A second dualistic answer to the mind-body problem is epiphenomenalism—the view that the physical can cause the mental, but the mental never can have an effect on the physical. In this view, the mind is alleged to be a simple byproduct of the body. The mind is given rise to by changes in the body. It could not exist independently of the body, in contrast to

Descartes's view. Mind is a mere epiphenomenon and without causal effi-
cacy of its own. T. H. Huxley, a nineteenth-century scientist who advocates
this view, likens the mental to the whistling sound produced by the steam
coming from boiling water in a kettle. The whistle is caused by the steam,
but it does not have any effect on the temperature of the water.[3] George
Santayana and C. D. Broad are two twentieth-century epiphenomenalists.

A third dualistic response to the mind-body problem is parallelism—the
view that neither the mind effects the body nor the body the mind. Male-
branche, Leibniz, Harald Hoeffding, and Friedrich Paulsen are parallelists.
These people reject any kind of causal connection between the mental and
the physical or between minds and bodies.

I suppose it would be logically possible for dualists to give a fourth
answer: minds affect bodies causally but not vice versa. Such a position,
as far as I know, has no name. Nor do I know of any philosopher who holds
it.

Let us consider now why Descartes's answer to the mind-body problem
is unsatisfactory. There are at least two objections. First, while he tells us
where these causal interactions occur—they are supposed to take place in
the pineal gland in the brain—this clarifies nothing and only increases
puzzlement. For it seems incomprehensible how they can occur anywhere.
Recall that the mental events are in no way physical and that they do not
take place in space. How then can they interact somewhere, like two billiard
balls colliding on a billiard table? Descartes admits the interaction is mysterious. It has to be, given his view of the mind and of the body. Of course
some might think this is a point in favor of Descartes's answer. For example,
one of the characters in Oscar Wilde's *The Picture of Dorian Gray* says,
"Soul and body, body and soul—how mysterious they were! Who could
say where the fleshly impulse ceased, or the physical impulse began? . . .
The separation of spirit from matter was a mystery, and the union of spirit
with matter was a mystery also."[4] If it is indeed a mystery, our answer to
the mind-body problem should acknowledge this fact. Not surprisingly,
however, most philosophers prefer unmysterious answers to the mind-body
problem. Certainly it does nothing to explain something to say it is a mystery. So we cannot really call Descartes's answer a solution to the problem.

Second, his interactionism seems to contradict tenet number 2, which
says that bodies and all bodily phenomena are explainable in terms of
physics but minds and mental events are not. The unextended mind's effects
on the body are not held to be subject to the laws of physics. So how can
minds have any causal impact on bodies? If they can, physics alone cannot
explain bodily phenomena, contrary to tenet number 2. By the same token,
if minds are effected by bodies, it seems they too are subject to the laws

of physics, again contradicting tenet number 2. In short, his philosophy becomes incoherent.

These two reasons give us ample grounds to reject Descartes's answer to the mind-body problem. We shall see in the next section how his dualism and interactionism also gives rise to an other-(human)-minds problem that he cannot solve, although there is an attempt to answer this problem in his writings. He argues for the positive thesis that there are human minds. He also tries to establish the unusual negative thesis that nonhuman animals— "animales" or brutes—have no minds. This is only one of four possible positions he could take. Another is that consciousness and mentality are common to both, though in varying degree, which is probably the view of most people. A third alternative is that both human beings and all other animals lack mentality. Finally, someone might hold what is perhaps the strangest view of all, namely, that the brutes possess mentality and consciousness but human beings do not.

The question now is this: Why, when Descartes is confronted by a bodily creature correctly described as a human being and also by a nonhuman animal, does he think he is entitled to say of the former that it has mentality and consciousness, while denying that the latter has any kind of mentality or consciousness; that nothing psychological can be ascribed to the animal, but only to the human being?

6.3 How Descartes's View Gives Rise to an Other-Minds Problem

Not only is Descartes's answer to the mind-body problem unsatisfactory, but his view gives rise to an other-minds problem as well, as the following premises make plain.

1. We have seen from tenet number 3 that Descartes thinks we get our psychological notions from the corresponding psychological phenomena. For example, I get the idea of pain from having it. And when I have an experience or thought, I know immediately, or directly, that I have it and exactly what it is (forth tenet). I have direct access and thus direct knowledge of my own experiences, feelings, sensations, thoughts, and the like.
2. But I do not, and cannot, have direct access to your pain or anger. I can neither have nor feel it. Nor can I experience anything else

that you experience: your tiredness, your happiness. This is be-cause no two people can have the very same feeling or thought. These are some of the ways in which minds are private for Des-cartes (fourth tenet). It is therefore only on the basis of your ob-served behavior, and on the basis of analogy, that I surmise, or infer, that you are in pain.

3. Moreover, I know from my own case that I am able to pretend to be in pain when I am not. This is because there is no necessary connection between certain behavior, say pain behavior, and being in a particular psychological state, for example, in pain. If others feel pain, there is no reason why they should not also be able to pretend to feel it when they do not. The same is true of other feelings and thoughts. (Of course, according to this view, if they are pretending to be in pain, they must have the concept of being in pain (by premise 1); hence they must once have been in pain, according to premise 1, even if they are not at this moment.)

4. This possibility of pretense shows clearly that there is a difference between the mental state, say of pain, and one of behavior. That is, pain is not to be confused with pain behavior. Nor does pain behavior by itself even imply that someone is in pain. (Premises 3 and 4 remind us that Descartes is no behaviorist.)

5. It is at this point that skeptics begins to draw their skeptical con-clusions. They say: it follows that we can never verify—or even confirm—our belief that someone else is in pain. These beliefs are not like the usual sort of inductive inferences. Given Descartes's view, we must admit that we can have no evidence for thinking that other people are in pain. Admittedly, if they are pretending to be in pain, they must have experienced pain in the past, ac-cording to the Cartesian, because they must have the concept of pain, which requires acquaintance with pain. But there is no way to ever tell whether another person is even pretending, or to dis-tinguish the appearance from the reality of pretending, when deal-ing with others. Thus we can have no evidence for ascribing pain or any other mental state to another person. Indeed, it appears we have no good reasons for believing that others have experiences of *any* kind, much less for believing that they feel or think what we feel or think when we observe their behavior to be the same as ours. For all we know, other human beings are robots and quite without feelings, sensations, emotions and thoughts. They may not even have any "inner" life. (Note: The skeptic does not even need

premise 3. That is, he does not even have to bring in the possibility of pretense. So even if there is no problem of pretense, Descartes still seems to have a problem of other [human] minds.)

Before we look at his actual proofs, we have to put things in context. In Descartes's *Meditations* he is trying to find what is metaphysically doubtful and what is not, so he can discover what he should believe. He says explicitly in the *Second Meditation* that he wants what is absolutely or metaphysically certain (HR 1, p. 150). Such certainty is contrasted with moral certainty, which is an old-fashioned name for probability (HR 1, pp. 104, 301). Descartes employs the following test questions: Can I find the slightest reason to doubt the matter under examination? Could it possibly be otherwise than I take it to be? Could I imagine the least doubt with regard to it? If not, I may continue to believe it. If I can find one of these reasons to doubt it, however, I must doubt it, at least until I can ground the belief on something else that is indubitable.

After establishing the *cogito, ergo sum* (I think, therefore I am) or the first principle of his philosophy, in his *Second Meditation,* Descartes tries to prove God's existence and finally the existence of physical objects. He offers three proofs for the existence of God, two causal ones in the *Third Meditation* and an ontological argument in the *Fifth Meditation*. The first causal argument contends that only God can be the cause of his (Descartes's) idea of God; the second, that God alone can be the conserving cause of Descartes's existence. In fact, both of these causal arguments already make essential use of the ontological argument, since to stop the causal regress, Descartes answers the question of what caused God by saying that God is his own cause. But God is his own cause only in the sense that his essence entails his existence, which is in effect the ontological argument. So if the ontological argument is flawed,[5] as I think it is, so are all his proofs for the existence of God and everything that rests on them.

For the sake of argument, however, let us temporarily grant that Descartes has succeeded in establishing that he exists as a finite thinking being and that a perfect God exists. A corollary is that such a God cannot be a deceiver, "since the light of nature teaches us that fraud and deception necessarily proceed from some defect" (HR 1, p. 171). This claim becomes an essential premise for his proof of the existence of physical objects that is given in the *Sixth Meditation* and for his proof of other human minds. He assumes that such a God guarantees the truth of all of our natural and incorrigible beliefs, since if he did not, he would be a deceiver. Again, let us suppose that Descartes has established the existence of physical objects.

We are now ready to deal with the proof of the existence of other human minds.

Descartes affirms, first, that he is spontaneously convinced, or naturally disposed, to believe, not only that physical objects cause his sense perceptions of them, but that various thoughts, feelings, intentions, and the like lie behind the actions and behavior of other people. That is, he thinks the belief is a natural one in the sense that it is part of human nature to have it. In other words, he could not not have it; it is an irresistible belief. Second, he contends that there is no way to discover such a belief to be false. In short, the belief is unfalsifiable, or incorrigible, in the sense of being beyond correction.

Descartes is next ready to show that certain corporeal objects—namely those that take a human form—have souls or minds (the positive thesis) and that nonhuman animals lack souls or minds (the negative thesis). It follows for him that the brutes have no thoughts, feelings, and the like.[6] Since his two contentions are connected, I shall consider the arguments for both the positive and the negative theses together.

Descartes does not give his reasons for the view he adopts in either the *Meditations* or in the *Principles of Philosophy*. But in his *Discourse* we find the main arguments for both his positive and his negative contentions. There he maintains, on the one hand, that machines and animals are indistinguishable. Consequently, there is no more reason to believe that nonhuman animals have reason than there is to believe that machines do. At least (he continues, surprisingly unskeptically) had we given machines the same outward form and organs, "we should not have had any means of ascertaining that they were not of the same nature as those animals." On the other hand, he maintains that, while we might make machines that resemble the human body and that imitate human actions, such machines would always be distinguishable from men—that is, they could never pass for them. This is because it is his view that we would always have "two very certain tests by which to recognize that, for all that, they were not real men" (HR 1, p. 116), which might be called a "language" test and an "action" test. They are both in fact behavioral tests—the language test merely appeals to a restricted set of actions (linguistic ones), whereas the action test examines a wide variety of nonverbal actions. These tests give an empirical character to Descartes's argument. He rests his case on an appeal to observable, behavioral evidence. On the basis of this evidence, he maintains that a real human being has a mind and, unlike the brutes, is not just a machine. For human beings pass both of these tests, while machines and other animals pass neither. For him, it is a natural and incorrigible belief, in the sense explained, to hold that nothing has mind or any psychological traits if it fails either of these tests, whereas anything that passes them must have a mind, consciousness, and all that is entailed by that.

Descartes finds that machines could not pass the language test, because "they could never use speech or other signs as we do when placing our thoughts on record for the benefit of others." He is aware that machines can be made that "utter words or even emit some responses to action on it of a corporeal kind, which bring about a change in its organs." He gives the example of a machine that asks—like the doll—"what we wish to say to it" or exclaims "that it is being hurt, and so on" if it is touched in a certain spot. He points out that this is not true conversation. And no machine could be constructed, he says, that would be able to arrange "its speech in various ways, in order to reply appropriately to *everything* [my emphasis] that may be said in its presence, as even the lowest type of man can do" (HR 1, p. 116). Machines may be capable of uttering words, but they cannot do it in the intelligent, flexible way human beings do, and it is only the latter discourse which is a sign of mentality, not the mere (mechanical) utterance of words.

Next he applies his action test to both men and machines to drive home the point that *l'homme* can never be a mere machine, contrary to La Mettrie's later contention.[7] Writes Descartes: "Although machines can perform certain things as well as or perhaps better than any of us, they infallibly fall short in others, by which means we may discover that they did not act from knowledge, but only from the disposition of their organs." That is, were reason the cause of the superiority, it would display itself in the performance of other tasks; but this does not happen. Therefore, the explanation of their excellence must be purely mechanical. The clock, for example, surpasses us in telling the time, but it is incapable of doing anything else. Hence we account for its superiority by pointing out how it is specially adapted for that particular action; we refer to the disposition of its wheels, weights, and so on. In contrast, human beings can not only tell the time and talk but can cope with all sorts of other situations and challenges. We can do this because we have intellect or reason, which Descartes regards as "a universal instrument which can serve for all contingencies." The mind for him is as a sort of jack-of-all-trades. He concludes "that it is *morally impossible,* that is, highly unlikely, that there should be sufficient diversity in any machine to allow it to act in all the events of life in the same way as our reason causes us to act" (HR 1, p. 116).

If Descartes were living today, three hundred years later, he would probably still insist that even our most highly complex computers lack the amazing versatility of even the most ordinary human being. For example, the so-called "thinking machine" that writes poetry is only capable of performing this one task, whereas the person who writes poetry understands the language, can use it on all sorts of different occasions, can add up a bill, do income tax, write letters, tell jokes, make dinner, and so on, which is one of the chief reasons we are inclined to ascribe rationality to people and not to automata. Accordingly (Descartes concludes), while it is proper to explain a person's voluntary actions by referring to his or her reason, we must always reject such explanations of a machine's performance. People are not mere machines. We may speak with the physiologists about "the machinery of the human body," but people have minds as well as bodies.

Descartes now goes on to apply his language and action tests to other animals in order to drive home his point that we are quite different from the brutes, who, in his view, are nothing more than complex automata. Using the language test, he finds no nonhuman animal is able to "arrange different words together, forming of them a statement by which they make known their thoughts," even though idiots can do this, according to him. He would surely agree with Alice's complaint that "whatever you say to [kittens], they *always* purr"; so you cannot keep up a conversation with them.[8] The carp also "bring nothing at all to a conversation."[9] Descartes might draw a different conclusion if ants traced messages in the sand at our feet reading "I am sentient; let's talk things over."[10] He says we cannot excuse the brutes either on the grounds that they lack the necessary organs, or are physically incapable of doing these things. For example, "magpies and parrots are able to utter words just like ourselves, and yet they cannot speak as we do, that is, so as to give evidence that they think of what they say." It's not weakness of intellect that makes the Dicky-bird "sit singing 'Willow, titwillow, titwillow,' " for he has no intellect at all. On the other hand, men who lack the organs needed for speech, that is, who are "born deaf and dumb," nevertheless acquire language. They "are in the habit of themselves inventing certain signs by which they make themselves understood." In Descartes's opinion "very little is required" to use language. Hence he concludes that not only do "the brutes have less reason than men, but they have none at all" (cf. HR 1, p. 117). In brief, the inability to talk—or to use language—implies the total absence of reason and everything psychological. The brutes lack this ability. Therefore, we can infer that they are altogether without the capacity to think, reason, or to feel anything.

Finally, Descartes applies his action test to the brutes, maintaining that they fail this too. For, he says, while "there are many animals which exhibit more dexterity than we do in some of their actions, we at the same time observe that they do not manifest any dexterity at all in many others." The nest building of many birds would be an example: some of them may surpass us in this but they cannot rise intelligently to other nonverbal tasks the way we do. The fact that they perform certain actions "better than we do, does not prove that they are endowed with mind." Because if they were, they should "have more reason than any of us, and would surpass us in all other things," and consequently at least have language. But we know that they do not come anywhere close to equaling us in most other activities. What is shown by these considerations, according to Descartes, is "that they have no reason at all, and that it is nature which acts in them according to the disposition of their organs, just as a clock, which is only composed of wheels and weights is able to tell the hours and measure the time more correctly than we can do with all our wisdom" (HR 1, p. 117).

So ends Descartes's proof of both his positive and his negative theses. It remains to examine in the next section the soundness of these demonstrations.

6.4 Some Objections to Descartes's Proofs

Again, let us suppose that we have been persuaded by Descartes that he knows of his own existence as a mental substance, of God's existence, and of the existence of physical objects. Let us also grant tentatively that he knows the principle of causality—that is, the principle that everything has a cause—since he assumes this principle in most of his arguments, including this one. He infers that our voluntary and intelligent behavior requires a mind as its cause, but the behavior of animals does not. What are we to think of his attempt to prove the existence of other human minds, or of people who are not mere automata, unlike the brutes? Has he established the indubitability of his two theses? I shall try to show why a consistent Descartes would not think so.

6.4.1 Two Objections of a Consistent Cartesian

A consistent Cartesian would find at least two flaws in Descartes's argument, even on the assumption that God exists and guarantees the truth of all of our natural and incorrigible beliefs. That is, his proof of other human minds fails judged by Descartes's own standards. He has not shown the matter to be absolutely or metaphysically certain. To see this let us grant that it is a fact that he is spontaneously inclined to believe in the passions, suffering, and thoughts of others when he sees them behave in certain ways. Most of us regard animals in a similar way. But is there any necessity in having such beliefs and attitudes? It might be seen as merely a deep psychological fact about (normal) human beings that, as presently constituted, they have a natural impulse to believe that people and animals have certain kinds of feelings, desires, and so on, when they act in certain ways. We know, however, that not everyone so regards people and animals. Some of the experimentalists at Port Royal—presumably influenced by Descartes's own skeptical argument—came to regard the cries of animals as of no account;[11] and some people living today—for example, idiots and some insane people—do not even recognize that other people have thoughts and feeling.

It is conceivable, then, that future experimentalists may come to regard the cries of human beings "as of no account" as well. So it cannot be indubitable to Descartes that he must have this particular belief. He himself might go insane, as he himself acknowledges in his skeptical argument from madness. Perhaps he will come to be like those people "whose cerebella are so troubled and clouded by the violent vapours of black bile," that he will one day come to believe that it is his own mind that is the likely cause of these ideas, maybe working through some faculty which is unknown to him (HR 1, p. 145). Indeed, it is conceivable for the Cartesian that people generally might come to abandon their present, contingent beliefs concerning the existence of other human minds, perhaps after lengthy exposure to philosophy courses that emphasize the skeptical tradition or after taking certain drugs. This is conceivable; therefore, on Cartesian principles, it must be viewed as possible. Hence it is not metaphysically certain or indubitable that his belief in other human minds is a natural belief, in the sense of being irresistible or an essential part of his nature.

Even if the naturalness of the belief were indubitable, however, this would not necessarily rescue Descartes's argument. For we must also know that the belief is unfalsifiable or incorrigible. This is because God's guarantee is only presumed to extend to beliefs that are *both* natural *and* incorrigible. Let us look next at some reasons for thinking that belief is in fact corrigible.

We have noted that Descartes is correct in insisting that machines are much more limited in what they can do than are people. This remains true today even in the midst of our computer revolution. We find that even the most highly complex computer lacks the versatility of the most ordinary human being. For example, the so-called "thinking machine" that can compose music in the style of Mozart is only capable of performing this one task, whereas the person who sings a song but cannot compose music, understands the language, can recognize faces, read a handwritten note, order hamburgers at a restaurant, add up a bill at the grocery store, and so on. Admittedly Descartes exaggerates a bit, remarking that "the lowest type of man" can reply *appropriately* to *everything* that may be said in its presence. This certainly is not true of idiots and imbeciles, no matter how generous the interpretation of the word "appropriately." Even normally intelligent people sometimes make stupid and inappropriate remarks. Indeed, Descartes's language test is here in danger of becoming so severe that no one will be able to pass it, neither people nor animals, if the requirement is to reply appropriately to everything said to you. Disregarding this objection, it still must be acknowledged that Descartes is pinpointing a very real difference between people and machines as we know them, as well as probably the chief reasons for ascribing rationality to the former but not to the latter. To this extent Descartes's position is certainly plausible and convincing.

But plausibility, as we have seen, can never be enough for Descartes. Indeed, it is something like a dirty word for him. His methodological requirements emphasize the need to go beyond mere probability if we are ever to attain knowledge of other minds. So conceding to him that it is "morally impossible"—that is, highly improbable—to make a machine that can match us in its verbal and nonverbal behavior is not to concede that we are essentially different from machines. We certainly have no such automaton at present and perhaps never will have. But from this it does not follow that it is inconceivable, or logically impossible, to have such an automaton. It is not like the claim that the sum of the interior angles of a Euclidean triangle is 180 degrees, which reduces to a tautology. Descartes leaves us, then, with the open possibility that someday we may be able to produce such a machine.[12] We already have chess-playing machines that "learn from experience"—that is, that are self-correcting—as well as "creative" machines that "compose" music, "write" poetry, and so on. The simple device of linking together our most highly developed automata forming one complex super-machine obviously would increase greatly the versatility rating of the resulting machine. It is not hard to entertain the thought that one day such a machine may equal, or surpass, our total performance.[13] No doubt there would be problems fitting such a machine into a human form. But again we can even conceive of arriving at a time in which miniaturization techniques would be sufficiently advanced even to do this. Consequently, Descartes is mistaken in thinking he has shown it impossible to develop a machine in the form of a man that would be indistinguishable from a true man. Consequently, he has failed to show that it is in principle impossible to explain human actions without making any reference to minds. For all we know, it may be that human actions, no less than those of the brutes, are all explainable simply in terms of "the dispositions of their organs," "the discharge of animal spirits," or, in more modern words, in terms of their "software," "wiring," "chips," and the like.

To drive home the point that Descartes's argument for other human minds is corrigible, just suppose that fifty years from now we discover how to produce computers with chips actually wired to mimic the nerves in the brain. Suppose further that these computers cannot be distinguished from us: in other words, that they pass both of Descartes's tests. We should then have sound empirical grounds for revising our present views in either of two ways. Either we would have to abandon the belief that such machines were mindless or we would have to conclude that the so-called people we meet are without minds. For God, being no deceiver, is not going to allow A and B to be different if they are indistinguishable. Nor would such a development make God guilty of having deceived Descartes. For if Descartes was in fact mistaken in his belief in other human minds, God could simply point out that this was his (Descartes's) fault: he should have foreseen the implication of his own admission that we only have moral assurance that people and machines are fundamentally different. From this it follows that the proposition is in principle corrigible, and therefore not subject to God's guarantee, judging by Descartes's own high standards of certainty.

We see, then, that using his methodology more rigorously than he does, Descartes would have to conclude that his argument for the existence of other human minds is inconclusive, even assuming he knows he is a thing that thinks, that there are physical objects, some of which take a human shape, and that God exists who vindicates our natural and incorrigible beliefs. The matter in question has not been shown to be absolutely or metaphysically certain. We shall see in the next section that additional Wittgensteinian criticisms can be made of Descartes's argument that do not depend on invoking the Cartesian notion of indubitability or metaphysical or absolute certainty.

6.4.2 Some Wittgensteinian Criticisms

There are several reasons why Wittgenstein would object to Descartes's arguments. First, he would object to Descartes's claim that to have a mind, or any psychological characteristics, it is necessary to pass the language test. Evidently having Descartes in mind, he writes:

> It is sometimes said that animals do not talk because they lack the mental capacity. And this means: "they do not think, and that is why they do not talk." But—they simply do not talk. Or to put it better: they do not use language—if we except the most primitive forms of language. (PI, §25)

Notice that Wittgenstein here agrees with Descartes that animals do not use language. Lately it has become a controversial topic whether there are any animals capable of using language. On the basis of recent research conducted with primates learning symbols and concepts from our language, as well as experiments with dolphins, some scientists have concluded that we are not the only creatures on earth capable of using language. Gorillas and chimpanzees who have been taught simple sign language seem to be able to express their emotions, desires, and interests and to take part in rudimentary conversations. Having a language, then, may no longer be viewed as an exclusive feature of human beings. Whether this is so is not a question to be settled here. But even if Descartes is right in maintaining that we are the sole language users, there remains Wittgenstein's objection that it does not follow that animals cannot think or have any psychological traits. The inability to talk, or to use language, in no way implies either the absence of reason, of consciousness, or of feelings.

Second, as regards what we call thinking, narrowly conceived, I think Wittgenstein would say there is much behavioral evidence for concluding that some animals have intelligence and that they can think, at least in rudimentary ways. Indeed, some of their nonverbal behavior is impressive, though Descartes does not seem to recognize this. Let me cite some evidence. Like us, animals adapt to new situations and learn from experience. For example, when young, we all learn how to walk on different terrains. We learn to avoid fire and precipices. Rats and dogs can both learn to open simple latches. That there is potential game at the watering hole is something the lion is taught by experience. And the macaque monkeys of Japan have even learned to use sea water to season sweet potatoes, passing their skill on to their children.

Moreover, there is evidence that some animals use tools and reason in simple, logical ways. For example, rats not only can learn mazes faster than retarded human beings who possess language, but they can learn to do things like gnaw telephone lines and use them as swings to cross expanses of water in sewers. Chimps both use and make tools, in a rudimentary sense—for example, when they strip twigs and use them to dig termites. Finches in the Galapagos also use twigs and cactus spines as tools "to pry grubs from a limb," in much the way a human being might use a crowbar to dig out roots. Again, the Egyptian vultures in Tanzania "pick up stones in their beaks and hurl them at ostrich eggs, breaking the shells and feasting on the contents."[14] Finally, the Stoics were probably the first to observe that a dog knows the argument form "disjunctive syllogism"—namely, if either *p* or *q* and one of these disjuncts is false, infer that the other one is true. For if the dog is sniffing down a trail that comes to a fork, if he does not find the scent down the one path, he will proceed down the other path. Many more examples could be given of seemingly intelligent animal behavior.

It is not to be expected that Descartes should have known about all of these particular cases. Yet it is curious that he never seems to consider *any* facts of this kind. That is, he ignores the many ways animals adapt to new situations, learn from experience,[15] seem to reason in a logical way, and apparently solve simple problems by trial and error.

This omission is connected with what we might call Descartes's careless application of his tests. We have seen that if we consult the available nonverbal behavioral evidence even superficially, we find that animal behavior displays many of the same signs of mentality that human behavior does. On the basis of a rough application of the action test, it seems that we ought to conclude, hypothetically: *if* the evidence presented shows that we have intelligence and reason, by parity of reasoning it also shows that many of the brutes do too, although to a lesser extent. It is reasonable to conclude that the evidence shows their ability to think and reason to be more limited than ours, but not that we have intelligence and they have none. As Hume observes, "A wise man . . . proportions his belief to the evidence."[16]

Finally, I think Wittgenstein would object to Descartes's requirement that the action test be passed in order to qualify for psychological characteristics. To see this, consider what Descartes is really doing with his tests. With them he effectively lays down the requirement that animals be able to do everything, or almost everything, we can do: otherwise they are not deemed fit to have consciousness and all that goes with consciousness. His demand is like Mr. Higgins's in *My Fair Lady,* who complains, "Why can't a woman be more like a man?" except that Descartes's complaint seems to be, Why can't brutes be more like human beings? Because they have no souls or minds, he quickly answers. Yet the sole reason he gives for offering this explanation is that they fail to match us in their actions, verbal and nonverbal.

I think Wittgenstein would find a muddle here. In a curious way, Descartes's position anticipates but also seems to caricature Wittgenstein's. For the latter also makes human beings and their actions central; they are the paradigm for things psychological. For example, Wittgenstein says "only of a living human being and what resembles (behaves like) a living human being can one say: it has sensations; it sees; is blind; hears; is deaf; is conscious or unconscious" (PI, §281). That is why we do not ascribe a sensation to a stone or to a number. So far the views of Descartes and Wittgenstein resemble each other. But there is a crucial difference. This is brought out by the fact that, in contrast to Descartes, Wittgenstein goes on to observe, "look at a wriggling fly . . . pain seems able to get a foothold here" (PI, §284). This is because the wriggling of the fly resembles some of our own (nonverbal) pain behavior; hence the plausibility in saying it too can be in pain. The same point holds for the dog who shows by his whining, cowering, and other behavior that he is in pain or afraid his master will beat him (PI, §650).

When dealing with the question whether a fly can feel pain or a dog fear, then, Wittgenstein sees no need to bring in Descartes's language or action tests. He is not tempted to ask, even rhetorically, whether he can have a conversation with a fly or a dog, or inquire whether they can do arithmetic, tell stories, ask questions, give orders, and the like. Nor does he consider whether they can tie shoe laces, solve puzzles, plan parties, play games, recognize faces, peel potatoes, or do any of the many other things we can do. Such questions would be out of place—absurd—from his point of view. Human behavior may be the paradigm, but, according to Wittgenstein, that means only that human behavior that is relevant to the ascription of the particular psychological predicate. And only certain behavior is relevant to the application of the psychological predicates "pain" and "fear." We must remind ourselves about what criteria we in fact appeal to when we ascribe specific psychological predicates. What holds true of "pain" and "fear" also holds for ascribing other psychological predicates, for example, "intention." Thus if we see an animal acting in characteristic ways that we do when we have an intention, we may describe it as having an intention too. In some cases, we might even say the animal and the human being have the same intention, at least up to a point. For example, it does not matter greatly if it is Daniel Boone or a cat stalking a bird; we may be able to say on the basis of this natural expression of intention—their stalking behavior—that they both intend to pursue their prey stealthily, under cover, probably for the purpose of killing it (PI, §647).[17]

A more thorough Wittgensteinian critique of Descartes's dualism will be given in the next chapter, which consists of a detailed refutation of the skeptical argument for other minds grounded on Cartesian premises.

Chapter 7

Wittgenstein's Refutation of Cartesian Dualism

One way in which Wittgenstein would attack the skeptical argument for other minds formulated in the last chapter is to refute its underlying Cartesian premises. This chapter will examine these criticisms. Seeing how Wittgenstein would reply to the skeptical argument will deepen our understanding of Wittgenstein's implicit critique of Descartes's dualism and also help to explain his own position, which is sometimes called the criteriological view. Here, in a slightly altered and expanded formulation, is the other-minds skeptical argument we have already been introduced to in the previous chapter.

1. I know what pain is—what experiences, feelings, sensations, thoughts, and everything else that is psychological are—only from my own case: from having pains, experiences, feelings, sensations, thoughts, and other psychological things. Indeed, this is how I acquire all my psychological and mental concepts, and there is no other way I could learn about such things. I just focus on the thing in question, giving myself a private ostensive definition of it. Claim 1, then, has to do with the acquisition of concepts or with concept formation. It is to be distinguished from the weaker claim that I only grasp the concept of pain, love, and the like if I have experienced these things.

2. I have access to my own thoughts, sensations, pains, experiences, and everything else that is psychological or mental. These are things I am directly acquainted with. But I never have access to, nor am I ever acquainted with, the feelings, sensations, pains, experiences, and thoughts of others. I never have direct access to other people's pains, experiences, emotions, or thoughts (Descartes's third tenet). I do not experience what you experience, supposing you experience anything. I cannot have your pain, I cannot think your thoughts, I cannot feel what you feel, for instance, your tiredness, your headache. I can only guess or surmise on the basis of observed behavior whether you are tired or in pain. It is on the basis of analogy that I infer such things in your case.

3. It follows from number 2 that I have direct and immediate knowledge of my own thoughts, pains, experiences, feelings, but I never have such knowledge of anyone else's thoughts, feelings. When I have these things, I know immediately—directly—that I have them (Descartes's fourth tenet). In summary, it is my access to my own thoughts and feelings that enables me to know (a) what it is to think or feel, (b) that I am thinking or feeling when I am, and (c) what it is that I am thinking or feeling on such occasions.

4. Moreover, I know from my own case that I am able to pretend to be in pain when I am not, for example, by groaning or crying out. This is because there is no necessary connection between certain behavior—for example, pain behavior—and being in a particular psychological state—for example, in pain. If others feel pain, there is no reason why they should not also be able to pretend to feel it when they do not.

5. This possibility of pretense, by itself, shows that there is a difference between the inward mental state and the outward behavior. For example, pain is not to be confused with pain behavior. Nor does pain behavior imply that someone is in pain, even though it implies, in the Cartesian view, that someone has once been in pain.

6. I can never verify—or even confirm or disconfirm—that other people are in pain, for all I can see is their behavior; I cannot get beyond that. The belief that someone else is in a certain mental state is therefore unlike the usual sort of inductive inference. It is not like my belief that there is a fire in the house next door because I see smoke coming from it. In that case, I can go and see whether there is a fire in the house; I can get beyond the smoke. I must conclude that I am totally lacking in good reasons or evidence for believing that others have experiences or thoughts of any kind. Nor do I have any reason or evidence for believing that they feel or think what I feel or think when they behave the way I do. For all I know, there is nothing but fear and confusion in my friends' minds when they act happy and talk lucidly; or worse, maybe their minds are quite empty or, indeed, they have no minds. For all I know, I am the only one who has feelings, sensations, thoughts, and the like, or anything "inner" or "mental." We may call this view *epistemological solipsism.*

7. But the situation is even worse than this. It seems I cannot even understand what it would be like for another being to be in pain, to have a thought, or the like, as we shall see below. Nor does the explanation by means of identity—"Well, it's just for the other to

have what I have when I have a pain, etc."—show how I can make sense of such a "hypothesis." We may call this more extreme view *conceptual solipsism*.

Let us consider next how Wittgenstein would counter most of the Cartesian premises of this argument. We shall see that he would disagree with every one of the first three claims.

7.1 Claim 1 Is Grammatical, Not Empirical

Let us begin by considering the status of the first premise of the skeptical argument. What kind of statement does claim 1 make? It certainly looks like an empirical assertion about how certain concepts are learned. It seems straightforward enough. The Cartesian seems to be saying that we have found this to be so from experience. But Wittgenstein warns against being deceived by the appearance of the proposition (PI, §295). He says "I know . . . only from my *own* case" is in fact a grammatical, not an experiential or empirical, proposition. I think what he means, at least in part, is that it is not something anyone discovered to be true on the basis of experience. Rather, its proponents think that that is the way it must be, just as you can only play patience or single solitaire alone. Thus he writes:

> What does it mean when we say: "I can't imagine the opposite of this" or "What would it be like, if it were otherwise?" —For example, when someone has said that my images are private, or that only I myself can know whether I am feeling pain, and similar things.
> Of course, here "I can't imagine the opposite" doesn't mean: my powers of imagination are unequal to the task. These words are a defense against something whose form makes it look like an empirical proposition, but which is really a grammatical one.
> But why do we say: "I can't imagine the opposite"? Why not: "I can't imagine the thing itself"? (PI, §251)

The point is that Descartes and other Cartesians cannot imagine learning these concepts in any other way than claim 1 says they are learned; it is not an empirical thesis.

In section 298 of the *Philosophical Investigations*, Wittgenstein makes it clear he rejects claim 1. He says it gives us no information. But, he explains, he is only rejecting "the grammar which tries to force itself on us here" (PI, §304). Rejecting the Cartesian outlook may make it seem he is adopting behaviorism, which of course he is not doing. As he says, what greater difference could there be than the difference between pain behavior accompanied by pain and pain behavior without any pain? We have already seen that Wittgenstein objects to philosophical behaviorism. (See Chapter 4.)

What he says in the next section, 305, is revealing: "What we deny is that the [Cartesian] picture of the inner process gives us the correct idea of the use of the word 'to remember.' We say that this picture with its ramifications stands in the way of our seeing the use of the word as it is." Indeed, it is his view that the Cartesian picture of the inner process doesn't give us the correct idea of the use of any word, including the word "pain." We say that this picture with its ramifications stands in the way of our seeing the use of the word as it is. I think Wittgenstein could accept this amended statement without any qualms. The same holds for the other psychological terms used in claim 1.

So far these considerations show he rejects claim 1. They also clarify the sort of a claim he takes it to be and what sort of claim he thinks it is not. In particular, he thinks it is a grammatical and not an experiential proposition. Grammatical propositions that you want to espouse, you feel must be true; you are convinced they could not not be true. Thus the Cartesian feels you could not learn the concept pain—and all other psychological concepts—any other way than claim 1 says. Notice that this by itself does not show that claim 1 is mistaken. For the proposition "One plays patience [single solitaire] by oneself" is also a grammatical proposition, but a grammatical proposition that is true.

7.2 The Impossibility of Ascribing Psychological States to Others

Let us turn now to Wittgenstein's actual argument against the first premise of the skeptic's argument. He cannot just say that we could not get the concept of pain as premise 1 maintains, because our concept of pain is public and it would not be if that premise were true. For that would be merely to assume one of the points at issue. Defenders of premise 1— Cartesians, Humeans, Russellians—could then assert the counterclaim that the concept of pain is basically private, as the passage suggests. Wittgenstein's line of attack is to show us that we could not get any concept this way. A fortiori, we could not get the concept of pain, thought, sensation this way.

Consider what is involved in fully having the concept of something, the concept of a cow or of red, say. If you have these concepts, you must be able to recognize instances of the concept—that is, cows and red things— as well as what things are not cows or red, assuming that you are in the proper circumstances. Obviously, if it is dark, you may not recognize the cow in the field or the red fire truck. Or if you have red glasses on, you may see something as red that is not. But blind people will not see the red object, or be able to distinguish it from things that are not red, no matter what the circumstances. For this reason they do not fully have our concept of red. Similarly, if you have the concept of pain, you must be able to recognize instances of the concept—that is, people who are in pain. But again this does not mean that you will never make mistakes. For example, you may not be able to tell that people are in pain if they hide it from you or you may think that they are in pain when they are not if they pretend they are. The same point holds for the concepts of having a thought, sensation, experience, and so forth.

Suppose it is true, as claim 1 has it, that when I feel pain, I am in direct contact with it, that I apprehend its nature by merely fixing my attention on it. Let me baptize the thing I feel as "pain." Can I now ascribe pain to others? Can I make sense of others being in pain? Wittgenstein would say I cannot make sense of another person's being in pain. Descartes would counter that I can.

Descartes would say there is no problem here, since all I have to do is suppose that the other person has the same kind of thing as I have (though not the same individual thing) when I have a pain (see PI, §350). In other words, I simply transfer the idea, the concept, of pain that I have to objects outside myself (see PI, §283). This is essentially Descartes's response to Wittgenstein's contention that I cannot make sense of others being in pain in the Cartesian view. It can be called the *explanation by means of identity*. If it is sound, it seems we need not accept the conclusion of the foregoing skeptical argument.

Wittgenstein counters that the explanation by means of identity is actually no explanation.

[The answer that] "if I suppose that someone has a pain, then I am simply supposing that he has just the same as I have so often had." . . . gets us no further. It is as if I were to say: "You surely know what 'It is 5 o'clock here' means; so you also know what 'It's 5 o'clock on the sun' means. It means simply that it is just the same time there as it is here when it is 5 o'clock." —The explanation by means of *identity* does not work here. For I know well enough that one can call 5 o'clock here and 5 o'clock there "the same time," but what I do not know is in what cases one is to speak of its being the same time here and there.

In exactly the same way it is no explanation to say: the supposition that he has a pain is simply the supposition that he has the same as I. For *that* part of the grammar is quite clear to me: that is, that one will say that the stove has the same experience as I, *if* one says: it is in pain and I am in pain. (PI, §350)

Yet we go on wanting to say: "Pain is pain—whether *he* has it, or *I* have it; and however I come to know whether he has a pain or not." . . . When you ask me "Don't you know, then, what I mean when I say that the stove is in pain?" —I can reply: These words may lead me to have all sorts of images; but their usefulness goes no further. And I can also imagine something in connection with the words: "It was just 5 o'clock in the afternoon on the sun"—such as a grandfather clock which points to 5. (PI, §351)

Wittgenstein's point is that just because some words lead you to have all sorts of images, or to imagine something in connection with them, it does not mean you understand them.

Perhaps what Wittgenstein is saying here will become clearer if I give another illustration, this one from a short piece by Lewis Carroll about two clocks. In it Lewis Carroll proves that a stopped clock is better than one that loses a minute a day.[1] Let us call the stopped clock clock A. A is exactly right twice every day. The other clock (clock B) is exactly right only once in two years. Which is better, a clock that is right only once in two years or a clock that is right twice every day? You say the latter. So A is better than B. But A does not go at all and B loses a minute a day. So you say B is better than A. Now you have contradicted yourself once.

You may object: But I cannot tell with clock A when it is the time that it says it is—that is, when it is right.

Reply: Well, suppose it points to 8 o'clock. Don't you see that the clock is right *at* 8 o'clock? So when 8 o'clock comes round, your clock is right.

I see that.

Okay. Then you've contradicted yourself *twice*.

Objection: But how am I to know when 8 o'clock *does* come? My clock won't tell me.

You've got to be patient. You know that when 8 o'clock comes, your clock is right. So just keep your eye fixed on your clock, and *the very moment it is right* it will be 8 o'clock.

Lewis Carroll, like Wittgenstein, is showing here just how empty this explanation by means of identity is. It really explains nothing. The objector is quite right to feel dissatisfied with the explanation given to him. For we still do not understand when Carroll's clock is right or when another person can have the same kind of experience we have, given the Cartesian assumptions.

To return to Wittgenstein's case involving psychological things, he points out that here we are not just trying to imagine pain in another part of the body, but in another subject. And the Cartesian is trying to do this "on the model of one's own." Wittgenstein replies:

> This is none too easy a thing to do: for I have to imagine pain which I *do not feel* on the model of the pain which I *do feel*. That is, what I have to do is not simply to make a transition in imagination from one place of pain to another. As, from pain in the hand to pain in the arm. For I am not to imagine that I feel pain in some region of his body. (Which would also be possible.) (PI, §302)

His view is that it is impossible to imagine pain I do not feel on the model of the pain I do feel, given the Cartesian assumptions.

In short, even if I could acquire the concept of pain—and all other psychological concepts—simply from having the thing, I still could not make sense of anyone else's being in pain, or thinking, or feeling, or experiencing something. Hence I could never understand second- or third-person ascriptions of psychological predicates. So the Cartesian view leads to conceptual solipsism, which in turn implies epistemological solipsism. From what has been said earlier about what is involved in having the concept of something, it also follows that I could not even be said really to have the concept of pain, since I would not then be able to recognize most instances of somebody's being in pain.

7.3 The Impossibility of Ascribing Psychological States to Yourself

But, comes the reply, I would still be able to recognize all instances of psychological things that are perceivable to me—namely, my own—whether I was in pain, had a thought, a sensation, an experience, and so forth.

Other people's pains, thoughts, sensations, experiences are not perceivable to me; hence I need not be able to recognize them. After all I am not required to be able to recognize cows and horses I cannot perceive in order to have the concept of these animals. Let us consider whether it is nevertheless true that I could at least ascribe pain, thoughts, and sensations to myself. Wittgenstein denies that I could if I acquired these concepts from contact with some private object of pain, of thought, and so on, which would explain why I cannot apply the concept to others either. Thus we get the strong conclusion that none of these psychological concepts could be acquired in the way imagined.

But why could I not acquire these psychological concepts as premise 1 alleges? Why could I not learn what pain is simply from having it? Suppose I have pain. Could I not then call what I have "pain"? And could I not then ascribe pain to myself? Suppose sometime in the future I say to myself: "Now I have pain again." How do I know whether I am using the term correctly? Whether I am calling the right thing "pain"? Maybe I am confusing it with something else. How do I know that it is the same thing I experienced before? That it is an instance of the same kind? Or that I have really named it? (See PI, §257.) If I reply that I remember it is, notice that there is no way this memory claim can be confirmed or disconfirmed.

There are several questions here. Two are: (1) Can I even name such a thing to myself if I cannot name it to others? Some think this is possible, that there is no problem here. (2) Even supposing I can do this, can I reidentify it without appeal to something public? By hypothesis, I have nothing external to appeal to in this view. But, then, I cannot call what I do justified, for "justification consists in appealing to something independent" (PI, §265). In short, I cannot tell whether I am using the term correctly. It seems I can just repeat my claim. But repetition of a claim in no way justifies it or shows it to be correct.

Wittgenstein asks us to imagine the following case.

I want to keep a diary about the recurrence of a certain sensation. To this end I associate it with the sign "S" and write this sign in a calendar for every day on which I have the sensation. —I will remark first of all that a definition of the sign cannot be formulated. —But still I can give myself a kind of ostensive definition. —How? Can I point to the sensation? Not in the ordinary sense. But I speak, or write the sign down, and at the same time I concentrate my attention on the sensation—and so, as it were, point to it inwardly. —But what is this ceremony for? for that is all it seems to be! A definition surely serves to establish the meaning of a sign. —Well, that is done precisely by the concentration of my attention; for in this way I impress on myself the connection between the sign and the sensation. —But "I impress it on myself" can only mean [here, in this context]: this process brings it about that I remember the connection *right* in the future. But in the present case I have no criterion of correctness. One would like to say: whatever is going to seem right to me is right. And that only means that here we can't talk about 'right.' (PI, §258)

That is, there is a distinction between thinking you are using a word in the same way, consistently, and hence as part of a linguistic practice, and really doing so; or between thinking you are right and being right; and, finally, between thinking you have reidentified something and really having reidentified it. Yet the Cartesian has no criteria for telling whether he has done these things; so he has destroyed these distinctions. Some think Wittgenstein is bringing in the verification theory here. But this is a mistake. The argument assumes no such theory; it presupposes no underlying general claim that statements are meaningful if and only if they are verifiable. Wittgenstein's point is simply that the distinction between following a rule and thinking you are following a rule is lost if there are no criteria for the former. This is because it is part of the notion of following a rule that you may think you are and be right or you may think you are and be wrong. In other words, the notion of following a rule is subject to both error and success. " 'Obeying a rule' is a practice. And to *think* one is obeying a rule is not to obey a rule. Hence it is not possible to obey a rule 'privately': otherwise thinking one was obeying a rule would be the same thing as obeying it" (PI, §202). The point Wittgenstein is making in PI, §258, is that the Cartesian speaker has no criteria of correctness. It follows that if you accept premise 1, you cannot recognize pain in yourself or in others. Therefore, you do not have the concept of pain. Consequently, claim 1 must be false.

Notice that this argument applies not only against the Cartesian view, but also against those who argue for a mixed position that there are two senses of "pain" and of other psychological terms, a public and a private sense of these terms. For these reasons, Wittgenstein considers that a person giving himself a private definition of a word is like your right hand giving your left hand money. Why can't it be done? He admits in PI, §268:

My right hand can put [money] into my left hand. My right hand can write a deed of gift and my left hand a receipt. —But the further practical consequences would not be those of a gift. When the left hand has taken the money from the right, etc., we shall ask: "Well, and what of it?" And the same could be asked if a person had given himself a private definition of a word; I mean, if he has said the word to himself and at the same time has directed his attention to a sensation.

Again, we could compare this private ostensive definition to the turning of a knob that looks as if it could be used to turn on some part of a machine, but that is really merely an ornament, not connected with the mechanism. This is a comparison he uses in PI, §270.

Neither can other people tell Cartesian speakers whether they are using the term correctly, for other people have no idea—and could not have any idea—what they are talking about. Premise 1, along with premises 2 and 3, gets into the idea of private language. Together they imply that psychological language is a private language, where by this is meant a language that not only is not understood by anybody else, but also could not be understood by anybody else. As Wittgenstein says: "The individual words of this language are to refer to what can only be known to the person speaking; to his immediate private sensations. So another person cannot understand the language" (PI, §243).

We have seen, then, that it is Wittgenstein's view that you cannot learn the concept of pain, and psychological concepts generally, through private ostensive definition. Nor can there be a private language, in the sense explained. In a genuine language, words are used according to rules and the conventions of the language. This, of course, in no way implies that Wittgenstein rejects the notion of ostensive definition or that he is committed to saying that ostensive definitions could not help someone to learn the meaning of a term. Such a definition might help you learn the meanings of the term "rock" and "beetle," for example.

What has been said connects up with the famous passage about the beetle in the box.

Now someone tells me that *he* knows what pain is only from his own case! —Suppose everyone had a box with something in it: we call it a "beetle." No one can look into anyone else's box, and everyone says he knows what a beetle is only by looking at *his* beetle. —Here it would be quite possible for everyone to have something different in his box. One might even imagine such a thing constantly changing. —But suppose the word "beetle" had a use in these people's language? —If so it would not be used as the name of a thing. The thing in the box has no place in the language-game at all; not even as a *something*: for the box might even be empty. —No, one can 'divide through' by the thing in the box; it cancels out, whatever it is. (PI, §293)

Nor will appeal to memory help answer these objections, for seeming to remember something must be distinguished from really remembering it. Our memories sometimes deceive. Wittgenstein writes, "Always get rid of the idea of the private object in this way: assume that it constantly changes, but that you do not notice the change because your memory constantly deceives you" (PI, p. 207). Again in PI, §260 he replies to the objection:

"Well, I *believe* that this is the sensation S again." —Perhaps you *believe* that you believe it!
   Then did the man who made the entry in the calendar make a note of *nothing whatever*? —Don't consider it a matter of course that a person is making a note of something when he makes a mark—say in a calendar. For a note has a function, and this "S" so far has none.

It is easy to misunderstand what Wittgenstein is saying here. You may object: but surely you do not always need the support of others. Robinson Crusoe, the shipwrecked sailor, was able to talk about his feelings and thoughts even while he was all alone. True. Wittgenstein would not want to deny that this is possible. We must remember, however, that Robinson Crusoe's language is not a private language. Nor is Wittgenstein maintaining that you can never have confidence in your memory. All he is insisting on is that there are independent checks on memory and that we do not always resort to what memory tells us as the verdict of the highest court of appeal. He gives the following example to show that we do not always resort to memory as the highest court.

What do we regard as the criterion for remembering it [the color that a word stands for] right? —When we work with a sample instead of our memory there are circumstances in which we say that the sample has changed color and we judge of this by memory. But can we not sometimes speak of a darkening (for example) of our memory-image [of our memory-image darkening with time]? Aren't we as much at the mercy of memory as of a sample? (For someone might feel like saying: "If we had no memory we should be at the mercy of a sample.") —Or perhaps of some chemical reaction. Imagine that you were supposed to paint a particular color "C," which was the color that appeared when the chemical substances X and Y combined. —Suppose that the color struck you as brighter on one day than on another;

would you not sometimes say: "I must be wrong, the color is certainly the same as yesterday"? This shows that we do not always resort to what memory tells us as the verdict of the highest court of appeal. (PI, §56)

In short, memory claims are corrigible and correctable by appeal to public things, which include physical phenomena and not just community responses. On the other hand, these public things are themselves sometimes corrected by memory, as in the case of the sample described above. Neither memory claims nor public things are immune from scrutiny and criticism. All the Cartesian users of "S" can do, however, is rely on their own memories, which are checked by each other. Wittgenstein says this is like buying several copies of the morning paper to assure yourself that what it says is true (PI, §265). If they were different papers, this would not be at all absurd. However, there is this difference from Descartes's situation: morning papers can themselves be checked by other things besides other newspapers; they can be checked by what people observe taking place in the world. Wittgenstein's point is not that you never know if memory is correct. (He is not a memory skeptic.) But rather that there are no checks on memory for the Cartesian. All we have are memory claims, which is not the way it is in reality.

Wittgenstein's conclusion is that the term "S" would have no use either in ascribing pain to others or in ascribing it to yourself. Hence you could not understand the meaning of the word "pain" as claim 1 says you do. "You learned the *concept* 'pain'," according to Wittgenstein, "when you learned language" (PI, §384). Not that Wittgenstein wishes to imply that it is impossible to learn language and not learn the concept of pain. It is entirely possible to learn language and still not learn the concept of pain, though it would be most unusual. His point is that you cannot fully learn the concept of pain if you do not learn a language. By parity of reasoning, the same would be true of "experience," "thought," "sensation," and so forth. Note that all these words are words "of our common language, not [ones] intelligible to me alone" (PI, §261). They belong to our shared, public language.

7.4 How We Get Our Psychological Concepts

Before we examine Wittgenstein's refutation of premises 2 and 3, let us consider how he would explain how we get our psychological concepts—of pain, for example—or how we find out what pain is. Wittgenstein offers a possible explanation. First he asks, how do words *refer* to sensations? He answers:

> There doesn't seem to be any problem here; don't we talk about sensations every day, and give them names? But how is the connection between the name and the thing named set up? This question is the same as: how does a human being learn the meaning of the names of sensations?—of the word 'pain' for example. Here is one possibility: words are connected with the primitive, the natural, expressions of the sensation and used in their place. A child has hurt himself and he cries; and then adults talk to him and teach him exclamations and, later, sentences. They teach the child new pain-behavior.
> "So you are saying that the word 'pain' really means crying?" —On the contrary: the verbal expression of pain replaces crying and does not describe it. (PI, §244)

In other words, there is natural pain behavior, which is publicly observable. Our pain language is connected to this publicly observable behavior. Wittgenstein also asserts: "Only of what behaves like a human being can one say that it *has* pains" (PI, §283). Thus pain is essentially related to human behavior, contrary to claim 1. But if my words for sensations are tied up with my natural expressions of sensation, then, according to him, my language is a public one. "Someone else might understand it as well as I" (PI, §256). The child falls down and begins to cry. We say he has a pain, and comfort the child. Later the child says "I'm in pain" on such occasions. If you doubt the existence of pain in this case, why not also in the first, where you only have the primitive, the natural, expression of pain? But the fact is you do not doubt it in either, at least not in a real case. As he says: "Just try—in a real case—to doubt someone else's fear or pain" (PI, §303). "I can be as *certain* of someone else's sensations as of any fact" (PI, p. 224).

7.5 Some Mistaken Views about Knowledge and Access

Let us turn now to Wittgenstein's refutation of some of the claims embedded in claims 2 and 3. Wittgenstein would say these passages reflect a mistaken view of knowledge. Consider first the claim that I have direct, certain, and immediate knowledge of my own thoughts, pains, experiences, feelings, but that I can only guess or surmise on the basis of your behavior whether you are sad, in pain, happy, etc. Writes Wittgenstein:

> If we are using the word "to know" as it is normally used (and how else are we to use it?), then other people very often know when I am in pain. —Yes, but all the same not with the certainty with which I know it myself! —It can't be said of me at all (except perhaps as a joke) that I *know* I am in pain. What is it supposed to mean—except perhaps that I *am* in pain? (PI, §246)

It is easy to misunderstand this passage. Some think he is saying, or implying, that perhaps you are in doubt whether you are in pain. Not at all. That would be absurd. It makes no sense, according to Wittgenstein, for you to doubt such a thing. You can doubt that other people are in pain but not that you are (PI, §246). He makes much the same point later in his *Investigations* when he writes

> that what someone else says to himself is hidden from me is part of the *concept* 'saying inwardly.' Only "hidden" is the wrong word here; for if it is hidden from me, it ought to be apparent to him, *he* would have to *know* it. But he does not 'know' it; only, the doubt which exists for me does not exist for him. (PI, pp. 220–21)

Why, then, does Wittgenstein say that you cannot say, except perhaps as a joke, that you know you are in pain? What could it mean other than that you are in pain? His qualification suggests it might be an emphatic and unusual way of simply saying you are in pain. Wittgenstein argues in support of his position this way: " 'I know what I want, wish, believe, feel, . . .' (and so on through all the psychological verbs) is either philosophers' nonsense, or at any rate *not* a judgment *a priori*" (PI, p. 221). Presumably it would not be a judgment a priori if we here used emotion words such as "love," "hate," etc., since it makes sense for me to doubt whether I am in love, whether I hate someone, etc. It is possible to be in error about such things.

But why should it be philosophers' nonsense to say that you know you are in pain? He gives the answer in the next sentence: " 'I know . . .' may mean 'I do not doubt . . .' but does not mean that the words 'I doubt . . .' are *senseless*, that doubt is logically excluded." I take Wittgenstein to be saying: "I know . . ." implies "I do not doubt. . . ." This in turn implies that the words "I doubt . . ." make sense if "I know . . ." makes sense.

Accordingly, "I know . . ." does not imply that the words "I doubt . . ." are *senseless*, that doubt is logically excluded. On the contrary. But these words are senseless in the case of your own present pain; doubt is logically excluded for you in such a case. You cannot be in error about your own present pain. It means nothing for you to doubt whether you are in pain. That is why

> if anyone said "I do not know if what I have got is a pain or something else," we should think something like, he does not know what the English word "pain" means; and we should explain it to him. —How? Perhaps by means of gestures, or by pricking him with a pin and saying: "See, that's what pain is!" This explanation, like any other, he might understand right, wrong, or not at all. And he will show which he does by his use of the word, in this as in other cases.
>
> If he now said, for example: "Oh, I know what 'pain' means; what I don't know is whether *this*, that I have now, is pain"—we should merely shake our heads and be forced to regard his words as a queer reaction which we have no idea what to do with. . . .
>
> That expression of doubt has no place in the language-game; but if we cut out human behavior [as the Cartesian does], which is the expression of sensation, it looks as if I might *legitimately* begin to doubt afresh. (PI, §288)

In short, it seems "I know I am in pain" either must be philosophers' nonsense or simply an emphatic way of saying "I am in pain."

Wittgenstein suggests a third possible interpretation of "I know I am in pain" in PI, §247. There he considers the statement that only you can know if you have a particular intention. He replies, "One might tell someone this when one was explaining the meaning of the word 'intention' to him. For then it means: *that* is how we use it. (And here 'know' means that the expression of uncertainty is senseless.)" By parity of reasoning, "I know I am in pain" might be taken as a grammatical statement, telling someone that here the expression of uncertainty is senseless.

Later in his *Investigations*, Wittgenstein also gives a second argument against saying "I know I am in pain" and in support of the parallel claim: "It is correct to say 'I know what you are thinking,' and wrong to say 'I know what I am thinking.' (A whole cloud of philosophy condensed into a drop of grammar.)" (p. 222). He writes: "One says 'I know [that]' where one can also say 'I believe' or 'I suspect [that]'; where one can find out [what one believes or suspects]" (p. 221). But it makes no sense to say "I believe or I suspect I am in pain" and then to find out that indeed I am.

We should not say, Wittgenstein concludes, that our own present pains, thoughts, intentions, etc., are known by us, unless saying this is merely an emphatic way of making the psychological statement or we mean by it the grammatical remark, "The expression of uncertainty is senseless here" or "Here it would make no sense to find out that it is or isn't so."

Notice that in all of these cases Wittgenstein always appeals to the way the word is actually used in the language-game that is its original home. We check what the philosophers say—for example, the Cartesian and the skeptic—by appeal to the way the word is actually used (PI, §116). For "philosophy may in no way interfere with the actual use of language; it can in the end only describe it" (PI, §124). Hence claims made about what we do and do not have "access" to (see premises 2 and 3) have to be checked by appeal to the way we use the word "access."

When we consider how we use the word "access," it becomes clear how Wittgenstein would refute the claims made about it in premises 2 and 3. He would say these premises reflect a misuse of that term. Consider some correct uses of the word "access": "The United States knows that in the event of a crisis it would have access to South Africa's facilities." "I'm going to go along with our leaders. They have access to information I don't have." "By eliminating some of the architectural barriers built into older buildings many handicapped students and faculty have gained increased access to campus buildings." Contrast now the way the philosophers use this word when they say: "Each of us has access only to his or her own mind. We never have access to each other's thoughts, sensations, pains, experiences, feelings." Here nothing would count as having access to another person's mind, to his or her thoughts, sensations, pains, experiences, or feelings. How unlike the correct uses! In every one of these cases it makes sense either to have or not to have whatever access is being discussed—that is, such access can be gained or lost. For example, even though I do not have access to information you have access to, it makes sense for me to have such access. And even though the United States has access at this time to facilities in South Africa, we can easily imagine losing such access. The same points apply to the other examples. We may conclude that the philosopher's use of the term "access" is different from the everyday use of the term, for it does not permit access to be something that can be gained or lost. The philosopher's use is really a misuse of the expression.

The confusion about access to psychological things arises out of another confusion and misuse of language involved in the second claim, namely, that I cannot have your pain, think your thoughts, or feel what you feel, for example, your tiredness, your headache. This assumption will be refuted in the next section.

7.6 You Can Have My Feelings; I, Yours

Most philosophers agree that we can have the same *kinds* of feelings, that is, those that resemble one another, but probably disagree that we can have the very *same* feelings, that is, feelings that are identical with one another. I think Wittgenstein would want to make both claims. The discussion that follows has four parts. In the first, I shall present and refute the main arguments against the possibility of our ever having the very same feelings. The next part consists of compelling arguments in support of this being possible, focusing on the case of pains. Essentially the same points seem to hold for other psychological concepts—thought, belief, intention, after-image, emotion, and the like. The third part offers replies to two possible objections to this view of feelings. The concluding discussion then provides an account of how we determine that two people have the same feeling when the feeling is a pain. The harder question of how we determine that two people have the same emotion is not discussed, but presumably Wittgenstein would answer it along similar lines.

Before discussing arguments for the two opposing views, it may be worth noting why people hold them. Some fear that if two people could have the same feelings, human beings would lose both their individuality and their privacy. Further, it is thought that we would no longer stand in the special relation we now stand to our own feelings—a relation in which, for example, it makes no sense for us to doubt our own pains, though we can doubt whether someone else is in pain. Again, it is thought that if two people could have the same feelings, our concept of what it is to be a person would be undermined. Some feel driven to insist on the privacy of experience because they are skeptical that anyone can have knowledge of another's experience. The privacy doctrine may also spring from a feeling of separateness or alienation that people sometimes experience.

On the other side, there is another fear. If we cannot share feelings, how can people ever be close to each other, avoid living in solitude, preserve a sense of community and a common language, or know what others are thinking and feeling? A person may not connect this fear with the philosophical problem of other minds and with the question whether there can be a private language. The issue here is whether psychological experiences and the like are private, in the sense that we cannot have the very same experience. I am convinced that the Wittgensteinian view of feelings—and of pains—that is presented here entails neither a loss of human individuality nor an invasion of privacy; it requires neither a revision in our concept of what it is to be a person, nor a change in the relation in which we stand to our feelings. The fear that it has these undesirable consequences has no sound basis.

7.6.1 Refutation of the Main Arguments against the View

Four objections to the view that we can have the very same feelings will be considered. First, you sometimes hear the argument: I cannot feel what you feel—for example, your tiredness, your headache—because if I feel anything, it is my feeling, and if you feel anything, it is your feeling. Generalizing, if I have something psychological, it is mine. My feelings and experiences are mine; yours are yours. Therefore, if I have something psychological, it cannot be yours. W. T. Stace seems to have such an argument in mind when he remarks: "In so far as I feel anger [or any emotion, pain, or experience anything], it is *my* anger [emotion, pain, or experience], not yours."[2]

Regarding the first premise, it is certainly true that if I have a feeling, an experience, or a thought, it is my feeling, experience, or thought. Thus it would be absurd to say, "I have a headache; I wonder whose headache it is." But from these trivial truths, or tautologies, it does not follow that *I* cannot also have the feeling, experience, or thought you have or that *you* cannot have the feeling, experience, or thought I have.

That my feelings are mine, and yours are yours is also a tautology that neither settles nor helps to settle the question being discussed. This premise plays a role much like Alice's final explanation of why she is different from Ada: "Besides, *she's* she, and *I'm* I."[3] Such a tautology gives us no reason to think that Alice is different from Ada. Indeed, a person could quite consistently say "I'm I," and then in answer to the question "Who's Ada?" reply, "I'm she." Even Alice—if she nibbled on more hallucinogenic mushrooms—might say and think this. Clever Elsie in the fairy tale of the brothers Grimm is similarly confused. She raises the ridiculous question "Am I myself or am I someone else?"[4] The question is an impossible one because of course she is herself—everyone is himself or herself—and not someone else. But this leaves unanswered the question who anyone is. Similarly, while each person's pains are his or her own—and mine are mine and yours are yours—this does not answer the question whether mine are also yours or whether we can have the same pains.

The fact is that things that I have and that are mine, in the sense that I possess or own them (my dog, my house, my bicycle), may also be yours, in the same sense of the word "yours," and vice versa. Even things that I have and that are mine, in what we may call the nonownership or non-possession sense of these words (my mother, my troubles), may also be yours, in the same nonownership sense of the words "have" and "yours," and again vice versa. In short, just because for some values of x, my (or your) having x, implies that it is my (or your) x, it does not follow that it is exclusively mine (or exclusively yours) and that you (or I) cannot also have it. The first argument, then, involves a non sequitur, and should be rejected.

Some will object that some of the things I mentioned (mothers, bicycles, dogs) are not comparable to feelings. For while they may be had by both of us and be mine as well as yours, such a possibility is ruled out in the case of feelings, or, more generally, in the case of things psychological; such things, if they are had by one person, cannot be another's. The trouble with this objection is that it merely assumes the point at issue and thus provides no argument in support of its conclusion that we cannot have the same feelings. Interpreting the second premise—that my feelings are mine, and yours are yours—as merely a way of saying mine are not yours and yours are not mine, again, just assumes the point at issue. Thus the first argument either involves a non sequitur or it begs the question.

A second argument you sometimes hear is that two people cannot have the same pain, because they are two people and one person cannot, at one and the same time, be another person. Or, putting it another way: since people are numerically different, their pains and feelings must also be different. Cavell suggests such an argument in his essay "Knowing and Acknowledging."[5] Stace, too, says, "I can never be you, nor you me" as a reason for concluding that the mental state I am aware of is mine and not yours.[6] Even more clearly and simply, A. J. Ayer asserts that when there are two persons, "we are to say that there are two feelings and not one, just because there are two persons."[7]

This kind of argument confuses the question of personal identity with the question of the identity of experiences or feelings. Certainly it is a different state of affairs if I have a pain or if you do, but that does not entail that we cannot have the same pain. It is also a different state of affairs if I am six foot tall or if you are six foot tall, but we can still be the same height, that is, both be six foot tall. So we cannot assume that when we say truly that x has the same pain as y, we are saying or implying that $x = y$; they may or may not be identical.

A third and similar argument is to be found in Plato. Sensations and the way something appears to two people, or even to one person, on different occasions, are never the same, since human beings "never remain in the same condition" and "there is all the difference in the world between one man and another."[8] Richard Hall, a colleague of mine, pointed out to me that this argument, unlike the previous one, seems to refer to the *qualitative,* rather than the *numerical,* difference of people. If we make the argument fully explicit, it would go something like this: (a) Having the same feeling requires that there be no qualitative difference in the condition two people are in; (b) there is always some qualitative difference in the condition two people are in; (c) hence you and I can never have the same feeling.

Even if premise (b) is true—and it is not evident that it is—premise (a) is not. For it is correct to say that two people can have the same experiences or feelings even if they are not in exactly the same qualitative condition. The fact that they differ in their blood pressure, for example, does not mean they cannot have the same feeling of nausea while eating treacle pudding. Similarly, we cannot assume that when we say that Joe has the same pain as Mary, we are saying or implying that there is no qualitative difference in the condition they are in; they may or may not be in the same condition. All of which is not to assert that questions of identity of the conditions that human beings are in are completely unrelated to those concerning the identity of what people feel. Change in blood pressure, posture, rate of respiration, and the like often affect our feelings.

A fourth and last argument contends that you and I cannot have certain feelings, for example, the same pain, since even if we both feel pain, say, in our legs, your pain will be in one place (your leg) and mine will be in another place (my leg); hence the pains will have different spatial properties. Using the principle of the indiscernibility of identicals—that is, if $x = y$, then $(F)(Fx$ if and only if $Fy)$[9]—we can now infer that no matter how alike, our pains cannot be identical since they have different spatial properties. Don Locke might accept such an argument, for he contends that our bodily sensations cannot be identical so long as they have different locations in physical space.[10]

Notice, first, that this argument cannot be used to show that we cannot have the same feelings, for some feelings, such as emotions, do not have any bodily location.[11] Second, the argument does not even establish its more modest conclusion, that is, that two people as a matter of fact never can have the same pain because their pains have different spatial locations. To show this, merely consider the case of Siamese twins. Suppose they are joined together just above the buttocks and a wasp stings them right where they are joined. Imagine that as a result they both feel a stinging pain at that place and that they sincerely describe their pain in the same way. In such a case the principle of the indiscernibility of identicals is not violated, for the twins feel pain in the same—and not just in a corresponding—place and they both agree on the properties of the pain. Thus our last argument also fails to show that two people can never have the same pain or even the same feeling of some other kind.

But this reply still grants too much to the argument. It leaves us only with the possibility that Siamese twins (and perhaps those with phantom limbs, and possibly a few others) may have the same pain. Wittgenstein suggests what is needed is a new philosophical perspective. Philosophers need to change their way of thinking about feelings, thoughts, and the like. In particular, they must resist their tendency to "try to find a substance for a substantive," which he says is "one of the great sources of philosophical bewilderment" (BB, p. 1). Instead of thinking of some entity that is someone's feeling, we should conceive of feelings as being (truly or falsely) predicable of people and other living organisms. We are not to think of them as things that can be pointed to, either inwardly or outwardly. Thus he says, "'Joy' designates nothing at all. Neither an inward nor an outward thing" (Z, §487). He also remarks, paradoxically, that pain "is not a *something, but not a *nothing* either!" (PI, §304). What he means is that it is not a something like a cow or a car, but it is not a nothing either, since it makes a difference if you have it. Sometimes the difference between having and not having a pain is slight, sometimes it is enormous: a pain can be inconvenient or horrible, even frightful. When people have a pain, however, this is not to possess or own something; in this respect, as well as others, it differs from having a vehicle or a ballpoint. When it is asserted that "Mary feels joy or pain," we avoid needless trouble, then, if we do not take this to imply that there are two things—Mary and the thing she feels, namely joy or pain. Such an assertion should be contrasted with, say, "John feels the table," which does imply that there are two things—John and the table he feels. Looking at feelings in this way, we shall no longer find it puzzling how people generally—and not merely Siamese twins—can have the same feelings.

7.6.2 Arguments in Support of the Wittgensteinian Thesis

It is widely agreed that two people can have the same feeling. But this is quite compatible with there being a sense of "same feeling"—individually or numerically—in which two people cannot have the same feeling. The present discussion aims to show that there is no such sense of "same feeling." Two arguments will be given.

First, it is significant that when you remark that you have the same pain as another person, or that you have the same pain as you had last week, you never add—at least not outside of the philosophy classroom—"Of course, my pain is not numerically or individually the same pain; it is only qualitatively the same, or the same kind of pain as yours, or as the one I had last week." Even philosophers when they leave the classroom or study never dream of applying such a distinction to feelings. "Numerically or individually the same pain" indeed! Anyone who talked that way to a neighbor, friend, or doctor we would regard as in need of instruction in how to speak the language. The expressions "pain" and "same pain" have no such use in English. But this is not true of physical things. When you say you have the same car Joe has, you may add, to prevent a misunderstanding, "Of course it's not *really* the same car. They're just exactly alike." This would be the case if there were two cars. Then they would be numerically distinct, that is, distinct in number.

What has been said about the use of the word "pain" is also true of the words "feeling" and "same feeling." This is not to deny that we sometimes speak of having the same *kind* of feelings, that is, feelings that resemble one another. For example, we may both have the same kind of headache (say, a tension or migraine headache) though we have different headaches—mine perhaps is throbbing and yours is not. Similarly, two tables can have the same kind of color—a pale one—though the colors are different; one may be yellow, the other pink. But if the headaches or colors are in every way qualitatively indistinguishable, we say they are one and the same headache, one and the same color. There remains no possibility of their now still being individually different headaches or different colors. We don't add, "Although indistinguishable, they are numerically or individually different colors, different headaches."

Contrast again the way we talk of bicycles, trees, chairs, and the like, and of having the same bicycles, trees, chairs. Here we find a preexisting linguistic practice in which a numerical/qualitative or individual/kind distinction is made. Not only may two trees differ in kind—one being a needle-leaved evergreen, the other, a broad-leaved evergreen—but they may also differ as individuals even though they belong to all of the same kinds and are qualitatively indistinguishable. For example, even if they are both needle-leaved evergreens, both spruces, and even both blue spruces, equally tall and with the exact same shape and color, we can rightly say they are nevertheless two trees and thus numerically or individually different from one another. It follows that the numerical/qualitative or individual/kind distinction has sense applied to trees. But it has no more sense applied to pains, or to feelings in general, than it does to colors or to heights.

Since this argument will not persuade those who think appeals to our use of language have no relevance to philosophy, I will shortly supplement it with a second, I hope conclusive, argument. Surprisingly, Cavell, who is himself a Wittgensteinian, seems unmoved by the above argument. He replies, in effect, that the question whether my headache is numerically identical with another's is intelligible and *can* be answered by each of us. He says simply: "The answer is, of course not!" even if the headaches are qualitatively the same. But it may seem pointless to us either to ask or to answer the question; and this, he contends, may fully explain why, outside of philosophy, we never say this sort of thing.[12] Note that Cavell's "of course" is merely another way of assuming the point at issue.

Let us inquire now what the criterion of identity of headaches is for philosophers who assert that two people cannot have numerically identical headaches. Judging from the four arguments given above, there seem to be four different possible criteria for two persons having numerically, or individually, the same headache. The criterion is either (1) that they be one person, (2) that there be no qualitative difference in the condition the people are in, (3) that when one of them has a headache, it not be his or her headache (this is in effect a denial of the first premise of the first argument in Section 7.6.1), or (4) that a person's headache not be his or her headache (that is, that the second premise of the first argument be false). But, as has been suggested, such criteria are all self-contradictory or otherwise impossible to satisfy. No doubt defenders of the numerical/ qualitative distinction applied to feelings would agree. They might say, "That is precisely why we can never have the same individual feeling: the criteria cannot (necessarily) be fulfilled." The second argument, which follows, shows that this will not do. It should settle the dispute.

Wittgenstein writes: "If as a matter of logic you exclude other people's having something, it loses its sense to say that you have it" (PI, §398). That is, if it is logically impossible for other people to have the individual feeling I have, then it loses its sense to say I have this individual feeling. By extension, if you exclude other people's having something by making it an absurdity for them to have it, then again it loses its sense to say that you have it. Saying "I have x" would have no function in the language if it were logically impossible or absurd for anyone else to have x. Thus saying "I have such and such a pain," implies it makes sense to think of other people's having such and such a pain. But the defender of the numerical/qualitative or individual/kind distinction applied to feelings makes it logically impossible or absurd for another to have individually, or numerically, the same feeling I have. Accordingly, such a philosopher is committed to the above antecedents. In such a view, it therefore loses its sense for anyone to say that I (or you) have an individual feeling or that I (or you) have a numerically different feeling. The moral is: the use of the words "pain," "love," and so on cannot be limited by a rule saying that no one else can (logically or without absurdity) have numerically or individually the same pain, love, etc., that I have.

7.6.3 Replies to Two Possible Objections

I would like now to anticipate, and reply to, two objections to this Wittgensteinian view. The first contends that our everyday language opposes the view being advocated here. This claim is based on the following considerations. It is alleged that there are certainly times when we refer to our feelings and describe them. Thus you may say, "the pain in my knee is sharp and intense." Moreover, particular feelings seem to last over time and to be subject to change. One says such things as, "The feeling persisted for hours, but sometimes it grew better and sometimes worse." Finally, it is asserted that feelings can be counted; so again they must be things. This seems to receive confirmation by the fact that a person may report there were three dull, throbbing headaches he or she had last week.

I believe the objector is misled by the surface grammar of our pain language and feeling language. It is true that we make statements reporting how many feelings, sensations, or pains were experienced over a certain period of time. But such assertions can be restated with no loss of meaning in words that speak about the number of times someone had a feeling. For example, the sentence "Three dull, throbbing headaches made it hard for me to concentrate on my work the last couple of days" can be translated into "At three different times during the last couple of days I had a dull, throbbing headache, making it hard for me to concentrate on my work." Similarly, talk about the feeling lasting and changing can again be paraphrased away, in this case into talk about somebody having a feeling for a certain time and then having a different feeling at another time.

Finally, while it is true that we talk about our feelings, if we ask what we mean when we do, we see that what we say is always elliptical for some statement about ourselves. That is, it is always legitimate to paraphrase away our reference to feelings. Putting it more technically, we do not have to quantify over them, committing ourselves to the existence of such entities. Thus the sentence "The pain in my knee is sharp and intense" can be translated into "I have a sharp and intense pain in my knee." I conclude that we need not refer to feelings in order to say what we want to, and that our everyday language does not commit us to the existence of such things.

I turn now to the second objection. If we agree with Thomas Reid—as we seem to be doing—and say that *"feeling a pain* signifies no more than *being pained,*"[13] and we treat other feeling predicates along the same lines, we are in effect interpreting feeling predicates as one-place predicate terms: they take exactly one subject or singular term. But then, Davidson suggests,[14] we are making our feeling language unlearnable. For we can certainly never learn the infinite vocabulary implied by this view.

While it is certainly true that we cannot learn an infinite number of feeling predicates, I do not think that the Wittgensteinian view defended here commits us to such a vocabulary. There are at least two reasons for saying this. First, it does not seem correct to interpret pain predicates as one-place predicates. They seem rather to be three-place predicates, since pains involve a living organism, a place or location, and a time. Hence if I say "Yesterday I had a mild throbbing pain in my elbow" and you say "This morning I had a mild throbbing pain in my knee," I believe we are both using the same feeling predicate, not two different ones. Second, I think that if we examine our actual feeling vocabulary—especially our language for talking about pains—we will be struck by its poverty rather than by its richness. In short, we are hardly dealing with an infinite vocabulary, and so with one that cannot be learned.

7.6.4 How We Determine That Two People Have the Same Pain

Now that it has been established that we can have the same feeling, let us turn to the questions how we determine that we do. When do we have identity of feeling, of sensation, or of emotion? What are our criteria of identity? Only a partial answer will be given to these questions. The discussion will be confined to the simpler case of pain, a sensation. But, as I have said, I think an answer along similar lines could also be given to the question: How do we determine that two people have the same emotion?

One way in which we determine sameness of pain is sameness of cause; that is, we look to see what caused the pains. Suppose, for example, that Smith's and Jones's wrists are simultaneously crushed by a heavy machine. The acute pain that results has the same cause, which gives us good reason to suppose that it is the same pain or at least that they experience very similar pains. However, sameness of cause does not necessitate sameness of feeling. Your headache and mine may both be caused by drinking a fifth of whiskey, yet our headaches may be quite different. Yours might be dull and throbbing; mine, sharp and piercing. So sameness of cause, though a criterion of sameness of pain, does not entail that we have the same pain. The fact that people have different pain thresholds implies the same point, namely, that the same cause may cause different pains in different people.

Furthermore, sameness of cause is not a necessary condition for sameness of pain. We might have the same headache, even though different things caused it.

A second criterion used to determine sameness of pain is identity of pain behavior. Thus if two dogs react in the same way, for example, both shrink back in pain and whimper when touched gently on the head, we are likely to conclude that they have the same pain. If we know that their pain was caused by receiving blows on the head of roughly the same force, we probably cease to have any doubt that they have the same pain.

With human beings also, the cause of pain and the pain behavior are relevant considerations for determining the identity of pain. But a new consideration enters: how the pains are described. Indeed, this is what we rely on mainly, though the claim needs qualification—sincerity and linguistic ability also have to be considered. I maintain that if two people are both fluent in the language, have roughly the same linguistic ability, and they both sincerely describe the pain they have in the same way, then they have the same pain.

There are a number of problems with this account. First, there is the question of whether two pain descriptions are the same. Obviously they are the same when the exact same words are used—for example, you describe your pain as throbbing and I do too. Using synonymous expressions in English or in some other language also makes them the same. But the descriptions are not the same if they are incompatible, for example, you say your pain is agonizing and I say mine is mild. For the pains to be the same, they must have the same intensity and the same quality, though it is not essential that they have the same duration or even, it seems, a corresponding location. Thus the pain in my elbow could conceivably be the same as the pain you have in your knee. It has already been implied that they need not have the same location when it was observed that other people besides Siamese twins could have the same pain. In this respect pains are like colors. Two flags—think of a painted Red Cross and a Swiss flag—may have the same colors at a given time even though one has those colors for a longer period of time than the other one and they are colored neither in the same nor in corresponding locations. So words that ascribe a different intensity or a different quality of pain to someone do not give the same pain descriptions. But it is not part of the description of a pain that a certain person has it at a certain time or place any more than it is part of the description of a color to say that a certain object has that color at a certain time and place.

A second question in this account concerns the matter of sincerity or truthfulness. It is sometimes hard to tell whether someone has given a sincere description of his or her pain. But there is reason to think we can sometimes know this. Suppose some "macho" type—Mary—describes her pain as rather faint, slight, as hardly noticeable, and another "nonmacho" type—Bob—describes his pain the same way. In the case of Mary, we have reason to suspect that the description may not be fully truthful or sincere, for we know that she likes to act as if she does not feel things and is given to playing a certain kind of role. I am supposing that Mary is fond of acting really gutsy and her favorite refrain is: "I'm no lilly-livered, yellow pantywaist or little lame kid!" Our suspicions will be reinforced if we know that she has just been badly burned in a way that normally causes intense pain or if we see her grimace as though in great pain when she believes no one is watching. To make the situation even clearer, suppose that we know that Bob received only a slight injury. Such causal and/or behavioral knowledge can help us determine whether the descriptions of the pain are open and fully sincere. In the case of Bob, we would probably conclude that the description was sincere; in the case of Mary, that there was a lack of openness and much role-playing. Hence we would most likely infer that they had different pains, even though they described them in the same way. For similar reasons, different descriptions do not imply that the pains are different. The problem is that one person's "slight" may mean another person's "severe," which is a problem psychologists face when they use questionnaires to construct psychological scales.

Consider another case. Suppose a hysterical hypochondriac, Harry, describes his pain as no longer bearable. Suppose we get the same description from another person, Nancy. Again, we are not forced to conclude that they have the same pain. For once more we may believe, on the basis of what has happened and their past and present behavior, that Harry is not describing his pain in a completely truthful manner: he exaggerates it because of his unmanageable fear. Harry may think that he is dreadfully sick and in need of immediate care. On the other hand, we have no reason to doubt the sincerity of Nancy's description. In this case we will again conclude that the two people probably do not have the same pain.

The point here is twofold. First, to bring out that such cases are not counterexamples to the thesis being defended here. For in both of them, one has reason to think that the pain descriptions are not sincerely or truthfully given by one of the persons involved. Second, we note that we have ways of detecting such lack of sincerity or lack of openness, just as there are ways of recognizing sincerity and openness, although we do not always, in fact, succeed in detecting these things.

As for having the same linguistic ability, this is admittedly a somewhat indeterminate notion. But there are clear cases as well as hard ones. We all agree that Archie Bunker's linguistic gifts fall short of Proust's. I think we also have a clear enough idea of what it means to be fluent or competent in a language. If two equally inarticulate people both sincerely described their pain as "a big one," my thesis does not force us to say they have the same pain. For it may well be that, if they were both fluent and competent in English, each would sincerely go on to ascribe quite a different quality, or character, to his or her pain. One might describe it as "a dull ache in my belly," while the other might say "it feels as if my joints are being torn apart." If so, we would rightly say that their pains were different.

I hope it is now clear that you and I can have the very same thoughts, feelings, desires, and so forth, and that we should therefore reject the fourth Cartesian premise of the skeptical argument for other minds, along with the first three. This should more than suffice to refute the skeptical argument and to expose some of the weaknesses of Cartesian dualism. The next chapter will discuss Wittgenstein's notion of a criterion. This is an important notion for him. Clarifying it will help explain Wittgenstein's philosophy, especially his philosophy of mind.

Chapter 8

Characteristics of Criteria

We have now seen how Wittgenstein could counter the argument for skepticism about other human minds. One conclusion is that there must be public criteria for the mental—for being in pain, thinking, etc. We cannot get these concepts—or any others—by just being in pain or thinking and giving ourselves private, ostensive definitions of these things. "An 'inner process' stands in need of outward criteria" (PI, §580). But what exactly are these criteria we cannot do without? How should we characterize them? This chapter will try to answer these questions. It deals with Wittgenstein's view of the mental, which is often called the "criteriological view," especially by those who do not confuse his position with behaviorism. Hence we have to get clear about what he means by this key term "criterion."

8.1 *Criterion For:* A Two-Place, Irreflexive, Nonsymmetrical Relation

We speak of one thing being a criterion of or for another thing. So *criterion for* is a two-place predicate or relation—it takes two things, two subjects or singular terms. For example, somebody's continuing a series correctly is a criterion of that person's understanding the system (PI, §146). What you say and do is the criterion for what mental image you have, for example, whether it is red or some other color (PI, §377). For instance, if in response to the question "What image do you have?" you paint a picture of a red one or say that you have a red one, you satisfy some of the criteria for having a red image. The account you give of your dreams and what you say you said to yourself in your thoughts are also criteria for what you dreamed and of what you said to yourself in your thoughts, respectively. In the last two cases Wittgenstein adds that truthfulness is a guarantee of truth (PI, p. 222).

Saying that one thing is a criterion for another also implies that the things are not identical. That is, *criterion for* is an irreflexive relation.[1] Finally, if X is a criterion for Y, then Y may or may not be a criterion for X. In other words, *criterion for* is a nonsymmetrical relation.[2] Thus moaning is a criterion for being in pain, but being in pain is not a criterion for moaning. On the other hand, being a closed figure with three straight sides is a criterion for being a triangle and being a triangle is a criterion for being a closed figure with three straight sides, since this is the definition of a triangle.

8.2 Often Several Criteria for the Same State of Affairs

Crying, groaning, saying "It hurts!" in English or "Me duele!" in Spanish are all different criteria for somebody's being in pain. Wittgenstein writes of the "great variety of criteria for personal *'identity'*" (PI, §404). And he observes that in different circumstances we apply different criteria for a person reading. So there is generally, if not always, more than one criterion for the same state of affairs. *Criterion for* seems often, if not always, to be a many–one relation, in the sense that there are usually many criteria for a given state of affairs.

8.3 Providing Evidence That Something Is the Case

If X is a criterion for Y, X is something by which we can tell whether Y is the case. As we have seen, normally your continuing a series correctly is evidence that you understand it; your saying you have a red image is evidence that you have such an image; and your saying you said such and such to yourself in your thoughts is evidence that you did. Similarly, under normal circumstances your saying you had a particular dream is evidence that you did have such a dream. Later, in Sections 8.6 through 8.8, we shall see that although a criterion can give us evidence, the evidence it provides us with is not any kind of evidence.

Discussing the notion of criterion, Kenny omits the qualification "under normal circumstances." He just says flatly, "If X is a criterion of Y, then it is a necessary truth that X is evidence for Y."[3] The qualification, however, is needed. Without it we would be committed to the view that we have evidence for saying that people in plays, movies, and on TV have certain thoughts, images, and dreams simply because of what they say in playing their roles.

8.4 A Criterion Neither a Necessary Nor a Sufficient Condition

You may have a red image and never say you have a red image. You may be a good opera singer, yet be unable to sing Wagner, even though being able to sing Wagner is a criterion of a good opera singer. You may understand the series but not continue it correctly, perhaps because—perversely—you want to fail your exam. You may also have a dream or say something to yourself in your thoughts without telling anybody about the dream or your thoughts. Maybe you are too embarrassed. Finally, the machine may be able to lift a ton, even though it never lifts anything that heavy. So a criterion for something is not always a necessary condition for it.

The following examples also show that a criterion for something need not be a sufficient condition for it. Saying you have a red image, or that you just had a certain dream or thought, does not establish that you do or did, for you may be lying. Similarly, continuing a series correctly may be the result of hypnosis; you may not actually understand how to do it. And the mere fact that a piston has been put inside a cylinder does not show that it fits the cylinder: it may have been forced in under great pressure or sit in there quite loosely. That is why Hacker correctly asserts that it is wrong to maintain "if *p* is a criterion for *q,* then *p* entails *q* . . . at least if [this is] made as a *general* claim."[4]

On the other hand, a criterion for something may be a necessary and/or a sufficient condition for something. For example, being a closed figure with three straight sides is a necessary as well as a sufficient condition for being a triangle, but it is also a criterion for being a triangle. And being a male is both a criterion and a necessary, although not a sufficient, condition for being a bachelor.

8.5 Satisfying a Criterion Not Logically Decisive

We have seen from the previous point that a criterion for something is not characterized as a sufficient condition for it. So in general, it is not logically decisive evidence in the sense of implying that for which it is evidence.

But there is another way in which it falls short of being decisive. Since there are often several criteria for something, it sometimes happens that someone may satisfy some of the criteria for some state of affairs, but not others, and perhaps even satisfy other criteria for *not* being in that state of affairs. For example, you may satisfy some of the criteria for liking some-one—you invite Sally to the prom—but you fail to satisfy other criteria for liking her—you never sit at her table at meals—and you satisfy other cri-teria for actually disliking her—you remark to your friends that she has an ugly disposition.

8.6 A Criterion Is Not Mere Evidence

At this point the reader may wonder how plain empirical evidence differs from a criterion, since such evidence too is not defined as being logically decisive or as being either necessary or sufficient for the obtaining of some state of affairs. Such evidence also provides us with reason to believe that something is in a certain state. Moreover, there can be different evidence for the same state of affairs. Indeed, *evidence for* seems also to be a many–one, two-place, irreflexive, and nonsymmetrical relation. I turn now to an important difference between a criterion and evidence, which I shall illus-trate with a few examples. Hereafter when I speak of evidence, I shall mean just this plain empirical evidence, and for the other sort I shall reserve the word "criterion."

In the *Blue and Brown Books,* Wittgenstein gives an example of some-thing that is evidence but not a criterion. Imagine that experience teaches us that having an inflamed throat is a symptom of angina. So finding some-one who has an inflamed throat is evidence for saying that that person has angina. But this is not a criterion of angina. Suppose now that medical science called angina an inflammation caused by a particular bacillus. Then finding that bacillus in someone's blood would be a criterion—as well as evidence—of angina. For "then to say 'A man has angina if this bacillus is found in him' is a tautology or it is a loose way of stating the definition of 'angina.' But to say, 'A man has angina whenever he has an inflamed throat' is to make a hypothesis" (BB, p. 25).

AIDS may provide us with a second example. Experience may have taught us that unbearable fatigue is a symptom of AIDS. Then finding someone who has unbearable fatigue is evidence for saying that that person may have AIDS, especially if he is also a member of a high-risk group (for example, he is a promiscuous homosexual or a drug addict). But this is not a criterion of AIDS. On the other hand, having certain immunity problems would be a criterion for having AIDS. But unlike the foregoing example, having certain immunity problems is not definitive of AIDS, since you might have AIDS and not at this time exhibit any immunity problems and you could have immunity problems that have nothing to do with AIDS.

Finally, let me give a third example, one having nothing to do with medicine. Someone might discover by experience that whenever I am in my office an old Raleigh bicycle is to be found leaning against Linton Hall. Then finding that bicycle there will be evidence that I am in my office. But this does not constitute a criterion for people being in their offices or even for me being in my office.

Notice that in all three of the examples given—having angina, having AIDS, being in the office—we have a fairly clear distinction between what is evidence and what are criteria. But this is not always the case. In diseases doctors are often not clear, Wittgenstein says, "which phenomena are to be taken as criteria and which as symptoms" (BB, p. 25). People also disagree about what is and what is not a criterion—for example, whether rapid eye movement is a criterion or merely evidence for dreaming, or perhaps neither. Maybe it was initially evidence but now it has become a new criterion for dreaming, just as the weight of an element was once evidence for its presence but now it is a criterion for that element. Wittgenstein recognizes that the language can change in this way, that there is sometimes a "fluctuation in grammar between criteria and symptoms," or between criteria and evidence. A good example of this comes from the early history of chemistry. Originally being an acid was defined as having a sour taste and being able to dissolve many metals. It was then discovered that a piece of metal dropped into an acid solution gives off hydrogen. Today acid is defined as a substance that generates hydrogen gas upon reaction with metal. As Wittgenstein says, "In science it is usual to make phenomena that allow of exact measurement into defining criteria for an expression" (Z, §438). This fluctuation in grammar, Wittgenstein says, "makes it look as if there were nothing at all but symptoms," or evidence, which is of course a mistaken view, according to him (PI, §354).

8.7 When X Is a Criterion for Y

Suppose Jones cries, groans, and says, "My stomach hurts." Imagine this happens in "normal circumstances"—that is, not in a play, movie, or on television. You only grasp the connection of these things to pain if you recognize that, in spite of their not being necessary or sufficient conditions of being in pain, they constitute something more than mere evidence of somebody's being in pain. You must understand that they have some sort of conceptual connection with pain. But what does this mean? That such behavior, in these circumstances, gives you grounds for thinking that somebody is in pain. Hacker puts the point well: "A criterion *p*," he says, "is a grammatically (logically) determined ground or reason for the truth of *p*."[5] Thus were Smith to object, "But what do cries, groans, saying it hurts, and so on have to do with a person's being in pain?" we would suspect that Smith does not fully understand what it means to be in pain. For the criteria for something are connected in meaning with what it means to be a thing of that kind. That is why when the criteria for Y change, Wittgenstein is committed to saying the meaning of "Y" changes.

Wittgenstein's view does not, of course, imply that you can always, or usually, define what it means to be "Y" by listing the criteria for it. As Wittgenstein says, for example, the word "pain" neither means crying nor the verbal expression of pain we sometimes replace crying with and that we learn as children (PI, §244). Pain is not pain behavior (PI, §304), though the latter is a criterion for pain. Nor does the word "pain" mean pain behavior. The criteriological position is not a form of behaviorism nor any other kind of reductionist view. (See the earlier discussions of behaviorism and identity theory in Chapters 4 and 5.) However, it can be called a form of quasi-behaviorism because, like the behaviorist, criteriologists recognize that pain behavior is a criterion for pain.

8.8 What "X Is Evidence for Y" Implies

Suppose scientists discovered that whenever people are in love their C-fibers fire, or that they have more of a certain chemical that is found in chocolate, or even more surprisingly, that their livers curl slightly. Curling livers, having a high dose of this chemical, and C-fibers firing would then become evidence for saying that people are in love. You could fully understand, however, what it means to be in love without knowing that these things give us evidence for saying people are in love. The meaning of "being in love" has nothing to do with such phenomena. That is why curling livers, having a high dose of this chemical, and C-fibers firing are not criteria for "being in love." In time they might, of course, become new criteria of love—just as we adopted new criteria for being an acid (see Section 8.6 above)—in which case the meaning of the word "love" and our concept of love would have changed. But as of now, biochemical or electrochemical processes and the shape of livers are not our criteria for being in love. We recognize that Shakespeare would not be judged to know less about what it means to be in love than we would because he was unaware of these "discoveries." This case contrasts, then, with the one mentioned in the previous paragraph, illustrating the difference between mere evidence and a criterion for something, and why it is important not to equate the notion of criterion with the notion of evidence. The test for whether X is a criterion for Y is always: could you completely understand the meaning of "Y" without having grasped the connection between X and Y? If the answer is yes, X is not a criterion for Y, though it may be evidence for Y. If the answer is no, X is a criterion for Y. Talk of *completely* understanding the meaning of an expression indicates that this notion is subject to degree: a person can understand the meaning of an expression to a greater or a lesser extent; it is not a matter of all or nothing.

It is a corollary from the present and the last two characteristics of criteria that the notion of evidence is less basic than the notion of criteria, since the former presupposes the latter. Certainly we cannot get evidence for some state of affairs until we understand what it means to be in that state of affairs. The next two characteristics are characteristics of mental or psychological criteria.

8.9 Criteria for Mental Events Not Always Directly Observable

Kenny notes that while, "most commonly, in the *Investigations,* a criterion is an observable phenomenon"—especially a person's behavior—"a criterion for a mental event need not always be something which is itself directly observable."[6] Sometimes a criterion may be a capacity. He bases this on the following passage from Wittgenstein: "How are we to judge whether someone meant such-and-such?—The fact that he has, for example, mastered a particular technique in arithmetic and algebra, and that he taught someone else the expansion of a series in the usual way, is such a criterion" (PI, §692). That is, a criterion for having meant such and such—for example, addition by the plus sign—can be an ability, the person's ability to do arithmetic.

8.10 Psychological Concepts Not Always Employed on the Basis of Criteria

When I say of myself, for example, that I am in pain, I do not apply the criteria of being in pain to myself to report that I am in pain, as I would in your case (PI, §404). As Wittgenstein says, I don't "identify my sensation by criteria" (PI, §290). Kenny sums the point up as follows:

> It is not part of Wittgenstein's thesis that a concept which has criteria is always employed on the basis of those criteria. The concepts of pain, of mental images, and of personal identify have criteria which Wittgenstein discusses at length; but none of these criteria, he says, are applied when a man says of himself that he has a pain or an image (§§239, 290, 377, 404).[7]

Shorter, unfortunately, overlooks this point, as we shall see in the next section. The discussion of Shorter's confusions should help clarify how we are to understand Wittgenstein's notion of a criterion and his view of the mental.

8.11 Shorter's Charge That Wittgenstein Is Inconsistent

J. M. Shorter says that Wittgenstein faces a dilemma: either he must abandon the claim that the connection between my pain and my behavior is a logical or conceptual one or he must give up his contention that my judgment that I have a pain is incorrigible. He must give up one or another or both of these most central tenets of his. I shall examine Shorter's arguments in support of these charges. We shall see that his criticisms depend on overlooking the previously mentioned characteristic of psychological concepts—namely, that they need not always be employed on the basis of their criteria.

8.11.1 The First Argument

Shorter gives the following reasons why Wittgenstein must abandon the claim that the connection between my pain and my behavior is a logical or conceptual one:

> The statement "I am in pain," made by me, contradicts the statement "He is not in pain," made about me by someone else. If one admits that the former is not about my behavior, how can one avoid the conclusion that the latter also is not about my behavior? But if the

latter is not about my behavior, how can it be maintained that the connection between my pain and my behavior is a logical one?[8]

The full argument can be seen most clearly if we lay out the following four statements:

1. "I have a pain," or "I am in pain." (*A* has a pain.)
2. "I have no pain," or "I am not in pain." (*A* has no pain.)
3. "He has a pain," or "He is in pain." (*A* has a pain.)
4. "He has no pain," or "He is not in pain." (*A* has no pain.)

The *A* indicates that the subject of all of these reports is one and the same person. Shorter's first argument is that, given that (1) and (2)—"I am in pain" and "I am not in pain"—are contradictory statements, and that (1)—"I am in pain"—is not about my behavior, we must conclude that (4)—"He is not in pain"—when said about me, is also not about my behavior. But if (4) is not about my behavior, Wittgenstein must give up the claim that the connection between my pain and my behavior is a logical or conceptual one. This is because statements (1) and (3) and statements (2) and (4) can be paired together as saying the same thing and statements (1) and (2) contradict each other just as do statements (3) and (4).

8.11.2 The Second Argument

Shorter gives the following reasons why Wittgenstein must give up his incorrigibility thesis:

(1) "I have pain," said by me about myself, is the contradictory of (2) "I have not a pain," said by me about myself. Therefore, since (3) "He has a pain," said about me by someone else, is also the contradictory of (2), (1) and (3) must both be the same statement. Consequently, if (3) is logically connected with certain behavioral statements, (1) must also have these connections. This makes it difficult to see how (1) can be incorrigible. If I can be mistaken about my own behavior, as is the case, and if there is a logical connection between my pain and my behavior, then, it would seem, I can be mistaken about my pain.[9]

We can summarize as follows. Since (1) and (3) are both the contradictory of (2), Shorter reasons that (1) and (3) are the same statement. His assumed principle is that two utterances make the same statement if they both contradict a third statement. But if (3) is logically connected with certain behavioral statements, (1) must also have these connections. Because I can be mistaken about my own behavior (the argument concludes), I can be mistaken about my pain, contrary to what Wittgenstein says.

The conclusion of the first argument is that we must give up the claim that the connection between my pain and my behavior is a logical or a conceptual one. The conclusion of the second argument is that we must give up the alleged incorrigibility of first-person, present-tense pain statements. We have seen it is plausible to say these are both Wittgensteinian theses. The first one is a logical or conceptual thesis. In opposition to the Cartesian outlook, it is that "the connection between mental states, on the one hand, and behavior and circumstances, on the other, is logical or conceptual, not contingent."[10] The second thesis is the incorrigibility thesis— that I cannot make a mistake about having a pain, or I cannot mistakenly utter statement number (1) if I understand what these words say.

Note the second thesis does not commit us to the view that we can know we have a pain. We have already seen that Wittgenstein thinks it is hard to make sense of such a remark. When Wittgenstein says: "It can't be said of me at all (except perhaps as a joke) that I *know* I am in pain. What is it supposed to mean—except perhaps that I *am* in pain?" (PI, §246), this is not a rejection of the incorrigibility of pain. As he says later in the *Investigations*:

> I can't be in error here; it means nothing to doubt whether I am in pain! —That means: if anyone said "I do not know if what I have got is a pain or something else," we should think something like, he does not know what the English word "pain" means. . . .
>
> If he . . . said . . . : "Oh, I know what 'pain' means; what I don't know is whether *this,* that I have now, is pain"—we should merely shake our heads and be forced to regard his words as a queer reaction which we have no idea what to do with. . . .
>
> That expression of doubt [whether I am now in pain] has no place in the language-game [of reporting my present pains]. (PI, §288)

That is also why I cannot say "I believe (surmise) that I am in pain" or "It seems to me I have a pain." I cannot be in error here because it makes no sense to be in error about my own present pain. Saying "I can't be in error here" is one way to formulate the incorrigibility thesis. There seems to be no doubt, then, that Shorter's attack applies against Wittgenstein. If the second argument is sound, his incorrigibility thesis must be given up.

It seems equally certain that Wittgenstein upholds the logical or conceptual thesis, at least if it is understood in the right way. He would surely reject it if it were taken to mean that "He has a pain" entails, or logically implies, specifiable behavioral statements—for example, wincing or moaning. For there is no contradiction involved in saying "He has a pain but he is not wincing or moaning." Nor do behavioral statements entail, or logically imply, that "He has a pain." Wittgenstein is not a behaviorist. As Malcolm observes, if we study the phenomenon of language, as it is, without preconceived ideas, we will learn that "the criteria for the use of third-person psychological statements are not related to the latter by an entailment-relation."[11] Summarizing these two points: the satisfaction of criteria for something psychological, even in normal circumstances, neither logically implies that that something obtains, nor vice versa. These points were already made earlier in this chapter when discussing the characteristics of criteria for psychological phenomena.

I shall now consider two possible objections to Shorter's arguments, a bad and a good one, beginning with the bad.

8.11.3 A Bad Objection to Shorter's Argument

You might think that Shorter's argument can be disposed of by showing that it involves two false premises: "I am in pain" and "He is in pain" are not the same statements, and "I am not in pain" is not the contradictory of "He is in pain." Shorter mentions this as an apparent way out of the difficulty he sees Wittgenstein facing: just reject these two key premises of Shorter's argument. That is, Wittgenstein could deny that "I have a pain," said by me about myself, makes the same statement as "He has a pain," made about me by someone else. Similarly, he might deny that "I have no pain," said by me about myself, is the contradiction of "He has a pain," said about me by someone else. Certainly the sentences are not synonymous.

In comparing (1) and (3) and contrasting (2) and (3), it is essential to distinguish the sentences from the assertions made with them at a particular time. This distinction is implicit in Shorter's discussion. Thus, even though sentences (1) and (3) do not mean the same thing—Shorter would agree they do not—it hardly follows that the two sentences cannot be used on some occasions to make the same statements. Alan Donagan rightly remarks somewhere that it is a "grammatical commonplace" that (1) and (3) can be used to make the same statement. It is equally obvious that (1) and (4) can be used to make contradictory statements, and they do just this in the cases Shorter imagines. Strawson echoes the point: "It is needlessly paradoxical to deny . . . that when Smith says 'Jones has a pain' and Jones says 'I have a pain,' they are talking about the same entity and saying the same thing about it."[12] Hence they are asserting the same thing. There is no reason to think Wittgenstein would disagree with these claims.

Shorter is also correct in holding that the statements made by (1) and (4) are contradictory, since they have opposite truth values. That is, if (1) is true, (4) is false, and vice versa. It seems, then, that this first objection has little merit, and that there is no reason to think that Wittgenstein would welcome this sort of defense of his views, or this line of attack on Shorter's criticism of him.

8.11.4 Shorter's Non Sequitur

But if we agree with Shorter (as we just have) that the statements made by (1) and (3) both contradict (2) and that (1) and (3) both make the same statement, mustn't we also agree with him that, since (3) is corrigible, (1) must be too? But then it seems it must be possible for me to be mistaken about whether I am in pain, contrary to what Wittgenstein says.

The trouble with this reasoning is that it rests on an equivocation. Consider the statement that (3) is corrigible. What could this mean? Two things. First, it is a way of saying that third-person present-tense pain statements are not beyond correction; so someone might discover that statement (3) is false when made by one speaker about another person. Second, the statement that (3) is corrigible might mean that even the speaker can be mistaken when he or she judges that "He has a pain," assuming that the speaker does not use the pronoun "he" in the fashion of de Gaulle to talk about himself.

Consider now first-person, present-tense pain statements. Are they corrigible in both these senses? No. Again, they are corrigible in the sense of not being beyond correction by somebody. So when a person says "I have a terrible headache," somebody else may well know, or discover, that this if false. It may be that the speaker is lying to get out of doing some unpleasant chore. But the statement cannot be corrigible in the second sense, for the speaker cannot be mistaken about having or not having a terrible headache. Shorter seems not to appreciate this distinction between two senses of corrigible. Thus he wrongly infers that because (3) is corrigible in both these senses—that is, it can be discovered to be false by another person as well as by the speaker—(1) must be corrigible in both these senses too. But this neither follows nor is true. Making the same statements with (1) and (3) does not make these two speech acts the same. We have seen that they are not. For one thing we do not assert (1) on the basis of observed behavior, whereas we do assert (3) on such a basis. Moreover, (1), unlike (3), is nonobservational, noninferential, and incorrigible for the speaker, even though there are public behavioral criteria for the statement made by (1). It is incorrigible and indubitable simply in the sense that the "expression of doubt [whether I am now in pain] has no place in the language-game [of reporting my present pains]" (PI, §288). The fact that I can be mistaken about my behavior and that behavior is criteriologically connected with (1), as it is with (3), does not make it possible for me to be mistaken about my pain. If we conclude that (1) is false, we must thus conclude that that speaker was not truthful or sincere when he or she asserted (1).

All Shorter succeeds in showing, then, is that Wittgenstein is committed to the view that there must be public and behavioral criteria for statement (1) as well as for statement (3). And that if (3) is conceptually connected with behavior, so is (1), since they make the same statement. Wittgenstein would not disagree. Indeed, he would insist on the point. From this correct view Shorter erroneously concludes that people who assert (1), like those who assert (3), appeal to public criteria when they assert (1), and that they can therefore be mistaken about (1), because they might make a mistake about whether the criteria have been satisfied. We have seen, however, that speakers of (1) need not make use of any criteria in order to assert (1). In this sense, we could say it is nonbehavioral or noncriteriological. Generalizing, while there are criteria for first-person, present-tense psychological statements, the speaker does not (normally) employ such criteria in making these statements, but we do employ these criteria when making the second– or third-person psychological statements. Shorter is overlooking the asymmetry of psychological verbs discussed in the chapter on behaviorism. Or as I say earlier in this chapter (Section 8.10), Shorter's criticisms of Wittgenstein are based on a failure to grasp one of the characteristics of criteria—namely, that a concept that has criteria need not always be employed on the basis of these criteria. It normally is not so employed in the first-person present tense when the verbs are psychological. Shorter wrongly assumes that because (3) is applied on the basis of behavioral criteria, (1) must also be so applied.

8.12 Summary of Wittgenstein's View of the Mental

The foregoing remarks about criteria—especially criteria for the mental—should not be taken to constitute a "theory" about the matter. It would be contradictory if they did, since Wittgenstein repeatedly says he has no theories (see Chapter 1). He would say what we have here are just a number of "grammatical remarks." They do not tell us anything we did not know all along, although we might have had difficulty articulating this knowledge.

We see that the relation between a criterion and what it is a criterion of cannot be reduced to a simple formula. The connection between the two is a complex matter. Further, when the criteria are criteria for the mental or psychological, two crucial points emerge, one negative, the other positive. First, the positive point. Satisfying such criteria, or enough of them in the right sort of context, entitles us to describe another person as being in pain, in love, or the like, in accord with the conventions of our language. In such a case, then, it simply does not make sense to ask whether the person really is in pain, say, unless the challenger has a special reason for raising a doubt about the matter. The relevance of this to the problem of other minds is obvious.

The second, negative point, is that satisfying such criteria never entails that someone is in a particular mental or psychological state. This is related to Wittgenstein's other belief that philosophers cannot give interesting truth conditions for psychological statements—for being in pain, being in love, having an opinion, and so on. Philosophers go wrong, accordingly, when they try to reduce psychological concepts to something else or to identify psychological phenomena with brain events, overt behavior, disposition to behave, or with anything else. You cannot say truly "*That* is what F is," where "F" is a psychological term. What philosophy should do, instead of trying to identify or explain the phenomena of mind, Malcolm observes, is to "*describe language*. It should remind us of what we say. It should bring to mind how we actually use the mental terms that confuse us philosophically."[13] When we do this, we see why behaviorism, identity theory, and Cartesian dualism must be rejected.[14] We also find that psychological concepts are family-resemblance concepts and there can be no illuminating philosophical theory of the mind.

Finally, when we pay close attention to our actual use of psychological language, we find that, though appeal to criteria always give us a reason for holding that another person is in psychological state F, given the right context, it is not normally a reason we have for saying of ourselves that we are in state F—in pain, in love, or the like. That is, the second– and third-person uses of psychological predicates are governed by criteria in a way the first person is not, as was noted in Section 8.10. This asymmetry in the use of psychological and mental predicates—between the first-person present-tense and second– and the third-person present-tense—we may take as one of the special marks of the mental. Physical predicates display no such asymmetry.

Some people regret this asymmetry. They wish that the grounds for saying that others are sad were the same as our reason for saying that we are—namely, because we feel sad. After all, we say that Jones is six foot tall for the very same reason we say that we are. Wisdom, a former student of Wittgenstein's, reminds us, however, that "the asymmetrical logic of statements about the mind is a feature of them without which they would not be statements about the mind, and that they have this feature is no more a subject suitable for regret than the fact that lines if truly parallel don't meet."[15] We have to accept the logic of our language, including the logic of our psychological language.

Part III, which begins with the next chapter, gives more examples of philosophers refusing to accept the workings of our language, even though they know perfectly well how to use the language. We continue to see Wittgenstein's methods at work, first applied to two historical and then to two more contemporary problems. Chapter 9 examines Augustine's discussion of and perplexities about time. Chapter 10, Descartes's treatment of the skeptical dream argument. These two great philosophers lived in the fifth and the seventeenth centuries, respectively, but their problems go back even farther. In Chapter 11, we turn to a contemporary of Wittgenstein, Bertrand Russell, and his theories of proper names. Probably no philosopher has been more influential in the first half of the twentieth century than Russell, unless it be his former student Wittgenstein. Moreover, his theory of logical atomism and theories of proper names bear a significant historical relation to Wittgenstein's own early thought. In Chapter 12, we see one of the brilliant younger philosophers and logicians of today, Saul Kripke, dealing with another important and persistent problem—making sense of rule-following. He relates his problem concerning rule-following to Wittgenstein's work, finding an alleged paradox there. We shall find that his discussion, like Russell's on names and descriptions, is still under the influence of more essentialist approaches.

Part III

Wittgenstein on Some Problems of Philosophy

Chapter 9

Augustine on Time

Time has often mystified philosophers. Saint Augustine, in Book 11 of his *Confessions,* one of the earliest important discussions of time (c. 397), asks "What is time?" He says when no one asks him, he knows; yet when someone asks him, he no longer knows. A lot of us could say the same thing. The problem of time first arises for him from the scriptural doctrine of creation. Objectors ask, "What was God doing before creation? How can we speak of an absolute beginning?" The bishop has an answer to these questions. But he himself is puzzled by the reality of the past and the future and how time is to be measured. Can what is not yet but will be—the future—and what is no longer but has been—the past—have any reality? If they do not, does only the present exist? Yet it seems to have no dimension. How then is time to be measured? These are some of Augustine's puzzles. The discussion nicely illustrates a philosopher grappling with what Wittgenstein calls a philosophical problem. For him, remember, "A philosophical problem has the form: 'I don't know my way about'" (PI, §123). Wittgenstein exposes Augustine's confusions and shows how the grammar of time can muddle anyone's thinking. I begin Part III with this discussion for several reasons. First, the topic of time is of major importance; no significant philosopher has ignored it. Second, Augustine's discussion of it is a classic. Finally, we know Wittgenstein always had a high regard for Augustine; he was one of his favorite authors. He often cites and responds to what Augustine has to say on time and language, something he rarely does with other philosophers.

The first part of this discussion lays out Augustine's analysis of time. The second part is a Wittgensteinian examination of this analysis.[1]

9.1 Augustine's Analysis of Time

According to Augustine, time was created by God, but he stresses that this does not mean it was created at any particular time. To say time was created at a certain time would be to contradict yourself, for then there would have to be a time before the creation of all time, which would be absurd. So, he argues, time could not have been made in time any more than heaven and earth were, or could have been, made in heaven and earth.[2] Augustine never doubts, however, that time was made, or that this belief of his makes sense.

While there is nothing temporally prior to the creation of time for Augustine, he maintains that eternity, or timelessness, is nontemporally, or logically, prior to the existence of time. God exists in such eternity, and his Word is coeternal with him. It is with this Word—which was of course not spoken in time—that God created heaven and earth and time. God's Word, then, is not like the words of man: it never began or ended; nor did it ever sound and pass away. Rather, it abides forever in utter silence and was spoken all together and is spoken eternally (pp. 248–49). For in eternity there is changelessness, and so, a complete absence of time.

This point of Augustine's that there cannot be time without change or movement deserves mention. He says, for example, that "times are made by the alteration of things" (p. 275) and that "without the variety of motions, there are no times: and no variety where there is no figure" (p. 278). It follows for Augustine that there could be no time before there was some creature possessing some form and changeableness.

In Augustine's view, failure to appreciate the wisdom of God and the distinction between time and eternity accounts for the following sort of vain question: "What did God do before He created the world?" (p. 251). Augustine rejects the question on logical grounds, pointing out that there could have been no *before* or *then* when there was no time (p. 252). The question, hence, he maintains, is wrongheaded.

In the beginning of his investigations of the nature of time, Augustine notes that "no time is all at once present." What happens, according to him, is that the time to come drives on the past and follows after it. "All past and to come is created and flows out of that which is ever present" (p. 251). What is more, he wants to say that if nothing passed away, there would be no past; similarly, that if nothing were coming, there would be no future; and that if there were nothing, there would be no present. These remarks indicate the rough picture of time Augustine starts out with. They also suggest, I think, the source of most of his ensuing difficulties.

Augustine proceeds to infer that since neither the past nor the future now are, neither exists (p. 253). He finds that even the present has a curious sort of existence since, like all time, it must become past, or tend not to be, if we are truly to say that it is time. He remarks that people talk about long and short times in regard to both the future and the past, in spite of the nonexistence of both the future and the past. He observes, for example, that a hundred years ago is thought to be a long time past, whereas a hundred years hence is thought to be a long time to come. But he asks himself how either the future or the past can be long (or short) if neither exists. Hence he proposes that we say that the past *has been* long and that the future *will be* long, rather than that either *is* long. But this raises the further question how it could be possible that the past be long. "Was it long when it was now past, or when it was yet present?" (p. 254). But when past, it was no longer, says Augustine: what does not exist cannot be long. Hence, he doubts whether it can be maintained that past time has been long. The alternative is to say that some present time was long—that is, it was long when it was present. For the present at least exists, even if very curiously it must (logically) continuously go out of existence. Accordingly, Augustine examines the present to see whether it could even properly be said to be long.

He discovers that no present can be long—that it does not seem to have any duration whatever. He comes upon this discovery by considering whether a hundred years could be present all at once. He thinks that they could not be, since we only live in one year at a time. Thus if we live in the first of one hundred years, the other ninety-nine are still to come. Or, if we are now in the second year, one year is past, another is present, and the last ninety-eight are still to come. Whatever year is now current, the other ninety-nine will either be past or future; therefore, a hundred years cannot be present all at once.

By the same argument, Augustine tries to show that even that year now current is not itself present (p. 255). For, he argues, if we are now in January of that year, the other eleven months still lie in the future; or, if it is now February, then January is already past, and ten months still lie ahead. Thus whatever the month current, the other eleven will either be past or future.

Employing the same argument, Augustine whittles down the time that is said to be present to the length of a mere day. Then he proceeds to argue that it cannot even be that long, since a day is not present as a whole any more than a hundred years, one year, or one month is. In particular, a day is made up of twenty-four hours, and only one hour is present at one time. The same argument of course applies to hours and minutes—indeed, to any length of time that can be mentioned. Augustine therefore concludes that only an indivisible instant of time may be called present (p. 255). But he laments that then the present has no duration; hence, that it cannot be measured. From the dimensionlessness of the present and the nonexistence of both the past and the future, the surprising conclusion follows that there does not seem to be any time that can be called long or that is measurable.

But, Augustine writes, we do compare and measure intervals of time, saying some are longer, some shorter, one is twice as long as another, and so on. The question is to explain how this can be: what time it is that we measure and how.

If it could be established that the future and the past do exist after all, this might be one way out of Augustine's predicament. Thus he considers two counterarguments to the nonexistence of the past and the future. One is that the future may be in "some secret place" (p. 256). It is suggested that perhaps the future becomes present by coming out of such a place, and then retires from the present into the past, which presumably is in another secret place. A second argument is that future things and events must exist now—otherwise, how can those who predict the future see such things now? And likewise, past things must exist: they must exist if they are to be discerned, and they must be discerned for people to talk about them.

Augustine replies to these arguments by inquiring where the past and the future are if they exist. Then he says that they cannot be wherever they are as *future* or as *past*; so the counterarguments do not establish the existence of either the past or the future. Writes Augustine: "If there they be future, they are not yet there; if there they be past, they are no longer there" (p. 256). Augustine takes it as axiomatic that whatever exists can only be present. Further, he contends that just because facts are related about the past, this does not mean that we must now discern things that are past (p. 257). For instance, the image of an adult's childhood can be present in the adult's memory without his childhood itself being present at the time he recalls it. Thus that we can talk about the past in no way proves its existence. Similarly with predictions: they have to do with future happenings, but only our thoughts about such happenings are present at the time of the prediction. What we see, according to Augustine, are the causes or signs of things to come, not the future things that do not yet exist. He gives as an example watching the day break with the belief that the sun is about to rise. Here what is seen is present and what is expected is future. Yet the expectation itself is present in the sense that in foretelling the sun's rising, you imagine it (p. 257), and this imagining is, of course, different from the actual rising of the sun that is still in the future.

For Augustine, then, the point holds that neither future nor past happenings exist. Accordingly, he believes that, strictly speaking, it is incorrect to say there are three times—past, present, and future. He allows that you may say there is a past in the sense that there is a present of things past— that is, memory. Similarly, he thinks it is all right to say that there is a present of things present, which he here calls "sight" and later (p. 267) "consideration"; and that there is a future, in the sense that there is a present of things future—that is, expectation. For such times do exist in the soul if nowhere else (p. 258). The point Augustine is insisting on here is that neither things to come nor past things now exist (a safe tautology, it would seem).

But there remains the problem of how we measure time. One possible answer he suggests is that we measure times as they pass (p. 259). This proposal seems to be the result of a process of elimination. We do measure time, says Augustine, and we can only measure what exists. But the future and the past do not exist; hence, we cannot measure things past and to come. The present, in turn, though it exists, cannot be measured since it has no duration. And this leaves us with time that is passing, and the question whether it can be measured.

One of the difficulties here, as Augustine sees it, is that we must measure passing time by some space of time (p. 259). Otherwise, he asks, how can we say the sorts of things we say about time—that two hours are twice as long as one hour or that it took x three times as long as y to do z? Further, such things can only be said about duration of time. But no time has yet been discovered that has any duration.

Dropping this problem for the moment, Augustine considers whether time could be defined as the movement of heavenly bodies. He does not think it can be, for two reasons. First, such a definition raises the question why time should be equated with the movement of the heavenly bodies and not with the motion of all bodies. Second, whether or not any more light came from heaven, we would still be able to measure "the whirlings of the potter's wheel" (p. 260). We could still say that it sometimes turned slower, sometimes quicker, and we would be speaking in time when we made such claims. Again, it is logically possible to say about the sun that it completed its trip in half the usual time. But this would be impossible if the motion of the sun itself constituted time. Finally, Augustine argues, the motions of the heavenly bodies cannot be time, since even if the sun stood still for the space of a battle, time would go on—the battle would still be waged in a certain amount of time.

More generally, Augustine contends that time is not definable as the motion of any body. For no body is moved except in time; and when a body is moved, we measure how long it moves by time. That is, we measure the time it takes from the time it began to move to the time when it stopped moving. Hence we must know when it began to move and when it ended if we are to measure how long it moved. Augustine's point is that the motion of a body is one thing and the measure of the duration of that motion is another. It is the latter that is time. But time cannot be equated with the motion of a body for still another reason: that we can measure how long a body stands still as well as how long it moves. Augustine therefore concludes that time cannot be the motion of a body.

To know what time is not, however, is still not to know what time is. Thus Augustine returns to the question how it is that we measure time. Apparently, he says, we measure a length of time by partitioning it into shorter lengths and counting the partitions (p. 263). For instance, we measure "the space of a long syllable" by saying that it is twice as long as another. But he says that in this way we cannot secure any certain measure of time, since a shorter verse, "pronounced more fully, may take up more time than a longer pronounced hurriedly" (p. 263). Time, then, seems to be some sort of protraction, but of what Augustine does not yet know.

It is clear for Augustine that no sense has yet been made of measuring the past, the future, or the present, for the reasons already given. The remaining alternative, already mentioned, is to maintain that we measure time as it passes, since this not only exists but endures, in contrast to the present, the past, and the future. But even here there are difficulties, according to Augustine, since if a sound never stopped sounding, we could never measure how long it sounded. That is, it has to pass before we can measure it, since what we measure is the space of time between its beginning and end. On the other hand, a sound that has ended no longer exists— so how can it be measured? Augustine faces the paradox that we cannot measure a sound until it has ceased to be, after which there no longer appears to be anything to measure. His problem is thus to explain how we can measure time if we cannot measure either the future, the past, the present, or passing times that have not yet ceased to be.

Augustine's solution of this problem involves the claim that time is a protraction of the mind itself (p. 264). Time seems to become something subjective.[3] What happens makes an impression on us that remains in our memory even after the event has passed (p. 266). According to Augustine, it is this impression that is still present that we measure when we measure time, "not the things which pass by to make this impression," since they are either present, past, future, or passing and hence unmeasurable. Augustine maintains that if his view is not correct—that is, if our impression is not time—then we do not truly measure time. Thus we are coerced into accepting Augustine's conception of time on pain of denying the obvious measurability of time.

Then there is the question of measuring silence. Suppose we claim that a particular silence was as long as some sound. It seems here we "stretch out our thought to the measure of" some hypothetical sound, in Augustine's view. For, he says, we can go over any "discourse or dimensions of motions" silently and in thought as well as vocally, "and report as to the spaces of time, how much this is in respect to that" (p. 266). He also believes that if a person decides to utter a sound of a certain length, he or she can, in silence, commit that duration of time to his memory.

Augustine then explains how the future passes away in the mind and how the past increases. He says the mind not only expects, but considers and remembers as well. What the mind expects passes through what it considers and into what it remembers. To illustrate how this happens Augustine recites a psalm. As he goes through it, however, his expectations gradually become memories. But his consideration is present with him all the time, and it is through this that "what was future, may be conveyed over, so as to become past" (p. 267). That is, as he goes through the psalm, his expectation diminishes and the content of his memory increases. Finally, after the psalm has been repeated, there is no more expectation, but his memory is extended over the whole psalm. Accordingly, a long future for Augustine is a long expectation of the future, whereas a long past is a long memory of the past.

So, after all, there can be long durations, and Augustine has managed to explain how time can be measured. However, the validity of his analysis must still be assessed.

9.2 Why Wittgenstein Would Reject Augustine's Account

As we have seen, Augustine maintains that time could not have been created at any time. This seems right. For it would certainly be self-contradictory to say that time was created, say, at time *t*. But couldn't we infer from this that it is senseless to maintain that time was ever created, that there was ever a beginning to time? Augustine in effect says, No: all that follows is that we must deny that the creation of time occurred in time. But this seems to presuppose that it is intelligible to say that an event can occur nontemporally, and I can make no sense of such an event. Suppose we ask: "When did God create time?" Augustine's answer would be: "In no time at all," and he would not mean by that that God made it in a jiffy! Consider the following dialogue:

"Such and such happened."

"When did it happen?"

"Not in any time. You see, it happened before there was any time."

"When was that?"

"When there was no time."

"Do you mean to say it didn't happen at any time at all?"

"Exactly."

"You mean then that it didn't happen?"

"No, no! You don't seem to understand. Before the creation of time, there was no time. It happened *then,* that is, before there was a *then.*"

Augustine himself speaks this way. That is, he cannot escape using temporal language that refers to a time in which he professes there was no time. For note how he stresses, "There was no *then, when* there was no time" (p. 252, my emphasis). And later, in reply to the question, "How came it into God's mind to make anything, having never made anything?" he writes that *never* cannot be predicated *when* time is not (p. 268, again my emphasis). Briefly put, we may object that Augustine's phrase, "when there was no time," is either self-contradictory or at best self-stultifying; and the same objection applies to his phrase "nontemporally prior." Wittgenstein says in this connection: "Philosophers who say: 'after death a timeless state will begin,' or: 'at death a timeless state begins' . . . do not notice that they have used the word 'after' and 'at' and 'begins' in a temporal sense, and that temporality is embedded in their grammar" (CV, 1932, p. 22e).

Perhaps Augustine would acknowledge the temporality of his statement. I fear that if he did, he might then explain it away as due to the inadequacy of our language. He might claim that, when he mentioned what came *before* all time, he did not mean to refer to "a time," but that words like "when" and "before" unfortunately seem to have temporality built into their ordinary usage. He might contend, finally, that even if it is impossible to say what he wants to say in our language, this is no refutation of what he is saying. For such a fact, if it is one, might only show that our temporal language does not properly reflect the wisdom and truth of God, which is eternal. Such arguments would be hard to answer only because we would no longer know what would count as an answer or criticism of Augustine's view. In short, whatever hinges primarily on a mystery and the ineffable wisdom of God has a kind of invulnerability, the invulnerability due to the cessation of philosophy.

I mentioned earlier that Augustine's picture of time is largely responsible for his difficulties. Writes Wittgenstein: "the ideas of the past, the future and the present in their problematic and almost mysterious aspect" can be "exemplified if we look at the question 'Where does the present go when it becomes past, and where is the past?'" (BB, p. 107). He says:

This question most easily arises if we are preoccupied with cases in which there are things flowing by us—as logs of wood float down a river. In such a case we can say the logs which *have passed* us are all down towards the left and the logs which *will pass* us are all up towards the right. We then use this situation as a simile for all happening in time and even embody the simile in our language, as when we say that "the present event passes by" (a log passes by), "the future event is to come" (a log is to come). We talk about the flow of events; but also about the flow of time—the river on which the logs travel. (BB, pp. 107–8)

Wittgenstein's point is that this analogy, which to some extent is built into our language, is a source of philosophical puzzlement. As he says, our very symbolism seems to permit such questions as, "Where does the flame of a candle go to when it is blown out?" or "Where does the light go to?" or "Where does the past go to?" (BB, p. 108).

The analogy suggests, further, that "past," "future," and "present" are the names of entities. Accordingly, Augustine tries to find out what they name, only to find that what is named either could not exist or exists so fleetingly that it could not have any duration. He concludes that past, present, and future must exist in the mind, for he can find nothing else that such words could name apart from some mental process. The following observation by Wittgenstein is most apt in this connection: "In our failure to understand the use of a word we take it as the expression of a queer *process*. (As we think of time as a queer medium, of the mind as a queer kind of being.)" (PI, §196). The essential thing is that these words could not be names, any more than "this" is the name of something. For a proper name such as "Smith" can be used in the phrase "This is Smith," whereas it would be logically odd to say "This is this," or "This is past (future or present)." Neither can we say "This is a year ago," "This is a year hence," or "This is now" (BB, pp. 108–9).

Unfortunately, Augustine's theory of meaning and the above picture are mutually reinforcing. In *Concerning the Teacher,* for example, he upholds the thesis that words signify things of some sort or another; and what they signify seems to be their meaning. But this ignores the fact that not all words are names. Furthermore, it is an erroneous theory of meaning, since even if all words were names, their meanings could not be identified with what they name. Otherwise, as Wittgenstein writes (PI, §40), a name would become meaningless if there ceased to be anyone who bore the name—for example, if the bearer of the name died; but this is not so.

To recapitulate: Augustine's original conclusion that the past and the future do not exist rests on both a faulty theory of meaning and on a particular picture of time that leads him to seek after some sort of entity that can be called "past" or "future." Not finding a physical entity, he postulates a mental one.

Of course Augustine is right that in a sense neither the past nor the future do exist. For example, the hundredth president of the United States does not now exist any more than George Washington does. Yet there can be facts about the future as well as about the past, and it is in this sense that both the future and past exist. Thus when an astronomer calculates an eclipse of the sun he does not think of the future as hidden from him because nonexistent. Nor does the historian think of the past as nonexistent, except in the trivial sense already mentioned.

Augustine's argument to show that no present can be long is dubious in yet another way. He starts out, as we have seen, by inquiring whether a hundred years can be present; then he considers whether one year, one month, one day can be present. Roughly, his argument is that none of these times can be present since they can always be divided into smaller units of time, only one of which will be present; therefore, the only time truly present is an indivisible instant of time; and this is unmeasurable because it has no duration. It is important to see that as Augustine whittles his way down from one hundred years to his indivisible instant, he is continually shifting and narrowing down his use of the word "present." To show that a hundred years cannot be present, for example, he argues that only one year is present at one time; then to show that one year cannot be present, he argues that only one month is present at one time; and so on. Thus he makes such contradictory claims as that the year now current is not itself present (p. 255), which is like saying that that year which is present is not present. But of course it is! What seems to allow him to make such self-contradictory remarks is the fact that the words "present," "current," and "now" can be used in a broader or narrower way. For example, it is perfectly correct to say that you are now living in that year and month in which you are reading this material and that the present century is the twentieth century. Such remarks are quite compatible with one another, unlike "what is present is not present." That is, the criteria of what is present are not fixed and rigid or unalterable: they depend on what we are interested in and on what we are talking about. Augustine makes it seem, however, as if no time can be called present unless it cannot be divided into smaller parts. Consequently, he unwittingly legislates that no time shall be called present unless it is an indivisible instant. The consequences of such verbal legislation he seems to appreciate: namely, that we can no longer find a time we can call present, since as soon as we hopefully begin to utter words of discovery, the moment in question will already have disappeared. But Augustine seems unaware that it is he who is distorting the use of the word "present" in this way, rather than explicating it.

Wittgenstein says some very pertinent things in this connection (BB, p. 25). He stresses that, in general, language is not used according to strict rules. More important, he sees that we can often create philosophical puzzles when we compare our use of words with one following exact rules; and he cites Augustine and his troubles with time as a case in point (BB, p. 26). According to Wittgenstein, what puzzles Augustine is the grammar of the word "time." Part of this puzzlement is due to a failure to appreciate how the word "now" or the word "present" is used. But Wittgenstein adds that it is also due to a conflict between two different usages of the verb "measure." According to Wittgenstein, Augustine constantly has in mind the process of measuring a *length*. The way to solve his puzzle, Wittgenstein therefore maintains, is to compare what we mean by "measurement" when it is applied, say, "to a distance on a travelling band" with the way it is applied to time. What he is saying is that we do not measure time the way we measure the length of some physical object.

In conclusion I want to examine the adequacy of Augustine's final explanation of time. As we have seen, he seems to think that time is a protraction or extension of the mind, a kind of mental impression. But there is an ambiguity in his account. For on one page (p. 266) Augustine speaks of measuring the impression things cause in us as they pass by, and he refers to such an impression as time. But then he would seem to have two different conceptions of time. Time is, as we just saw, an impression, and time is the measure of motion. For he distinguishes that in terms of which we measure the motion of a body from the motion of the body; and it is the former that he calls time (p. 262). By parity of reasoning, he should claim that the means by which we measure an impression is time, and so it is not to be identified with the impression itself. But if this is his view, he still owes us an explanation of time; all we know is that we can measure our impressions by it.[4]

Augustine's second, and apparently final, conception of time he states explicitly: time is a mental impression. Perhaps Augustine would contend that this is his only conception of time, and that what seem to be two views can be shown to be one as follows: time is a mental impression, yet any such impression can be measured by "shorter" impressions; elsewhere (p. 263), Augustine speaks of measuring time by partitioning it. However, if this is his reply, it might be asked how shorter impressions can measure longer ones. Furthermore, in what units do we measure those shorter impressions? Once more we seem to involve ourselves in a kind of regress. To say that we just know how "long" our impressions are would of course be no answer; certainly not one Augustine ever accepts in any other part of his investigation of time.[5] Augustine's account becomes even less clear and satisfactory when we remember that talk about the "length" or "shortness" of impressions must be taken metaphorically, and that, since he does not conceive of the mind as a physical object, he would never want to maintain that it could ever be literally protracted or extended. Thus we see that, preoccupied with time as length but unable to find such a length, Augustine internalizes time along with its mental and immaterial measuring-stick. But Wittgenstein would say that such a measuring-stick ceases to measure.

Augustine's final position, however, is limited by more than lack of clarity. For suppose we agree that we have both an idea of five o'clock and an idea of an hour. Presumably, for him, such ideas need not involve any reference to clocks or to any other instrument we ordinarily use to measure time. If so, it seems fair to object, as Wittgenstein does (BB, p. 106), that Augustine's idea of five o'clock and of an hour are "in need of explanation," since our ideas of five o'clock and of an hour certainly require some reference to clocks or at least to some instrument for measuring time. Writes Wittgenstein: "If there did not exist all the connections that give our measure of time meaning and importance" (that is, if there were no clocks or there were no need ever to use them to tell the time, etc.), then "the measure of time would either have lost its meaning (like the action of delivering check-mate if the game of chess were to disappear)—or it would have some quite different meaning" (RFM, pt. V, §15, pp. 173–74).

It would seem, then, that our measure of time is not Augustine's. Consequently, our notion of time is not his either, even though there may be similarities between the meaning he gives to time and what we do. For example, on Augustine's theory we could have a notion of the same time, of before and of after, which would in many ways resemble our present notion of the same time, of before, and of after. For to some extent we can—without clocks—perceive, remember, and expect, what will precede or follow or happen at the same time as something else. But when it comes to something more complicated, like telling the time correctly, Augustine's theory of time lets us down, since it cannot make any sense of such a notion. Wittgenstein considers the following objection that a twentieth-century Augustinian might make in reply to what I have just said: "But surely I can appeal from one memory to another. For example, I don't know if I have remembered the time of departure of a train right and to check it I call to mind how a page of the time-table looked" (PI, §265). Wittgenstein counters that it is not the same here. "For," he writes, "this process has got to produce a memory which is actually *correct*. If the mental image of the time-table could not itself be *tested* for correctness, how could it confirm the correctness of the first memory? (As if someone were to buy several copies of the morning paper to assure himself that what it said was true.) Looking up a table in the imagination is no more looking up a table than the image of the result of an imagined experiment is the result of an experiment." Hence it won't do just to say our memory preserves a picture of what has been seen before, or of what happened and how long it took— "allowing us to look into the past (as if down a spy-glass)" (PI, §604).

If Augustine were to reply that we know whether our internal measure of time is correct from the truth that teaches within, or from the immediate certainty of inner experience, or through faith in Christ, this would in no way do away with the need for some outer criteria of accuracy and correctness. As Wittgenstein observes: "The statement 'These ticks follow at equal intervals' has got one grammar if the ticks are the ticks of a pendulum and the criterion of their regularity is the result of measurements which we have made on our apparatus, and another grammar if the ticks are ticks we imagine" (BB, p. 171). In the latter case there are no ticks, for we only give a picture—a metaphor—when we talk of an inner clock; hence the ticks we imagine are neither public nor in any objective sense measurable, unlike the ticks of a real clock. Augustine's account of time fails to recognize that our notion of time involves real clocks or other instruments for measuring time. By identifying time with things that exist "in the soul" (p. 258)—with our expectations, memories, and consideration of duration—he breaks these connections. Consequently, the measure of time has either lost its meaning (like delivering check-mate without a game of chess) or it has some quite different meaning. Our measure of time is not Augustine's. So our notion of time is not his either.

We have seen that several things led Augustine to develop this erroneous view. To begin with, there is his picture of time as like a river with logs floating down it: those logs that have all gone towards the left are past events; those logs up towards the right, and still to pass by, are future events. Such a picture, coupled with the surface grammar of our language, seems to permit—and even to invite—such questions as, "Where does the present go when it becomes past and where is the past?" His theory of meaning reinforces this inclination, since he held that words signify things of some sort or another and that what they signify is their meaning. Thus "past," "future," "present," like all other words, he takes to be names of entities, even though they are in fact not names. Not finding a physical entity that can be called "past" or "future," he postulates a mental one, making these things subjective, or things that merely exist "in the soul" (p. 258).

Augustine's confusions about the grammar of the word "time" reveal themselves in other ways as well. In his account of the creation of time, for example, and what came *before* all time, we saw that he did not grasp that he could not escape the temporality embedded in the grammar of his own remarks. Further, when looking for a time that can be called long, he confused the measurement of time with the measurement of a length. Thus Wittgenstein would dissolve some of Augustine's puzzles by reminding him of what we mean by "measurement" when it is applied to lengths and what it means when it is applied to time. Finally, he would point out that Augustine unwittingly legislates that no time shall be called present unless it is an indivisible instant. Such linguistic legislation distorts the usage of the word "present," which can be used in a broader or narrower way. That is, the criteria of what is present are not fixed and rigid and unalterable: they depend on what we are interested in and on what we are talking about. In short, Augustine presents Wittgenstein with a fine example of a philosopher bewitched by language. He also confirms Wittgenstein's observation: "When we do philosophy we are like savages, primitive people, who hear the expressions of civilized men, put a false interpretation on them, and then draw the queerest conclusions from it" (PI, §194). Descartes (in the next chapter) will confirm this as well.

Chapter 10

Dissolving the Dream Argument

10.1 The Argument

The dream argument[1] goes back at least to the time of Plato. We find it in the *Theaetetus,* as part of Plato's refutation of the view that knowledge is perception. Theaetetus agrees with Socrates that what appears to a dreamer is not real. He maintains that "dreamers believe what is false . . . [for example, when they] think they have wings and are flying in their sleep." Consequently, perception in a dream is not knowledge. But (he continues) none of us can be sure that any of our perceptions are not dream perceptions. Maybe all or some of them are dream perceptions. At least Theaetetus says he cannot "see by what evidence it is to be proved [whether we are asleep or awake, dreaming all that passes through our minds or talking to one another in the waking state], for the conditions correspond in every circumstance like exact counterparts." Socrates apparently accepts Theaetetus's conclusion that we cannot be certain we are not dreaming.[2] To my knowledge Plato nowhere attempts to refute this argument.

Roughly a generation later, about the time of Aristotle, Chuang Tzu, the great Chinese Taoist, also expresses doubt about whether we can ever be certain we are awake. "Perhaps you and I are dreaming," he writes, "and have not wakened."[3] He rightly contends that while we dream "we do not know that we are dreaming," even if we dream that we are dreaming. "Only after we are awake do we know we have dreamed" (p. 189). But since there seems to be no certain way of telling whether we are awake, we can never know when we have dreamed. Chuang Tzu illustrates the difficulty: "Once I, Chuang Chou"—this was his private name—"dreamed that I was a butterfly and was happy as a butterfly. I was conscious that I was quite pleased with myself, but I did not know that I was Chou. Suddenly I awoke, and there I was, visibly Chou. I do not know whether it was Chou dreaming that he was a butterfly or the butterfly dreaming that it was Chou" (p. 190).

These two examples show that the dream argument goes back to ancient times and was taken seriously by major philosophers in both the East and the West. Descartes's version of the argument, which is probably the most famous, serves a new purpose in showing that a particular class of perceptual judgments is not indubitable. But the argument remains basically the same.

In his First Meditation, Descartes inquires whether there are any philosophical reasons to doubt perceptual judgments of the form "I see (hear, feel) such and such," where the such and such is something physical, nearby, and easy to perceive. He has already concluded that he cannot trust such judgments if the such and such is "hardly perceptible or very far away," since his senses have sometimes deceived him about such matters. At first he is tempted to respond in the manner of G. E. Moore: Surely these hands and this body are mine and I am here, seated by the fire, attired in a dressing gown, with these papers before me. One must be insane to doubt such matters, or at least it seems only madmen do in fact have doubts of this kind.[4]

Unlike Moore, however, Descartes quickly subdues the temptation to admit perceptual judgments of nearby physical objects as indubitable. Speaking now with more metaphysical rigor, Descartes introduces his dream argument. He contends that possibly he is only dreaming that he is perceiving a fire, attired in a dressing gown. Not only could this happen, but he claims that it has happened to him and indeed that "on many occasions I have in sleep been deceived by similar illusions." Descartes justifies his present doubt, then, by observing that "manifestly . . . there are no certain indications by which we may clearly distinguish wakefulness from sleep." The experience of seeing a real fire is not clearly distinguishable from dreaming that we are seeing a fire. To generalize: we can be in one and the same qualitatively indistinguishable perceptual state whether we are dreaming or awake. The conviction about what we are perceiving is therefore inconclusive, and it is always possible that we are mistaken about the matter—even if the perceptions seem to be of a nearby physical object that is easy to perceive. Descartes thus concludes that possibly he is asleep and "neither our hands nor our whole body are such as they appear to us to be."[5] Maybe we are always dreaming.

10.2 Two Answers That Will Not Do

Before presenting a refutation of the dream argument, I want to discuss two unacceptable answers to it. The first tries to defeat the argument by establishing that I am awake and not dreaming on the basis of some sort of evidence. The second tries to defeat the dream argument with an argument from contrast or from correlative terms.

10.2.1 The Appeal to Evidence

A necessary premise of the dream argument is that *there is no evidence I can appeal to, at time* t, *to establish whether I am awake or dreaming at time* t. Theaetetus and Descartes make the premise explicit; it seems to be implicit in Chuang Tzu. One of the most common responses to the dream argument is to contend that this premise is false. Such a response is unsuccessful.

Consider a Humean who proposes to dispute the premise on the grounds that we have an internal criterion of the difference between impressions and ideas. He may quote with approval Hume's remark that impressions and ideas differ in "the degrees of force and liveliness with which they strike upon the mind."[6] This may tempt him to conclude that I have the following test to determine whether I am awake or dreaming at any given time: all I need do is check the vivacity of my perception; if my perception is, say, of a fire and the perception is vivid and has a great deal of force and liveliness, then I can be sure that I am not dreaming that I am perceiving a fire; I really am perceiving it and hence I am awake. This approach to the problem, however, fails to appreciate the force of the skeptic's counter that it is possible to have dreams that have much "force and vivacity." This is obviously possible, since if any waking experience has a certain quality, I can always dream that I have an experience that has that very same quality. Thus Hume's internal evidence is inconclusive. Hume himself implied as much when he observed on the second page of his *Treatise*: "In sleep . . . our ideas may approach to our impressions . . . [and] it sometimes happens, that our impressions are so faint and low, that we cannot distinguish them from our ideas." Appeal to the vivacity of our perceptions cannot settle the question whether our perceptions are waking or dream perceptions for another reason as well. If it is uncertain whether we are now dreaming, then, if we are consistent, it also ought to be uncertain whether we are now applying the test to our perceptions or only dreaming that we are doing so. But dreaming that we are applying a test is not applying a test. So, it cannot be certain that we have even applied the Humean test, much less passed it.

In his book *Dreaming*, Malcolm shows that the last objection also applied to the use of any coherence principle to find out whether I am awake or dreaming.[7] Several eminent philosophers—Descartes, Leibniz, Pascal, Russell, Ayer—have thought that the way to answer the question is to employ a criterion of coherence, consistency, or agreement. Descartes, for example, makes use of such a criterion in his Sixth Meditation. Roughly, the test is: if the perceptions cohere with one another, I am awake; if they fail to cohere, they are dream perceptions. For instance, if my memory can connect the perceptions one with another, or with the whole course of my life, I am not dreaming. But again, there is the objection that incoherence, while characteristic of many dreams, is no more essential to a dream than is lack of vivacity. A second decisive objection to such a test is that it is always possible to dream that I am remembering the connection of one perception with another or with the whole course of my life. That is to say, it is possible to dream that my perceptions cohere; hence reliance on coherence settles nothing. The point may be generalized: no test can get me out of such a doubt, for it is always possible merely to dream that I have applied the test that shows my perceptions to be veridical.

In his reply to Malcolm, Ayer shows he does not appreciate the force of this last objection. For he writes that it is a mistake to think that the coherence test is worthless just because it is inconclusive.[8] A test can be useful even if inconclusive. The general point may be accepted. But Ayer fails to see that if we genuinely doubt whether we are now awake or only dreaming, then we must also doubt whether we have just now applied or only dreamed that we applied our test. Accordingly, neither the coherence nor any other test can get us out of the doubt. No matter what the test, we always confront the same difficulty: assuming an acceptance of the initial doubt, we must, if we are consistent, also doubt whether we have carried out the test. Hence Ayer cannot conclude that his "test" provides him with even an inconclusive reason to cease questioning whether he is awake or dreaming. We do not conclude on the basis of any argument that it is highly probably that we are awake and not dreaming. Indeed, if we begin by doubting whether we are awake—if this is accepted as a genuine doubt— no appeal to any tests or evidence will ever make it more probable, or inductively support, that we are awake rather than dreaming. The point is nicely illustrated in a passage from "The Poet," the last of Isak Dinesen's *Seven Gothic Tales*.

"Listen, Madame Fransine," he said, "I dreamed of you two nights ago." At this she smiled, but was much interested. "I dreamed," he said, "that you and I were walking to a great seashore, where a strong wind was blowing. You said to me: 'This is to go on forever.' But I said that we were only dreaming. 'Oh, no, you must not think that,' you said. 'Now, if I take off my new bonnet and throw it into the sea, will you believe that it is no dream?' So you untied your bonnet and threw it from you, and the waves carried it far away. Still I thought that it was a dream. 'Oh, how ignorant you are,' you said, 'but if I take off my silk shawl and throw it away, you must see that all this is real.' You threw back your silk shawl, and from the sand the wind lifted it and carried it off. But I could not help thinking that it was a dream. 'If I cut off my left hand,' you said, 'will you be convinced?' You had a pair of scissors in the pocket of your frock. You held up your left hand, just as if it had been a rose, and cut it off. And with that—" He stopped, very pale. "With that I woke up," he said.[9]

I conclude that Theaetetus is quite right: there is no non-question-begging way I can tell that I am now awake and not dreaming.

Let me mention two provisos at this point, to forestall a possible misunderstanding. First, I am not denying that there are differences between dreams and waking experiences. In dreams physically impossible, absurd—and even logically impossible—things can happen. In a dream a human being can turn into a butterfly or be identical with a chandelier. Wives can change their husbands into giant pastrami sandwiches. With hot mustard. Woody Allen recounts how in a dream his laughter turned to tears and "then into a serious ear infection."[10] In dreams it is possible at one and the same time to be a corpse in a coffin and a person not in the coffin. (Professor Isak Borg had such a dream in Ingmar Bergman's *Wild Strawberries*.) I say it is possible to dream such things, because if someone on awakening sincerely reports that he did, we all accept that that is what he dreamed. That is, we accept sincere or truthful dream reports as true regardless of their content. Note a distinction here. I am not saying that "I dreamed that *p*" and "It is not the case that I dreamed that *p*" can both be true. They cannot both be true, since they contradict each other. What I am saying is that reports of the form "I dreamed that *p* and not-*p*," or those reducible to this form, can be true and will be true if reported sincerely or truthfully. Such reports are not self-contradictory, even though what follows the words "I dreamed" is self-contradictory or is reducible to a formal self-contradiction.

Contrast now our reaction to sincere reports of waking experiences. We do not always accept them as true. Indeed, we shall insist that they are not true if we think the experiences described could not have happened or if we think the descriptions of them are self-contradictory. If someone reports that yesterday he had an exciting conversation with a logician who happened to be, literally, a caterpillar or that he got his fifth divorce after being married only twice, we know the reports could not be literally true. Accordingly, if someone believes that he did something and that he did not merely dream he did it, and, if he becomes persuaded that such things never happen or are impossible, he now has reason for thinking he may have dreamed it. Thus I may believe that as a child I visited a fabulous city constructed only of emeralds in which everything appeared green. Later, upon reflection, I may become convinced that the quantity of emerald required to make such a city was too vast to be real: hence I may come to believe that I only dreamed that I visited such a city. This later conviction may or may not be correct. Perhaps I didn't dream it, but my belief was based on a story I read as a child.

I have mentioned a few specific ways in which dreams and dream reports *can* differ from waking experiences and reports of waking experiences. From this it of course does not follow that physically impossible, absurd, or logically impossible things must occur in dreams. Dream occurrences *may* be very plausible, coherent, logical. Hence the absence of absurdity and the occurrence of what is logically possible does not guarantee that the experience is a waking one and not a dream experience. Yet the difference cited helps to explain how appeal to evidence may show that I did not dream something I thought I dreamed. If I am awake at time t_2, I may at that time gather evidence supporting the conclusion that I dreamed that a particular thing happened at some earlier time t_1. In such cases it is legitimate to talk about gathering inductive evidence. Indeed, the evidence will be inductive in the sense of being inconclusive. For even if such an event could not have happened, it does not follow that I dreamed that it happened. As we have seen, I may have read about it or it may even have been a hallucination.

There may still linger a temptation to think that if what I said is true, while there is indeed no evidence I can appeal to, at time t, to prove that I am awake at time t, there is a way of proving, at time t, that I am dreaming at that time: all I need observe is that what seems to be happening is absurd or logically or scientifically impossible. But that won't help, as Chuang Tzu recognizes, for if I am in doubt about whether I am dreaming, I must also doubt that I am observing something.

10.2.2 A Simple Contrast or Correlative Argument

I want now to show that a simple contrast or correlative argument also fails to defeat the dream argument. This kind of argument goes as follows: It cannot be that we are always dreaming, for "dreaming" and "not dreaming" are correlative terms. If the first is meaningful, the other must be too, and vice versa. Hence the first applies to something only if the second does, and conversely. Put more generally, if "F(a)" makes sense, it cannot be the case that $(x)F(x)$, for "not-F" must also make sense; hence "not-F" must apply to something. (Compare Butler's short answer to the psychological hedonist.)

There are several reasons why this argument fails. First, it gives *me* no assurance that I am not now dreaming. All it concludes is that *everybody* is not *always* dreaming. But this conclusion is compatible with my always dreaming. So the argument will not get Descartes out of his skeptical doubt. Finally, the argument involves a non sequitur. Even accepting its first premise that "F" is meaningful if and only if "not-F" is meaningful, it does not follow that "F" applies to anything, in the sense of being true of that thing. It is easy to see this if we replace "F" by "mortal." It is certainly intelligible to say that a human being is not mortal—is not-F—yet we don't think this is true of any human being. So a simple contrast or correlative counter to the dream argument does not even succeed in showing that not everybody is always dreaming.

10.3 Refutation of the Dream Argument

10.3.1 A Dilemma

The first good objection to the dream argument that I want to consider is grounded in Wittgenstein's thought, and takes the form of a dilemma. The argument seems to force us to choose between two equally unacceptable alternatives. First, if we accept the extreme doubt that we are not now perceiving this table, on the grounds that possibly we are now dreaming, by parity of reasoning we must also doubt whether we understand the words we are using to express our alleged doubt. After all, it is no less an empirical fact that particular words mean what they do rather than something else or that they are used in such and such ways rather than in other ways. Moreover, such facts are no more certain than the fact that I now see a table. If I therefore profess uncertainty about the latter, because I might only be dreaming, surely I ought to claim to be uncertain about the meaning of these words as well. This is a point Wittgenstein makes in *On Certainty* (see OC, §456). Perhaps these words are meaningless or express something quite different from what I take them to express. Thus if Descartes is consistent, his professed doubt should defeat itself by making him doubt his very doubt.[11]

It might be objected that skeptics can go on doubting that they are awake on this first alternative so long as their doubt does not depend on language and they do not express their doubt in words. In replying to the objection, I shall not try to settle the question whether we can think and doubt without using language. But even supposing we can, to doubt that we are awake and not dreaming we must at least have the concept or idea of dreaming and of being awake. And it is no less an empirical question whether we do or do not have such concepts. Thus if I can doubt that I am now awake, how can I consistently keep from doubting that I have the requisite concepts to entertain such a doubt? Maybe I am only dreaming that I have such concepts. But dreaming that I have a concept is not the same thing as having that concept; nor does it imply that I have it: I may or may not. So, if I now doubt—even silently and nonlinguistically—that I am awake, if I am consistent, I will go on to doubt that my silent doubt is a genuine doubt. So the first alternative again leads to a destruction of the initial doubt. I am assuming here the principle that if I doubt that p, then I cannot doubt that I doubt that p, or, if anyone sincerely was uncertain that he had a particular doubt, we would conclude that he did not have that particular doubt.

We know that Descartes's initial doubt is not quite so hyperbolical as I am maintaining that it should be. He never goes on to doubt his own doubt. Instead, he takes for granted that he understands what it is he doubts, that he knows what it is to doubt, to know, think, exist, and so forth. He wrongly and inconsistently thinks he can doubt whether he perceives his hands, his body, the papers in front of him, and yet can avoid doubting whether the word "hand" has the particular meaning he thinks it has. Thus he does not push his alleged doubt far enough. Had he, he would have seen that it was equally doubtful whether he was even entertaining the doubt he thought he was. That too might only be part of a dream. So he should have thrown out his so-called initial doubt as itself doubtful. Put in a word, the first alternative points out that the professed doubt the dream argument gives rise to is self-defeating. Finally, it seems to lead to an infinite regress of doubts, each doubt undermining the doubt that precedes it. At any given moment we may be left with some doubt, but in the next breath we will destroy it as well.

Let us turn now to the second alternative. If we grant that Descartes understands the relevant words and possesses the concepts needed to express his doubt that he is awake, consistency will require that he admit that he has no such doubt after all. Accordingly, the second alternative returns us to the commonsense view that there is no doubt that we are awake, which contradicts one of the conclusions of the dream argument. To see this let us grant that the proponent of the dream argument understands the meaning of words like "hand" and "blue." Then he will know that it is correct to say of things such as my hand, "That is a hand," and of a blue color, "This is blue." In short, if we allow Descartes to have language and to understand the meaning of his words and to have certain concepts—and we have seen he must have such understanding if he is to entertain his initial doubt—then it will follow that he will be able to make many correct and true judgments that belie that he doubts that he is awake or that he doubts that he is now perceiving some nearby physical object.[12] (I am of course not saying or implying that if he understands these words he will never be hesitant to apply them to what he sees nor that he will never make perceptual errors. But he will only hesitate to judge a thing to be a hand, say, if he has some special reason to think that what looks like a hand really is not a hand.) It is for this reason that Wittgenstein says: "If I make certain false statements, it becomes uncertain whether I understand [those statements]" (OC, §81). Or putting it positively, in some cases: "The *truth* of my statements [or better, my recognizing them to be true] is the test of my *understanding* of these statements" (OC, §80). For example, if I understand the word *table,* I will recognize that what I see before me is a table, or I will recognize the truth of the statement "What I see before me is a table," assuming I am now in a normal state, the illumination is adequate, and the like. This, incidentally, helps explain why Wittgenstein writes: "I am not more certain of the meaning of my words than I am of certain judgments" (OC, §126).

There is a possible reply Descartes could make at this point, although I do not want to deal with it here. He might concede: I admit I am now perceiving a hand. There is a sense in which I never did doubt this. I never did doubt it practically; I only doubted it metaphysically. A counter to this could involve trying to undermine his distinction between metaphysical and practical doubt. The distinction seems a phony one.

But to return to the dilemma. We saw that Descartes's dream argument forces its proponent to choose between two equally unacceptable alternatives. On the one hand, there is the first alternative: If we doubt the truth of all of our perceptual judgments because we may now be dreaming, we must doubt that we understand what it is to doubt such matters or any others; so accepting our doubt we must doubt it, which undermines our initial doubt. On the other hand, there is the second alternative: If it is beyond doubt that we understand the conclusion of this dream argument and that we possess the relevant concepts to entertain the doubts it leads us to, consistency will require that we abandon our doubt that we can never be certain of the truth of our perceptual judgments along with our doubt that we are now awake. On the basis of these considerations we ought to reject Descartes's dream argument.

10.3.2 A Reductio ad Absurdum

Another powerful Wittgensteinian objection to the dream argument takes the form of a brief *reductio*. If we accept the argument, we must, if we are consistent, doubt everything. Anything and everything comes to be subject to doubt for the reasons already given in the last section. The argument leads to complete skepticism. But, as Wittgenstein observes, "a doubt that doubted everything would not be a doubt" (OC, §450). This is because "the game of doubting itself presupposes certainty" (OC, §115). Thus Descartes's doubt that he is awake rests on his certainty that he once dreamed that he was sitting in front of his fireplace, attired in his dressing gown, and so on. Hence, "a doubt without an end is not even a doubt" (OC, §625). I take Wittgenstein to be making a conceptual point here: the concept of doubt is parasitic on that of belief. Doubt presupposes belief, because we always need grounds or reasons for doubt (see OC, §122); that is, the doubt of p must rest on the belief that some q.[13] It follows that complete or total skepticism is an incoherent notion. Since the dream argument implies total skepticism, the dream argument must be rejected.

10.3.3 The Skeptic's Question Is Senseless

This third and final objection to the dream argument is directed at the meaningfulness of the philosophical question "Am I now dreaming?" The question assumes that either I am now dreaming or I am not now dreaming: the questioner wants to know which it is. The objection, put very roughly, is that "I am now dreaming" is senseless. (I shall qualify this claim shortly.) Hence the disjunction "Either I am now dreaming or I am not now dreaming" is also senseless. Here I am employing a principle endorsed by Hempel and others, namely, that if a sentence "S" is without sense, then "Either S or not S" is also without sense.[14] I conclude that the question must also be senseless.

Strictly speaking, however, it is not correct to say "I am now dreaming" is senseless. What I mean to say is that it is senseless unless it is used in certain ways. The first-person present tense of the verb "to dream" has various uses. "I dream" may be used to inform someone that I do dream. "I am dreaming" is sometimes also used as an expression of surprise or amazement. Thus a colleague told me he thought he was dreaming when late one night he saw a neighbor of his apparently watering his lawn with a hose in the middle of winter in Michigan! (He found out later the neighbor was making an ice-skating rink for his children.) "I am dreaming" may function as an exclamation like "My God!" "I'm dreaming!" or "I must be dreaming!"—perhaps millions of people uttered such words when they heard that Indira Gandhi, the prime minister of India, was slain by two of her own bodyguards in New Delhi, on October 31, 1984. The first person present tense may be used metaphorically as well, that is, as hyperbole. If one day I woke up in Tahiti, saw the sun rising out of the ocean, the fishermen pushing their boats into the surf, and myself surrounded by incredibly beautiful people who informed me that I was now the ruler of their island, I might wax extravagant and say "I'm dreaming." The locution "I dream of . . ." in turn functions to express a desire or wish. We can imagine a rubber fetishist saying to his psychiatrist, "I dream of Jeannie in a rubber bikini wearing rubber longjohns and a rubber raincoat." Were Martin Luther King to remark, "I dream of a time when all men will be brothers," we would know he is expressing an ideal as well as a hope and a wish. If Stravinsky says, "I dream of creating new forms of music," we can take this as an expression of a wish or longing, or even as an expression of a plan. Finally, we sometimes say, "I am dreaming again," or "I'm dreaming; I can't afford that," when this is elliptical for, roughly, "I am imagining things," or "I'm being unrealistic." I believe that in all of these uses of "I am dreaming" the speaker could go on to assert: "Well, I'm going to sleep now," which shows very clearly that he never for a moment thought he was claiming, literally, that he was now dreaming, for that would imply that he already was asleep. (Notice: I am not discussing daydreaming here.)

We have seen the ways "I am dreaming" can be used and ways "Am I dreaming?" might be used. We can imagine occasions on which these words can be meaningfully uttered, and we can paraphrase, at least roughly, what would be conveyed by them. So it is certainly reasonable to hold that the sentences are meaningful. They are meaningful because they can be used in these different ways. Suppose, however, that someone uttered these sentences and that he denied he meant them to be taken in any of these standard ways. We would be bewildered. We would perhaps admit that what he said sounded okay and that it was grammatically well formed, but that we could not understand it since the speaker rejected all of the standard interpretations. I believe we would eventually conclude—and I think rightly—that the person had lapsed into nonsense.

This brings me back to the main point: When philosophers ask, "Am I dreaming?" they do not mean it in any of the ways suggested. Nor do they use "I am dreaming" in any of the ways we have allowed as legitimate. For these reasons, as well as those given earlier, we may conclude that their use of the question is senseless.

10.4 Seven Possible Objections

In this last section, I shall try to anticipate and answer some possible objections to the third and last argument. This is to adopt a largely negative strategy, which might be viewed as a very Wittgensteinian thing to do. That is, the main "proof" of the thesis should be obvious outside the philosophy classroom if all of the philosophical objections can be explained away.

10.4.1 Proof That the Philosopher's Use of "I Am Dreaming" Is Meaningful

The following "unassailable proof" may be offered to show that "I am dreaming" is meaningful when used by the philosopher:

1. The negation or denial of every true sentence is meaningful and false.[15]
2. Every sentence that is false is meaningful.[16]
3. The sentence "I am not now dreaming" is true, where "I" is understood to refer to me now.
4. Therefore, if I say "I am now dreaming," it is false. (By 1, 3.)
5. Therefore, if I say now "I am dreaming," what I say is meaningful, whether or not I mean it in any of the ways mentioned above. (By 2, 4.)

Reply. The first premise is ambiguous and may be taken in either of two ways, both of which must be rejected. We may take it as claiming, first, that if any true sentence is prefaced with the words "It is not the case that," or some synonymous expression, the resulting sentence will be false and meaningful. Second, we may take it as claiming that every statement has a negation in the sense of denial—namely something that counts as an action of negating it. If we reflect on the sentences "I am not dead," "I am conscious," and even perhaps "It's not the case that I believe falsely that Michigan has little sunshine," I think we will see that the first premise is false, on either interpretation. For the statements made with these sentences do not have negations, in the sense of denials, that is, anything that counts as an action of negating them. Moreover, the sentences "I am dead," "I am unconscious," and "I believe falsely that Michigan has little sunshine" are not both false and meaningful, though I grant that "I am dead" is meaningful in much the same sort of way "I am dreaming" is meaningful. Other criticisms could be made of this argument, but this suffices to refute objection 1.

10.4.2 The Sentence "I Am Dreaming"
Can Literally Ascribe Dreaming to Me

We can literally ascribe dreaming to others in the present tense by saying "He (or she) is dreaming." Therefore, I must grant that the sentence "I am dreaming" can also literally ascribe dreaming to me. Taking "dreaming" as a one-place predicate and "he," "she," and "I" as terms that refer to individuals, we may be tempted to say that "He (or she) is dreaming" is meaningful if and only if "I am dreaming" is meaningful and that the predicate must be able to function in the same way in both cases.

Reply. The objection involves at least two mistakes. First, as Strawson has pointed out in his article "On Referring," we should not speak of "I," "he," and "she" as referring to particular persons; rather, it is *we* who refer to particular persons *by using* such referring expressions. Second and more importantly, the objection contains a non sequitur. For it is not even the case that if something of the form "He is *F*" is meaningful, the expression "I am *F*" must also be meaningful, much less mean in the same way. Proof by counterexample: "He believes falsely," "He is dead," "He is unconscious," these are all meaningful statements. Yet it is nonsense to say "I believe falsely (am dead or am unconscious)."

10.4.3 It Makes Sense to Ascribe Dreaming to Myself

Suppose while I am dreaming I say, "I am dreaming." Then I say what I might say later of myself, namely, "I was dreaming," or I say what another person says if he says of me, "He's dreaming." I make the same assertion, affirm the same proposition. Hence it must have the same truth value. A fortiori, it has a truth value and it is meaningful for me literally to ascribe dreaming to myself.

Reply. What is being overlooked here is that when I utter these words while I am dreaming I do not make any assertion, I do not affirm any proposition; hence I cannot have made the same assertion that someone else made or that I might make at some other time. I could not, since, by hypothesis, I am dreaming; I am asleep and not conscious. Merely uttering these words is not to make an assertion. To make an assertion a person must be conscious and mean to say what he (or she) says. That is why Wittgenstein writes: "Someone who, dreaming, says 'I am dreaming,' even if he speaks audibly in doing so, is no more right than if he said in his dream 'it is raining,' while it was in fact raining. Even if this dream were actually connected with the noise of the rain" (OC, §676). Even if he shouted these words, or uttered them with great emphasis, if he is dreaming, he still can have no idea what the is saying. Hence he cannot ask a question either. John Locke seemed to recognize this point: "If . . . any one will be so skeptical as to distrust his senses, and to affirm that all we see and hear, feel and taste, think and do, during our whole being, is but the series and deluding appearances of a long dream, whereof there is no reality; and therefore will question the existence of all things, or our knowledge of anything: I must desire him to consider, that, if all be a dream, then he doth but dream that he makes the question."[17]

10.4.4 Saying "I Am Dreaming" When
I Am Dreaming Is Both True and Meaningful

Let us grant, if I am dreaming, I cannot make an assertion, cannot affirm any proposition or ask any questions. Yet the words I utter, namely, "I am dreaming," are true or at least express a proposition that is true. So in one sense of "say," what I said is still true and meaningful. Likewise, if I uttered the words "I am not dreaming," while dreaming, my words would be false or express a proposition that is false. So, again, in one sense of "say," what I said would be meaningful. The same goes for the utterances of parrots even if they cannot make assertions, the words they utter can be true or false or express a proposition that is true or false.

Reply. I said in answer to objection 2 that we should not suppose that linguistic expressions refer to or mention things. It is more accurate, as Strawson stressed, to say that referring is something that people do with referring expressions.[18] This objection is also guilty of anthropomorphism. It assumes either (1) that sentences are true or false or, alternatively, (2) that they express something—namely, propositions—that is true or false. You might as well say that a shovel is shoveling. The simple truth is that neither is a shovel shoveling nor does a shovel shovel. But people use shovels to shovel. Similarly, they use sentences to express propositions, to make assertions, that is, to say something true or false. It is a mistake, however, to think that the sentences themselves do this or that they are true or false. Strawson reminds us that what can be said of a sentence cannot necessarily be said of the use we put it to, and conversely.[19] For example, the sentence may be composed of seven words, but we do not say that the assertion is composed of seven words. It is the assertion we make and can make with the sentence that is true or false, not the sentence.

10.4.5 I Can Believe and Even Know That I Am Dreaming While I Am Dreaming

Even granting that while dreaming I cannot make an assertion and that the words I utter when I am dreaming will fail to express a proposition, it might still be objected that surely I can believe I am dreaming while I am dreaming. And of course if I had such a belief, I would be quite right, for it would be a true belief. Moreover, I may also want to say that the dreamer is in a position to know whether this is a true belief, that is, to know whether he is dreaming or not. "He ought to know," we might say of him. Well, if he is sure that he is dreaming and he is dreaming at the time that he is sure that he is dreaming and we grant that he has a right to be sure of it, then at least on one plausible account of knowledge[20] we are committed to saying that a person can know that he is now dreaming, contrary to the view expressed here.

Reply. It is a mistake to think that a dream belief is a belief. It is no more a belief than a birthday suit is a suit. If someone reported that he dreamed he believed he was Hitler, we would not infer that he ever believed he was Hitler even if we accepted his dream report as true. Nor is the dreamer in a position to know anything, including whether or not he is dreaming, for he is asleep and hence not in a position to know anything. To say "he ought to know" is absurd for the same reason: it disregards the obvious fact that he is asleep and therefore not conscious. It may be that we can know he is dreaming when he is dreaming, but it cannot be said of him at all that he knows he is dreaming when he is dreaming.

10.4.6 The Awake May Sometimes Doubt They Are Awake

Suppose that the sentences "I am not dreaming" and "Am I now dreaming?" cannot be used in a literal way to make an assertion or to ask a question when we are asleep, since nobody makes assertions or asks questions save when awake. This leaves open the possibility that we can use them to make an assertion or to ask a question when we are awake. Again, suppose that dream doubts and dream beliefs should not be confused with real doubts and beliefs; and hence that we should not infer that a person once believed that he was dreaming merely because we know he dreamed that he believed that he was dreaming. People who are awake may nevertheless sometimes believe that they are dreaming. Thus my colleague might dispute the interpretation I gave of his remark "I must be dreaming," made when he observed the strange behavior of his neighbor. Could he not maintain that what he saw was so surprising and unusual that he momentarily believed that he was dreaming or at least that he might be? After all, it is neither a logical truth that we are not dreaming, nor a sense-data statement; consequently, we can doubt it, and we will if we have specially good reasons to.

Reply. It is a philosophical error to think that everything neither a logical truth nor a sense-data statement can be doubted. Moore has shown us, in his "Defense of Common Sense," that there are many empirical propositions that cannot be doubted. My contention is that "I am not now dreaming" should be included among these indubitable empirical propositions. Thus if anyone said he thought he was dreaming or that he doubted he was awake while he was awake, we would interpret his remark in one of the ways I have mentioned. If the speaker objected: "No, I really do, literally, believe that I am now dreaming," and he persisted in this line, we should think something like: He doesn't know what these words means and must intend to say something radically different, or, more likely, that he is not being serious and wants to pull our leg. We might take his words to be symptomatic of some mental disturbance, but more likely they would reflect a certain philosophical training. I do not believe, however, that we would ever—at least outside of a philosophy classroom—take the speaker to be expressing a genuine doubt that he is awake. There can be no such doubt, because nothing counts as, or is accepted by us as an instance of, such a doubt.

10.4.7 A Fregean Argument

A follower of Frege, who thinks that the sense of a sentence is dependent on the sense of its primary parts,[21] may develop this counterargument: If a sentence has sense, all of its primary parts must have sense. "Mary believes I am now dreaming" has sense. "I am now dreaming" is a primary part of this sentence. Accordingly, "I am now dreaming" must have sense; and this sentence literally ascribes dreaming to the speaker.

Reply. Independently of the problem of primary parts, I think it is clear we should reject the Fregean principle. For a sentence can be meaningful even though one of its primary parts is without sense. Proof by counterexample: "He believes I am unconscious" and "She believes I am dead" are both meaningful sentences. Yet "I am unconscious" and "I am dead" are without sense, taken literally, for they have no use in the language. We cannot give a story within which such remarks can be imagined to function in a literal way.

I have now considered seven objections to the thesis that "I am now dreaming" is without sense unless it is taken in one of the ways suggested; hence, that the philosopher's question "Am I now dreaming?" is without sense. I hope we are now convinced that there is no problem left, even though there is no evidence we can appeal to in order to establish, and no ways we can prove, that we are not now dreaming.

In the next chapter, we move to a twentieth-century Cartesian—Bertrand Russell—and to the topic of proper names. Russell's theories of names will be given a close Wittgensteinian examination.

Chapter 11

Russell's Theory of Proper Names

In his lectures on logical atomism of 1918, Russell tries to set forth "a certain kind of logical doctrine, and on the basis of this a certain kind of metaphysic."[1] His aim is to explain language and thereby reality. The account of proper names is an important part of this enterprise. Sentences he analyzes in terms of their truth conditions. In the resulting analyses, many denoting phrases—definite descriptions and grammatically proper names—cease to be treated as semantical units; they are paraphrased away in the analyses.[2] To make sure that analyses finally terminate, Russell introduces the notion of logically proper names, which are names that guarantee that something corresponds to them. Together with predicates or relational terms, they form atomic propositions—the only true subject-predicate statements, according to Russell. The terms in these statements are supposed to stand in a perfect one-to-one relation with particulars and universals, which are nonlinguistic entities, and his fundamental "logical atoms."

Russell, then, has a double theory—two theories—of proper names: one, for what he calls *genuine or logically proper names*; another, for *grammatically proper names*. He finds logically proper names in the language we speak, but they also belong to the logically perfect language, or ideal language, he is constructing. The second theory is about those things that "pass for names in language, like 'Socrates,' 'Plato,' and so forth."[3] These are grammatically proper names or the things we habitually call proper names. He gives one account of the first sort of proper names—of genuine or logically proper names—and a totally different account of the second sort—grammatically proper names. We shall now take a closer look at both theories, beginning with the former.

11.1 Russell's Theory of Logically Proper Names

According to Russell, a logically proper name has the following characteristics:

1. (a) It has meaning, (b) even in isolation, or when it stands alone (R, pp. 202, 253).
2. (a) He defines logically proper names as "words for particulars" (R, p. 200). (b) A particular is one of the "terms of relations in atomic facts" (R, p. 199). Particulars are sense-data, "such things as little patches of color or sounds, momentary things" (R, p. 179). (c) What the name denotes or stands for—a particular—is its meaning (R, p. 201). That is, he gives a referential theory of the meaning of logically proper names.
3. No question as to the existence of N can arise if "N" is a logically proper name, since "N" will then always have a denotation (R, p. 250). (This follows from (1) and (2).) That's why Existential Generalization (EG) is a valid rule of logic for sentences involving genuine proper names. That is, if a predicate "F" truly applies to *a,* where *a* is a genuine proper name, there is something that is F. That is, Fa implies $(\exists x)Fx$.
4. To understand a logically proper name it suffices to be acquainted with the particular (R, p. 202). This is because the particular is the denotation, and hence the meaning, of the proper name; and acquaintance gives direct and certain knowledge of the thing with which you are acquainted. (Russell calls this sort of knowledge "knowledge by acquaintance.") Moreover, since the denotation is the meaning of the word, and since you cannot know this denotation in any way except by acquaintance, you cannot understand the proper name unless you are acquainted with what it denotes. In short, acquaintance with the denotation is both necessary and sufficient to understand "N," where "N" is a logically proper name. It is a corollary that you cannot name anything with which you are not acquainted.
5. Only words like "this" or "that" can be logically proper names in our everyday language and they only are if they are used to stand for a sense-datum (R, pp. 201, 203), that is, a particular. "This" and "that," when so used, do not mean the same thing to the speaker and to the hearer, because no two people can be acquainted with the same thing. In an important way particulars are private. That is why "if you try to apprehend the proposition that I am expressing when I say 'This is white,' you cannot do it," when I am using "this" as a genuine proper name (R, p. 201). Also, because "this" stands for one particular one moment and for another particular a few seconds or a couple of minutes later, since such particulars only have a fleeting existence (R, p. 203), even

the speaker will no longer apprehend the proposition that he or she expressed a couple of minutes ago with "This is white." Logically proper names are ambiguous proper names (R, p. 201): they stand for many different things at different times and in different uses.

11.2 Russell's Theory of Grammatically Proper Names

Russell's account of grammatically proper names, of words that pass for names in the language, contrasts sharply with his theory of logically proper names.

1. (a) Grammatically proper names, for example, do not have meaning. It follows that (b) they do not have meaning in isolation, or when they stand alone, unlike logically proper names.
2. Consequently, grammatically proper names are not logically proper names (R, pp. 200–201). They cannot be because they do not denote particulars. The things they purport to denote—things like Socrates, Plato, Times Square, France—are things nobody could be acquainted with, since they are complicated systems of classes or series. For example, we "might identify Socrates with the series of his experiences" (R, p. 191). Not being particulars, things like Socrates, Plato, Times Square, France cannot be named, strictly speaking (R, p. 187). For Russell, only particulars have proper names in the logical and strict sense. We have seen that he defines logically proper names as "words for particulars" (R, p. 200).
3. With such so-called proper names, questions as to the existence of N can always arise since "N" in these cases never names or stands for anything. Existential statements involving such names can be either true or false.
4. You can never come to understand a grammatically proper name by becoming acquainted with its denotation or referent, because it does not have one to be acquainted with. According to Russell, Washington and Wittgenstein, for example, are not the sort of things you can be acquainted with. As we have noted, they are not what he would call particulars, since they are alleged to be complicated systems of classes.

5. Grammatically proper names are really abbreviations or short for descriptions (R, p. 200). Thus "Socrates" is to be replaced with something like "the teacher of Plato"; "Plato," with "the author of the *Republic*"; "George Washington," with "the first president of the United States." Such replacements are definite descriptions, as contrasted with indefinite descriptions like "a president of the United States." In short, to give the sense of "Socrates is wise" you first replace "Socrates" with a definite description and then simply analyze the resulting sentence in accord with Russell's theory of descriptions.[4]

11.3 How the Later Wittgenstein Would Criticize Russell's Theory

I shall try to bring out next what Wittgenstein's explicit and implied criticisms of Russell's view are in his later philosophy, especially in his *Philosophical Investigations*.

11.3.1 One Big Criticism of Russell's Picture of Language

Let us look first at the second page of Wittgenstein's *Investigations*, where he discusses what can be referred to as Augustine's conception or picture of language. According to this picture, the words of the language name objects; so sentences are just combinations of such names. Every word is viewed as having a meaning, which is correlated with the word. Indeed, the meaning "is the object for which the word stands" (PI, §1). Words are names and what they name is what they mean. Consequently, we know that they must name something and if we are acquainted with what they name, we know what it is that they mean. Baker and Hacker nicely summarize this conception "in three theses: (i) every word has a meaning; (ii) this meaning is something correlated with the word; (iii) it is the object for which the word stands." They say these theses "are an integral part of what Wittgenstein calls 'Augustine's conception (or description) of language.'"[5]

Wittgenstein opposes this picture of language in his later philosophy. He denies that this is the essence of language and even that language has an essence, in the sense that there is one thing languages have in common that makes them all languages (PI, §65). First, not everything in a language must be a word. For example, Wittgenstein would include the color samples that one person shows to another as part of the language, even though "they do not belong among the words." He says, "It is most natural, and causes least confusion, to reckon the samples among the instruments of the language" (PI, §16). Second, Wittgenstein denies that all words are names. See, for example, section 27 of the *Investigations,* where he gives a list of exclamations and asks the reader, "Are you inclined still to call these words 'names of objects'?" So there are at least two flaws Wittgenstein would find in the Augustinian picture of language.

How does this apply to Russell and his theory of proper names? Russell would agree that not all the words in our language are names. Indeed, he seems to push this thesis even further than Wittgenstein, denying that the words we call proper names in our language really are genuine proper names. (See claim 2 above.) Nevertheless, when we get to the final analysis of our language using Russell's theory—when we arrive at the basic atomic statements our language is analyzed into—we get something very much like the Augustinian picture of language. The following quotation from Russell's *Philosophy of Logical Atomism* should help to bring this out.

> The reason that I call my doctrine *logical atomism* is because the atoms that I wish to arrive at as the sort of last residue in analysis are logical atoms and not physical atoms. Some of them will be what I call 'particulars'—such things as little patches of color or sounds, momentary things—and some of them will be predicates or relations and so on. (R, p. 179)

So his logical atoms are basically two kinds of things: particulars and relations. (Predicates we can think of as just being one-place or monadic relations.) He speaks of these things as being different sorts of simples: particulars are one kind; qualities and relations, another sort (R, p. 270). He says:

> In a logically perfect language the words in a proposition would correspond one by one with the components of the corresponding fact, with the exception of such words as 'or,' 'not,' 'if,' 'then,' which have a different function. In a logically perfect language, there will be one word and no more for every simple object, and everything that is not simple will be expressed by a combination of words, by a combination derived, of course, from the words for the simple things that enter in, one word for each simple component. (R, pp. 197–98)

At the level of the atomic proposition there will be no logical connectives—words like "or," "not," "if," "then"—since these are only used to form molecular statements by connecting together other statements. The logical connectives are never themselves constituent parts of atomic statements. Here we only find proper and common names. The proper name stands for a simple, which is a particular; the common name—"horse," "red," "love"—signifies, or stands for, a relation. There is a nice one-to-one relation between them just as in Augustine's picture of language. I think the later Wittgenstein would criticize Russell—as well as Wittgenstein's own earlier view—for both having a similarly misleading picture of language. This, then, is one big criticism of Russell's theory: he overemphasizes the naming relation in explaining language—in his analysis of our language—even while he radically downplays the naming relation in discussing our ordinary language in its unanalyzed form.

11.3.2 Wittgenstein's Criticisms of Russell's First Set of Claims

Let us consider now the more specific criticisms Wittgenstein makes, or his view implies, of the first set of claims, namely, that a genuine or logically proper name has meaning, even in isolation, or when it stands alone (R, pp. 202, 253), whereas grammatically proper names do not.

The later Wittgenstein never seems to discuss the question whether proper names, as such, have meaning. But many of his remarks imply that the things we call proper names—grammatically proper names—have meaning as much as any other words do. There are at least four reasons for saying this. First, he says, "one can ostensively define a proper name" as well as other things. That does not of course mean that it will always be understood. Writes Wittgenstein, another person "might . . . take the name of a person, of which I give an ostensive definition, as that of a color, of a race, or even of a point of the compass. . . . [A]n ostensive definition can be variously interpreted in *every* case" (PI, §28). Second, he writes: "We may say, following Russell: the name 'Moses' can be defined by means of various descriptions. For example, as 'the man who led the Israelites through the wilderness'" (PI, §79). If a word is definable in either of these ways, it seems it must have a meaning. Third, he implies in many places (for example, PI, §41) that even if use and meaning are not identical, words that have a use in the language have a meaning. This is sufficient for having meaning. Proper names surely have a use in the language; therefore, they must have meaning. Finally, even more conclusively, Wittgenstein actually speaks of the meaning of a proper name (PI, §43) and, more specifically, of the meaning of "Mr. N. N." (PI, §40); so he is committed to the view that they have meaning.

But does it follow from this that Wittgenstein thinks that a grammatically proper name ever has meaning in isolation? No. And I doubt that he thinks they do. For he says he agrees with Frege that a word has "meaning only as part of a sentence" (PI, §49). Wittgenstein observes:

Naming and describing do not stand on the same level: naming is a preparation for description. Naming is so far not a move in the language-game—any more than putting a piece in its place on the board is a move in chess. We may say: *nothing* has so far been done, when a thing has been named. It has not even *got* a name except in the language-game. This was what Frege meant too, when he said that a word had meaning only as part of a sentence. (PI, §49)

Since Wittgenstein holds that this is true in general about words—that they only have meaning as parts of a sentence—he must also think it true of Russell's logically proper names; that is, they cannot have meaning in isolation. But would the later Wittgenstein at least acknowledge that Russell's logically proper names have meaning when they are not in isolation? I don't think so. For one thing, he would contend there are no rules governing the use of such names. The so-called rules he would call "private rules," since there is no distinction here between thinking you are following the rule and really doing so. But thinking you are obeying a rule by itself does not imply that you are. Moreover, with genuine rules there are always public ways of determining whether someone is obeying or not obeying a particular rule (PI, §201). We do not have such criteria here. Wittgenstein would therefore deny that such so-called private rules are real rules (PI, §201).

To summarize Wittgenstein's implied comment on the first set of claims: he would say Russell is wrong to deny meaning to grammatically proper names; the things we habitually call proper names have meaning as much as any other words do. He would also think Russell is mistaken both in attributing meaning to logically proper names and in holding that they can have this meaning in isolation. According to Wittgenstein, no words have meaning in isolation; so Russell's logically proper names do not either.

11.3.3 Wittgenstein's Criticisms of Russell's Second Set of Claims

Consider next the second claims, that genuine or logically proper names stand for particulars that constitute their meaning, but grammatically proper names stand for nothing. It is pretty certain Wittgenstein would not want to deny that the things we call proper names *may* stand for, or denote, things, leaving undefined for the moment what sorts of things. For this is merely to say that we sometimes use them to refer to things. (Whether they always denote or name something will be considered under the third claim.)

But could the denotation of either a logically, or a grammatically, proper name—the thing it stands for, when it stands for something—ever constitute its meaning? Wittgenstein implies an answer to this in section 40.

> It is important to note that the word "meaning" is being used illicitly if it is used to signify the thing that 'corresponds' to the word. That is to confound the meaning of a name with the *bearer* of the name. When Mr. N. N. dies one says that the bearer of the name dies, not that the meaning dies.

Note the generality of Wittgenstein's claim: he says the word "meaning" is being used illicitly whenever it is used to signify the thing that "corresponds" to the word. The point is not restricted to grammatically proper names. So he is committed to criticizing Russell's theory of logically proper names for confusing the meaning of a name with the bearer of the name. It misuses the word "meaning." Incidentally, the early Wittgenstein himself makes essentially the same mistake. For at that time he held both that a name means an object, and the object is its meaning (TLP, 3.203).

11.3.4 Wittgenstein's Criticisms of Russell's Third Set of Claims

Claims number 3, you will recall, were these: if "N" is a genuine or logically proper name, no question as to the existence of N can properly arise. But if "N" is a grammatically proper name, the question as to the existence of N can always properly arise. (Note: Russell is talking about the existence of N, not the word "N." We mustn't confuse a person with his name.)

Well, section 40, already referred to, at least suggests, if it doesn't imply, that N may not exist even though "N" is a grammatically proper name. Section 79 makes it even clearer that he would agree with Russell on this point about grammatically proper names. He speaks there of the meaning, or meanings, of the negative existential statement "Moses did not exist." It is clear that he does not regard this statement, which commences with the grammatically proper name "Moses," as either meaningless or necessarily false. It could be either true or false.

That does not tell us, however, how Wittgenstein would react to Russell's other claim about logically proper names necessarily having a denotation, or to his own similar early view in the *Tractatus* that you cannot question or deny the existence of the simple objects that genuine names stand for.

Some passages in the *Investigations* may wrongly give the impression that Wittgenstein continues to hold this earlier view in his later philosophy: namely, that if a name is meaningful it must name something. For example:

"What the names in language signify must be indestructible; for it must be possible to describe the state of affairs in which everything destructible is destroyed. And this description will contain words; and what corresponds to these cannot then be destroyed, for otherwise the words would have no meaning." (PI, §55)

But notice that this passage is in quotes. It does not necessarily reflect his own present view. Wittgenstein has to be read with great care. What we in fact have here is his own previous opinion (see TLP, 2.0271) and that of Russell in his logical atomism, which the later Wittgenstein is attacking.

Again, another passage that could lead an unwary reader astray occurs in section 57, which begins: " 'Something red can be destroyed, but red cannot be destroyed, and that is why the meaning of the word 'red' is independent of the existence of a red thing.' " Note that Wittgenstein again puts quotes around this passage; that usually indicates that the quoted passage does not reflect his own present opinion.

Consider still a third misleading passage, beginning at section 58: " 'I want to restrict the term "*name*" to what cannot occur in the combination "X exists".' " Again, we have the warning sign of quotation marks. More important, this remark is incompatible with his later discussion of existential statements involving proper names like "Moses" (PI, §79). We have already seen that he does not regard such statements as meaningless; they can be either true or false. In fact, the passage in section 58 actually expresses a view of the *Tractatus* and of Russell's *Philosophy of Logical Atomism* that he is attacking in his *Investigations*.

Could the later Wittgenstein nevertheless agree with Russell's view that there are proper names that must name something if they are meaningful? I doubt it. He speaks mockingly of "the conception of naming as, so to speak, an occult process. Naming appears as a *queer* connection of a word with an object" (PI, §38). Russell (and early Wittgenstein) are free, of course, to stipulate that by a genuine or logically proper name they mean something that has to have a denotation. But that leaves open the question whether there are such names or ever could be. That is, because a philosopher makes it true by definition that such proper names always have de-notations, it does not follow that there are any names of this kind. We shall return to this topic in discussing the fifth group of claims.

11.3.5 Wittgenstein's Criticisms of Russell's Fourth Set of Claims

The view of the later Wittgenstein also indicates partial opposition to, as well as partial agreement with, the fourth set of claims—that is, that all we need fully to understand a genuine proper name is to be acquainted with the particular it stands for, that we cannot really name things we are not acquainted with, that we are not acquainted with the things that gram-matically proper names purport to name, and that we need more than acquaintance with particulars to understand these words that we habitually call proper names.

As for the first point that all we need fully to understand a genuine proper name is to be acquainted with the corresponding particular—to focus our attention on it—we have already noted some of the ways we may fail to grasp ostensive definitions. For example, we may take an ostensive definition of a person's name, or of a number, to be the name "of a color, of a race, or even of a point of the compass." To understand the ostensive definition "that is called 'two'" (PI, §28), as someone points to two nuts, or an ostensive definition of "red," we need to have the concepts of number and of color, respectively. For an ostensive definition tells someone the use of a word only "if the place is already prepared," in which case the indi-vidual "is already master of a game" (PI, §31). Putting the point another way, we may say that naming cannot be merely a two-place relation as Russell supposed, anymore than ownership (think of "N owns a house") can be a simple two-place relationship. For, just as ownership involves reference to the law, naming involves reference to the rest of language and other extra-linguistic circumstances.[6] We have to know about such matters before we can grasp any ostensive definition of a proper name, even our own private, inner ones, if there are such private ostensive definitions. So acquaintance—taken in either the everyday or in Russell's technical sense —is not a sufficient condition for understanding the meaning of a genuine proper name.

Wittgenstein would also object to Russell's claim that we cannot really name things we are not acquainted with and that we cannot be acquainted with the things that grammatically proper names purport to name, at least if we are to use "name" and "acquainted with" in the usual way. And, he would ask, rhetorically, how else are we to use these words, or any others?

Recall that he wants to get philosophers "to bring words back from their metaphysical to their everyday use" (PI, §116). Surely it would be absurd to imply that Russell was not—and could not have been—acquainted with Wittgenstein, when he himself tells us that getting to know him was one of the most exciting experiences of his life! A person is precisely one sort of thing we can be acquainted with.

I imagine Russell would agree that this is true of what *we* call naming or being acquainted with something, but not for what *he* means by these terms. He is using "naming" and "acquaintance" in a technical sense, which is different from what they commonly mean. He might reply to Wittgenstein's criticism much the way Humpty Dumpty replied to Alice, when she pointed out to him that he was not using the word "glory" correctly, or the way the rest of us do. " 'When *I* use a word,' Humpty Dumpty said, in rather a scornful tone, 'it means just what I choose it to mean—neither more nor less.' "[7] So, it could be argued, these Wittgensteinian criticisms do not apply to Russell's theory of logically proper names and to his doctrine of acquaintance. They might be seen as just misunderstandings.

This answer has a certain force. However, we must ask whether any word could be used in the way Russell says genuine proper names are used. It is unlikely that Wittgenstein would think so, because Russell's account of logically proper names commits him to a private language—that is, a language that is logically impossible for others to understand—and Wittgenstein denies that there can be such a language. But we will return to this point in considering Wittgenstein's criticism of the fifth set of claims.

Russell is right, however, in Wittgenstein's view, to suggest that it is a mistake to think that acquaintance—in either his technical sense or ours— is "the only thing necessary" to grasp completely, or fully to understand, a grammatically proper name. We have already seen that being acquainted, in our sense, with what we call the referent of a grammatically proper name does not guarantee that we will understand that name. It is also not necessary. For, as Wittgenstein says, we can define a grammatically proper name "by means of various descriptions" as well as ostensively. Thus we can understand the meaning of the name "Moses" without ever having met the man. Most of us understand the name, but obviously we have never met him. The same is true of any other grammatically proper name. As Kenny says: "Most of us know perfectly well who it is that we are talking about when we use the name 'Adolf Hitler' without having made the acquaintance of the bearer of that name."[8] In short, taking acquaintance in any normal way, it is neither necessary nor sufficient for understanding what we call a proper name. Wittgenstein would agree with this much of the fourth set of claims.

11.3.6 Wittgenstein's Criticisms of Russell's Fifth Set of Claims

Let us begin with the fifth claim that words like "this" and "that" are the only words that could be logically proper names in English. The sections in which Wittgenstein discusses this claim are numerous, and it is clear that he opposes it. He speaks of it as a "queer conception [that] springs from a tendency to sublime the logic of our language," for example, to search for a hidden essence of language. He suggests we only produce confusion when we call the words "this" or "that" names. Many things are called "names" but not these words, though he admits that,

> in giving an ostensive definition . . . we often point to the object named and say the name. And similarly, in giving an ostensive definition for instance, we say the word "this" while pointing to a thing. And also the word "this" and a name often occupy the same position in a sentence. But it is precisely characteristic of a name that it is defined by means of the demonstrative expression "That is N" (or "That is called 'N'"). [But we never] give the definitions: "That is called 'this,'" or "This is called 'this.'" (PI, §38)

It seems we ought to if "this" were really a genuine proper name. The conclusion of Wittgenstein's reductio is that "this" and "that" are not the only genuine proper names. "This" and "that" are not names at all. It is a misnomer to call such things proper names or any kind of name. "This" is no more a name than "I" is the name of a person or "here" of a place. But all three of these words "are connected with names. Names are explained by means of them" (PI, §410).

Suppose Russell admits that the singular terms "this" and "that" are not like ordinary names, even when they are used to designate sense-data. He might reply that this is beside the point, for he is objecting to what is ordinarily called a name. Wittgenstein recognizes that this is what he is doing. That is why he raises the question why a philosopher might want to object to what is ordinarily called a name (PI, §39). He thinks we can begin to understand why a philosopher might want to do this if we look at an example, such as, the grammatically proper name "Excalibur." This is a proper name in the ordinary sense for a fictional sword; it would not qualify as one of Russell's genuine or logically proper names. Speaking of the mythical sword Excalibur, Wittgenstein explains the sort of reasoning underlying Russell's theory of proper names.

The sword Excalibur consists of parts combined in a particular way. If they are combined differently [say all broken up] Excalibur does not exist. But it is clear that the sentence "Excalibur has a sharp blade" makes *sense* whether Excalibur is still whole or is broken up. But if "Excalibur" is the name of an object, this object no longer exists when Excalibur is broken in pieces; and as no object would then correspond to the name it would have no meaning. But then the sentence "Excalibur has a sharp blade" would contain a word that had no meaning, and hence the sentence would be nonsense. But it does make sense; so there must always be something corresponding to the words of which it consists. So the word "Excalibur" must disappear when the sense is analyzed and its place be taken by words which name simples. It will be reasonable to call these words the real names. (PI, §39)

I said that here we have the sort of reasoning underlying Russell's theory of proper names. But it also undergirds Wittgenstein's own earlier *Tractatus* view, which is similar in certain respects.[9] It explains why they both think in the first quarter of the century that there had to be names for simples, names that had guaranteed referents that were not themselves further analyzable. Russell wanted to say "this" and "that" were the only true proper names, provided they were used to refer to sense-data with which we were immediately acquainted. The later Wittgenstein points out, then, that Russell's erroneous theory of logically proper names is not the result of a discovery he has made, but is rather a consequence of his philosophical requirements, the idea of the philosopher that it must be like this, that it has to be like this.

In sections 38 and 45 of the *Investigations,* Wittgenstein gives two additional reasons why Russell may have chosen "the demonstrative 'this'" for the special role of being the only genuine proper name. First, demonstratives and names are similar in their surface grammar: as we have seen, they often occupy the same position in a sentence (PI, §38). Second and more important, Wittgenstein says the demonstrative "this" "can never be without a bearer" (PI, §45). This second claim is doubtful, at least if we take "bearer" to mean "referent" rather than "term for a referent." I may speak of "this wastepaper basket in the corner" even though there is none there; perhaps it is a hologram or I am hallucinating. Still, what is right about Wittgenstein's remark is that I will not use the word "this" without being prepared to say what the particular this is and without pointing to something that I presume to be there. So there is always the assumption that it has a bearer. Perhaps this is all that Wittgenstein means here. He continues: But these facts do "not make the word into a name. On the contrary: for a name is not used with, but only explained by means of, the gesture of pointing." Wittgenstein is here giving another reductio of the view that "this" could be a name.

Suppose Russell replies: Well, I'm saying it can be used as what I call a logically proper name, not that it is the sort of thing that we call a name; I am not an ordinary-language philosopher. Granted, but just saying it could be so used doesn't show it could be. Russell's interpretation of logically proper names commits him to the existence of a private language. He himself admits only you can understand what you are saying when you use a logically proper name, and even you cannot understand what you are saying for more than about a couple of minutes at most (R, pp. 197–98, 201). Wittgenstein repudiates the possibility of such a private language, since language must be characterized by agreement in definitions (PI, §242). It involves rule-following. And we cannot make sense of rule-following in the case of private language. In a so-called private language we have only private rules, which are not rules. We cannot (logically) fail to follow them; we cannot get it wrong. But if we cannot (logically) get it wrong or cannot violate a rule, we cannot get it right either or actually follow a rule, since these are correlative notions. So Wittgenstein would not agree with Russell that it is even possible, much less desirable, to construct his "perfect language." It would not be desirable because this "language" would be useless. It could not be used to communicate anything. How could you possibly use it? What for? We have seen you could not use it to say anything intelligible to anyone else. Nor could you yourself understand what you had just said a couple of minutes later; so you could not even use it for purely personal purposes, for example, to keep a diary. In short, you could not use it in any way. Again, Wittgenstein would have to conclude this is no language: the words in it have no use, hence they have no meaning.

Let us turn now to the other claim in 5—that grammatically proper names are really abbreviations for descriptions. Section 79 is the most relevant passage on this in the *Investigations*. As we have seen, Wittgenstein is there discussing what it may mean to say "Moses did not exist." He says you may explain what you mean when you say this by bringing in definite descriptions, for example, you might say "I mean the man who as a child was taken out of the Nile by Pharaoh's daughter." But is this what it means? The problem is you may substitute many different descriptions for "Moses" here, with the result that this could amount to several different assertions. "Moses" does not function like the word "bachelor" or "geometrical circle." A person who has one definite description in mind—"the recipient of

the Ten Commandments"—would be maintaining something quite different from someone else who had a different definite description in mind—
"the historical founder of Israel." The assertion would have different truth
conditions.

I take it that Wittgenstein is here criticizing Russell's theory of proper
names. For Russell's theory requires that our use of names be governed
by rigid rules, whereas in fact our use of proper names is not governed by
such rules. Nor need it be, according to the later Wittgenstein. He says
proper names do not need fixed meanings, any more than tables are restricted to having three legs, since if they have four they might wobble
occasionally. They might indeed wobble, but this does not mean we cannot
use them (PI, §79). (Compare Waismann on the open texture of language.[10])

If someone were to reply: Just put into your definite description what is
essential and leave out what is incidental, Wittgenstein has the ready counter: "Where are the bounds of the incidental?" (PI, §79). I think that he
is saying here that appeal to the notion of what is essential will not help
Russell with the problem of finding the right definite description for a
grammatically proper name, for that simply raises the question what is
essential to being N, where "N" is a grammatically proper name, and what
is not. Nor will it help Russell's theory to string together all things that are
uniquely true of the bearer of the name, for then no human being could
possibly understand a proper name—only God could—which is a reductio
of such an answer. In short, Russell does not really tell us how to analyze
statements of the form "N is F," where "N" is a grammatically proper name.
When he tells us to replace "N" with a definite description—something of
the form "the such and such"—this only tells us what our analysis should
look like, the form it should take, not what the analysis should be. In fact,
he never gives us an analysis of grammatically proper names, since he does
not tell us how to pick out the correct definite description from the many
competing ones, he does not give us the criteria we need for selecting the
right description to substitute for our grammatically proper names. Indeed,
he cannot satisfactorily deal with this problem.

Some people in the Russell tradition think Quine solves this problem.
He suggests a way in which we can get rid of grammatically proper names
like "Pegasus."[11] All we need to do is invent some new predicates, for
example, "is-Pegasus" or "pegasizes." "The noun 'Pegasus' itself could
then be treated as derivative, and identified after all with a description:
'the thing that is-Pegasus,' 'the thing that pegasizes.'" However, if we ask
what does such a new predicate mean, or when does it truly apply to
something, we quickly go in circles. For the answer is: when it is identical

with Pegasus. We can understand why Peter Geach concludes, "Quine's thesis that [proper] names are theoretically dispensable is pretty well empty."[12] So neither Russell nor Quine has shown us how we can get rid of grammatically proper names.

In the next chapter, we turn to another twentieth-century logician, Saul Kripke, who thinks Wittgenstein has uncovered a new skeptical paradox involving rule-following.

Chapter 12

Saul Wittgenstein's Skeptical Paradox

Reading the *Philosophical Investigations,* Saul Kripke was impressed by a skeptical argument he says is neither Wittgenstein's nor his own; it is "rather Wittgenstein's argument as it struck Kripke."[1] Taking a suggestion of William Callaghan's, I call the proponent of this argument and problem "Saul Wittgenstein" or "SW" to prevent his being confused with his less paradoxical "brother" LW. For the benefit of those who have neither heard Kripke's stimulating talk nor read his published version of it, I will outline SW's arguments and position. (It is possible that Kripke would not accept my account of them. If so, I ask that the arguments and views be considered on their merits, independently of Kripke, and for the light they may shed on Wittgenstein and skepticism.)[2]

SW's bizarre conclusion is that there is no such thing as following a rule; hence there is no language, no meaning, no nothing—not even tiddledy-winks—for language, science, games, as well as many other activities, require that you be able to follow rules. Kripke maintains that a central task of the *Investigations* is to offer a solution to this new paradox. He characterizes LW's proposed solution as a skeptical one, remarking that it is in this respect like Hume's "solution" to the problem of induction. His contention is that it is a skeptical solution because, like Hume, LW does not think the skeptic is wrong: in a way he accepts SW's doubts. Thus (Kripke continues) rather than offer a refutation of SW, LW presents an alternative picture by focusing on the questions: Under what conditions would you say, or when are you justified in saying (and when are you not justified in saying), that somebody is following a rule, or has learned, say, addition? and, What role do such things play in our lives? (pp. 86–87).

Kripke is right that LW does offer an alternative picture and focuses on different questions. Yet it is misleading, if not positively false, to say that LW offers a "skeptical solution" to SW's paradox, since he in no way accepts SW's doubts and in fact implies that the skeptic is wrong. Saying he offers a *skeptical solution* mistakenly suggests *that* solution is unsatisfactory, or at least that he is dissatisfied with it and that it is not as good as the "solution" he wanted to find. Kripke himself remarks that a skeptical solution fails to show "that on closer examination the skepticism proves to be unwarranted"; it concedes "that the skeptic's negative assertions are unanswerable" (p. 66). I would like to make three points in this regard. First, LW's view of philosophy commits him to a rejection of the skeptic's position—in his view, philosophical problems are merely pseudo problems and skepticism is a confused position. Second, LW's writings contain an implicit dissolution of the paradox. Finally, I try to point out what I take to be the main lesson to be derived from Kripke's discussion of Wittgenstein on rules and private language—namely, that there is nothing that is common and peculiar to instances of following or obeying a rule, whether the rule be that of addition or any other rule.

12.1 Saul Wittgenstein's Skeptical Arguments

SW begins his argument by pointing out that all the calculations that people have performed have been with numbers smaller than some number n. Simplifying, let us suppose that for me $n = 57$. Suppose now that I give 125 as the sum of 68 plus 57, believing (a) that 125 is the sum of these numbers and (b) that my calculation accords with my previous intentions as to the use of the plus sign or with what I previously meant by " $+$."

SW grants that (a) is true, for he does not begin by questioning mathematics (p. 13). But, he objects, either I *am* mistaken about (b) or I *may be* or *could be* mistaken about (b). Skeptic number one says: in accord with my previous intention, I "should have said '5'" (p. 15). He charges that I had a bizarre experience—under the influence of LSD, in a frenzy, or something—that resulted in a sudden change in my usage or in my misinterpreting my previous ideas. By " $+$ " I had not previously meant addition; "I always *meant* quus" (p. 9), or " $\oplus$," where $x \oplus y =_{df} x$ plus y if x and y are less than 57, and otherwise equal 5. He might equally well have said that I meant any of an infinite number of other functions, either mathematical or nonmathematical. For example, I might have meant the "many" function, where x many $y =_{df} x$ plus y if x and y are less than 57, and otherwise equal many; or I meant the "cross" function, where x cross $y =_{df} x$ plus y if x and y are less than 57, and otherwise equal the sign of the cross. Perhaps realizing that, logically speaking, there is no end to the number of functions I might have meant, the more moderate skeptic I designate skeptic number two more cautiously inserts "maybe," or some synonymous expression, into the extreme claims and arguments of skeptic one. That is, "perhaps in the past I used 'plus' and ' $+$ ' to denote [the quus] function" (p. 8; see also pp. 13, 15).

These initial formulations of SW's problem make it sound like a purely epistemological problem: How can I know—can I ever *know* (pp. 12, 21), *establish* (p. 21), or *justify* (pp. 13, 23)—what rule I am following or what I mean by a word? Yet SW's problem is not "merely an epistemological problem" (p. 38). He wants also to raise a doubt about the related metaphysical issue—whether there is a fact about me meaning addition by "plus," and if so, what the nature of that fact is. Presumably it is such a fact about me, and only such a fact—whatever it is that constitutes my meaning addition by the plus sign—that will settle the epistemological question of what I meant by " + ." SW uncritically assumes that an answer to the metaphysical query necessarily answers the epistemological one.[3]

12.2 Why LW Cannot Accept SW's Skeptical Position

We have seen from Chapter 1 that ever since the *Tractatus,* Wittgenstein has held that philosophical problems result from misunderstanding our language. (See TLP, 4.003, 4.0031, 6.5, 6.51, and 6.53.) Philosophical problems and paradoxes have "the form: 'I don't know my way about'" (PI, §123). They are always symptomatic of some misunderstanding of the language, never genuine problems. The "solution," or rather dissolution, of such pseudo problems is achieved by discovering how and why the logic of our language has been misunderstood. This is done by engaging in a linguistic investigation directed at uncovering the mistake and its causes, replacing wild conjectures and explanations "by quiet weighing of linguistic facts" (Z, §447). The philosopher reminds us of these facts (PI, §127). For the problems in philosophy are solved "by looking into the workings of our language, and that in such a way as to make us recognize those workings. . . . The problems are solved, not by giving new information, but by arranging what we have always known" (PI, §109). Wittgenstein's stated aim is to eliminate these philosophical muddles by removing the misunderstanding (PI, §109), or, more colorfully, "To show the fly the way out of the fly-bottle" (PI, §309). He wants to teach us to recognize such disguised nonsense for what it is—patent nonsense—for example, to show us that "skepticism is *not* irrefutable, but obviously nonsensical, when it tries to raise doubts where no questions can be asked" (TLP, 6.51). Although *complete* clarity is Wittgenstein's professed aim, this is only in the sense that he wants the philosophical problems to disappear completely (PI, §133). It is evident that LW's view of philosophy commits him to a rejection of SW's skeptical paradoxes and of his skeptical doubt.

12.3 The Dissolution of SW's Paradox

Before dealing directly with SW's paradox, it may be instructive to see how LW attacks a closely related paradox in PI, §201. "This was our paradox," he writes: "no course of action could be determined by a rule [call this C], because [P] every course of action can be made out to accord with the rule." Kripke quotes this sentence (p. 7), but fails to follow it up with the next sentence in which LW resolves the paradox. Wittgenstein's resolution: "The answer was: if everything can be made out to accord with the rule [P], then it can also be made out to conflict with it. And so there would be neither accord nor conflict here."

How are we to understand Wittgenstein's cryptic reply? I take him to be giving a reductio of the false premise, P, that every action can be made out to accord with any rule. This premise was used to support the paradoxical conclusion, C, that no action can be determined by a rule. We are to suppose that P is true only to show that it cannot be. Supposing P, we get the surprising and absurd result that smoking and not smoking, for example, can both be made out to accord with the rule "no smoking." But then both smoking and not smoking must also conflict with the rule, since, by definition of "accord" and "conflict," what is in accord is not in conflict, and vice versa. Generalizing, we arrive at the absurd conclusion that whatever we do—whether it be A or not-A—it will be both in accord and in conflict with some rule, which makes a hash of the distinction. P, then, cannot be true because it implicitly denies that there is a distinction between actions that are in accord and those that are in conflict with a rule. Yet it is a fact that if a certain action, A, is in accord (or in conflict) with a rule, then there is another type of action, not-A, that is not in accord (or in conflict) with that rule. The paradox in PI, §201 depends on overlooking this grammatical fact about rules.

But LW also takes issue (PI, §§198, 201) with a particular conception of what it is to act according to a rule. In this conception, every action according to a rule is an interpretation of it by some other rule; so there cannot be a way of grasping a rule that is not an interpretation of it. This leads to an infinite regress. If to act according to a rule you must always interpret it by some other rule, then the same goes for acting according to that second rule; and so on without end. It will then be impossible to act according to a rule, contradicting the grammatical fact mentioned above— that if a certain action, A, is in accord (or in conflict) with a rule, then there is another type of action, not-A, that is not in accord (or in conflict) with that rule. LW concludes section 201 by pointing out that what we call "obeying a rule" and "going against it" are ways of grasping or understanding a rule that are not interpretations of it. Obeying a rule is a custom (use, institution) (PI, §199). He remarks earlier (PI, §85) that a rule is like a signpost. It may sometimes leave room for doubt about the way I have to go, and thus require an interpretation; but it does not have to raise doubts and thus always require an interpretation. And it is in order if, under normal circumstances, it does not leave room for doubt about the way I have to go (PI, §87). Wittgenstein is not saying that there is a time when rules cannot (logically) be further interpreted. But rather that often their further interpretability does not even occur to us. In such cases we simply act either in accord or not in accord with a rule without interpreting it and, a fortiori, without interpreting it by reference to some other rule. (See, for example, his *Philosophical Grammar*, sec. 99, p. 147.)

In section 220, LW also rejects C, or the claim that no rule can determine an action. He writes that a certain action may be logically determined by a rule, or in some sense necessitated, whether or not it is causally determined. Thus if asked to write down the sum of 68 plus 57, those who have mastered the use of the plus sign will recognize—if they are reasonably good adders, attentive, and so on—that there is a sense in which they must (logically) write down "125" as the answer. But that does not mean that someone who can add is causally determined to write down this number. A person who has mastered the use of the plus sign may refuse to add these numbers, or, being a bad or careless adder, give the wrong sum. Incidentally, it was failure to recognize this distinction that led Thor in *What's New, B.C.?* to pass the ball after going beyond the line of scrimmage in an American football game. He had been told you cannot do this. Misunderstanding, Thor said he wanted to see if he could—whether it was possible for him to do it. I turn next to the criticism of SW's skeptical argument.

12.3.1 A Refutation of Skeptic Number One

This skeptic supplies no reason for supposing that I had a bizarre experience, took an intoxicant drug, or worked myself into a frenzy, resulting in my misinterpreting my previous ideas and in a sudden change in my usage. He does not claim to have seen me taking acid, acting funny, frothing at the mouth, blacking out, and so on. There is only the suggested argument that all these things could have happened. As he says, "the skeptic's hypothesis is not logically impossible. . . . [I]t does not seem to be a priori impossible" (p. 9). But it is not a good argument to say "So-and-so happened because it is not a priori impossible or it is logically possible that it did." That is why the following dialogue is ridiculous. "Why should I believe what you said?" Answer: "Because there is no contradiction in it." If that were accepted as a good reason to believe something, you would have an equally good reason to believe its negation, assuming the original proposition is not a logical truth; so such so-called reasons cancel each other out. Moreover, if we had to doubt everything that is not logically true, we would have to doubt all empirical propositions—not just the proposition (b) that my calculations accord with my previous intentions as to the use of the plus sign or with what I previously meant by " + ." We would therefore have to doubt the proposition that we understand anything, which in turn would mean that we would have to doubt that we can entertain any doubt, which is absurd and ultimately undermines the doubt we are trying to profess (OC, §§111, 450). In short, we neither give a reason for believing a proposition by establishing that there is no contradiction in it nor for doubting one by showing that it is not logically true. Finally, it is worth noticing how inconsistently unskeptical skeptic number one is about my previous intentions. If he is really persuaded by the suggested argument, he should not talk so knowingly about my previous intentions. A skeptic who was firmly convinced that we cannot know what we previously meant by a sign would not claim to know what someone meant by it. I charge that skeptic number one's position both lacks support and is incoherent.

Surprisingly, SW seems to agree. For he goes on to remark: "Of course this bizarre hypothesis, and the references to LSD, or to an insane frenzy, are in a sense merely a dramatic device" (p. 10). His point is that the rule exhibited by my previous calculations "could just as well have been the rule for quaddition (the quus function) as for addition. The idea that in fact quaddition *is* what I meant, that in a sudden frenzy I have changed my previous usage, dramatizes the problem" (p. 11). So the skeptic, in his more cautious mood, does not really want to say I meant quus rather than plus any more than he wants to say I meant plus rather than quus: he does not know what fact would establish any claim of this kind (p. 13). Let us therefore dismiss skeptic one as not the real SW. His role was merely to introduce some drama into the discussion.

12.3.2 A Refutation of Skeptic Number Two

By one interpretation, this skeptic's position is trivially true. He says I might or could have been mistaken about (b), that my usage might have changed suddenly. This is true; these are logical possibilities. But if he wishes to contend that this fact gives me a reason to doubt my previous intentions, what I previously meant by " + ," and that it is therefore an open question what I meant by it, then his position merely repeats the bad arguments that were criticized in the previous section. Apparently, then, skeptic number two can be dismissed along with skeptic number one. Neither has yet given an acceptable reason in support of doubting our past intentions. But as LW stresses, doubts and suspicions require grounds (OC, §§4, 458, 323). Until SW provides us with a good reason to doubt what we meant by "plus," we have no skeptical problem that needs to be solved.

It may be objected that this reply to the skeptic takes the easy way. What I ought to do is to give reasons showing that my calculation accords with my previous intentions as to the use of the plus sign or with what I previously meant by " + ." If my past calculations are equally compatible with both hypotheses, is it not arbitrary to say I meant plus rather than quus? Moreover, I must make my case in a non-question-begging way. Thus I cannot just assume that I remember, in the success sense of the word "remember," that I meant to add and not to quus. Skeptic number two can be interpreted as implying that this challenge cannot be met, even when no limitation is put on the kinds of evidence that can be cited. To see whether this is so, let us first ask what the criteria are for the way a sign is meant.

LW answers: "It is, for example, the kind of way we always use it, the way we are taught to use it" (PI, §190). Again, in reply to the question, "How are we to judge whether someone meant such and such?" he says, "The fact that he has, for example, mastered a particular technique in arithmetic and algebra, and that he taught someone else the expansion of a series in the usual way, is such a criterion" (PI, §692). Well, judged by the usual standards, I long ago mastered the use of the plus sign, and I have even taught someone else how to use it in the usual way. Indeed, I learned how to add in the second grade, and to follow the rule of addition is simply to do what I was taught to do then when given addition problems. My teachers, parents, classmates, and I all agree on this. But I did not learn how to quus until 1976—many years later—when I heard Kripke's talk. Moreover, my learning how to quus depended on my already knowing how to add, since Kripke explained, and even defined, quusing by comparison to the notion of adding.

It might be thought that this point is undermined by the fact that Kripke could have defined plusing by reference to quusing and some other function, say, glusing, where x glus $y =_{df} x$ plus y if x and y are greater than 57, and otherwise equal 5. Since we know from Kripke that x quus $y =_{df} x$ plus y

if x and y are less than 57, and otherwise equal 5, Kripke could now define plusing by reference to quusing and glusing as follows: x plus y $=_{df} x$ quus y if x and y are less than 57 and x glus y if x and y are greater than or equal to 57. What we should notice, however, is that the function glusing was itself explained to us here by reference to plusing; so the whole discussion still presupposes that we begin with an understanding of what it is to plus.

There may be a temptation to object that I have made use of various success words when marshalling my evidence for saying I learned how to add. I said, for instance, that I "mastered" the use of the plus sign, was "taught" and "learned" how to add in the second grade. Accordingly, it may seem that I am violating the stricture mentioned above against assuming the point at issue against SW. But this is not so. Although I did use these words in their success sense, the evidence cited in no way implies (b), for I may not have meant addition by " + " yesterday, a year, or even ten years ago, even though I did mean that in elementary school and once mastered the use of the plus sign.

But then is my evidence not inconclusive and weak as well, and my conclusion arbitrary? No, to both questions. First, the word "arbitrary" does not signify "inconclusive," in the sense of not being logically demonstrable. To say that something is arbitrary is to say that it arises from will or caprice, or that it is random and without reason—and none of this applies to the case under consideration. Second, my evidence is not weak, since it includes not only what I was and was not taught and what I learned, but also the way those fluent in the language would describe my actions. A natural description would be to say that I was adding when I did those past calculations, not that I was quusing, despite the fact that either rule would have given the same results. And if the dramatic number-one skeptic comes back to browbeat me into saying I was actually quusing, we should note how misleading his description of my act is, since it is clear that I did not quus intentionally and I was at no time aware that that was what I was doing.

Finally, I shall refute the skeptic's contention that maybe, all along, I was nevertheless—albeit unconsciously—following the rule of quusing. Two tests together suffice to show that I was not. First, if I was quusing, then I previously took " + " to mean "$\oplus$." Accordingly, I should have answered yes to the question whether $x + y + z$ could ever equal $x + y$, where x, y, and z are all positive integers; for example, $100 + 100 + 1 = 100 + 100$. But if I denied, as I undoubtedly would, that $x + y + z$ could ever equal $x + y$, if x, y, and z were all integers greater than 0, surely this would be strong evidence for saying that I did not previously mean "$\oplus$" by "$+$." Note that while this argument rules out that I was quusing and some other things, it does not rule out an infinite number of other possibilities.

Consider now the second test. Suppose, again, that I had been following the rule of quusing. Then after I heard Kripke's lucid formulation of the rule, would I not have recognized that this was the rule I was following all along? Yet I say I did not recognize this. Indeed, when informed of this rule of quusing, I sincerely denied that I was ever trying—consciously or unconsciously—to make my conduct conform to it. This fact, together with the results of the other test, normally suffice to eliminate quusing as the rule I was following when I performed my past calculations. By a similar line of argument we can eliminate, one by one, the other possible hypotheses imaginative logicians like SW might come up with, even though, taken individually or together, passing the two tests fails logically to imply that I was adding. I conclude that it is certain, that is, beyond doubt, that I meant addition by the plus sign when I carried out those past calculations.

This rebuttal, of course, hinges on there being a clear distinction between acting in accord with, and acting in obedience to, or following, a rule. (We already find this distinction in LW's *Philosophical Grammar*, §61, p. 101.) At least two things seem to differentiate these from one another. First, when you follow a rule, the rule guides your behavior; thus it plays a causal role in bringing about what you do. ("Reasons as causes.") Such is not the case when you merely act in accordance with a rule. To illustrate: some may wish to say that Alexei Karenin *acted in accordance with* the dictates of his religion when he decided not to cast off Anna Karenina, who had committed adultery; yet these people would be making a mistake if they added that he also *followed* the dictates of his religion in adopting this course of action. For he decided on it first as the best way of making Anna suffer for having destroyed his honor. Only afterwards did it occur to him that this course of action was also in accord with his religion. Excluding the possibility of backward causation, then, such considerations obviously could not have played any causal role in producing his decision.

Second, you either know right off what rule you are following or you come to know it simply by being presented with a reasonably clear statement of the rule. Thus if I sincerely denied that I had been trying to make my past behavior conform to a rule clearly presented to me, this would normally suffice to establish that I had not been following that rule. But this response would not even be relevant to the question whether my previous behavior was in accordance with the rule.

12.4 Nothing Both Common and Peculiar to Following a Rule

SW, if I understand him correctly, would object that the answer given still does not constitute a deductive, a priori argument that when I give 125 as the sum of 68 + 57, my calculation accords with what I previously meant by " + ." My sincerely claiming that I remember I meant to add does not prove that I did. Again, if it is a fact that I said to myself yesterday that I then intended to add the smaller numbers, I may yet never have had such an intention, for I may in the past have meant by "adding" what I now mean by "quusing." As LW himself remarks, even thinking you are obeying a rule does not imply that you are (PI, §202). Indeed, citing all my thoughts, experiences, calculations, behavior, along with the beliefs and experiences of others, does not logically imply that I am not mistaken about my past intentions and past usage, since the totality of such evidence is logically compatible with the hypothesis that by " + " I previously meant the quus function.

This last point is correct, and in section 185 LW suggests he agrees. But it is a mistake to suppose that, because LW mentions no fact, or nontrivial truth conditions, that could prove whether a person meant "quus," "plus," "cross," "many," "blue," or something else by the plus sign, he must somehow accept SW's doubts and concede to him that there is no fact that I meant "plus." That would be like saying there is no fact that someone has a headache if we cannot, as seems to be the case, give nontrivial truth conditions for someone's having a headache. As McGinn says, "irreducibility is not obviously or uncontroversially a good reason for pressing a claim of non-factuality."[4] Moreover, a matter that is not beyond all *possible* or *imaginable* doubt need not be doubted and indeed may be beyond doubt (PI, §§213, 84). It may even be known, for as Hamlyn rightly observes, "what we claim to know must be true and based on the best of reasons. But by the best of reasons is not meant proof."[5]

Moreover, since it is true that I did mean "plus," there is, to use Kripke's word, the *echt* fact that I did, and no reason to think that LW would deny such a truism. "It is true that *p*" and "It is a fact that *p*" are just alternative ways of saying the same thing, as Kripke himself seems to acknowledge (p. 86). So even if LW agrees "with the skeptics that there is no 'superlative fact' (PI, §192) about my mind that constitutes my meaning addition by 'plus' and determines in advance what I should do to accord with this meaning" (p. 65), this in no way implies that LW must hold that there is no fact about my mind—or better, about me—that constitutes my meaning addition by "plus." The qualifier "superlative" should not be ignored. Unfortunately, Kripke seems to suppose that it does imply that there is no fact about anyone's meaning some definite function by a certain sign (p. 65; see also pp. 69, 71). It is significant, however, that he can nowhere quote any actual denial by LW that there are such facts. This is because no such quotations are to be found in Wittgenstein's writing. It would also be inconsistent for LW to deny this, for the following reasons that Kripke himself mentions:

> In denying that there is any such fact, might we not be expressing a philosophical thesis that doubts or denies something everyone admits? [The denial would thus contradict PI, §599, quoted in Section 1.2. Further:] We do not wish to deny the propriety of an ordinary use of the phrase 'the fact that Jones meant addition by such-and-such a symbol,' and indeed such expressions do have perfectly ordinary uses. (p. 69)

In summary, a crucial difference between LW and SW is this: while LW holds that there must be a way of determining whether you are obeying a particular rule (PI, §202), SW requires that this way constitute a logical proof. He wants some sort of reductive account of what it is to mean something by a sign or word. He is not content that we have criteria for meaning addition by " + " or for following a rule. That there are tests, such as those mentioned, to differentiate between the plus and the quus hypotheses does not satisfy him. It still leaves him with his initial doubt. Like the foundationalist, SW wants to obtain the unobtainable. Hence he demands nontrivial truth conditions for following a rule, such that, if they are satisfied, the rule must (logically) be followed, and if not, the rule must (logically) not be followed. Similarly, he wishes to be told what is common and peculiar to meaning addition by the plus sign. In effect, SW either wants these things to be defined the way we define what it is to be a circle or at least to be given interesting truth conditions for them, as we do for combustion. (Obviously, we can provide trivial truth conditions, such as Jones means addition by " + " if and only if Jones means addition by " + .")

The implied answer of LW is, first, that this cannot be done (see PI, §§138–242). (His remark that following a rule is a practice [PI, §202] is not meant as a definition.) We cannot give that sort of definition of meaning addition by the plus sign or of what it is to follow a rule, or even give the truth conditions for somebody's doing such things, any more than we can define, or give truth conditions for, a game, edibility, selfishness, and countless other things. Indeed, the point holds generally for all family-resemblance predicates. In all of these cases there is also an infinite possibility of defeasibility.

Kripke, in agreement with LW (see Chapter 4), points out, for example, that we cannot give a dispositional analysis of what it is to follow the rule of addition, arguing that such an analysis is subject to the fatal objections both that it overlooks the fact that adders make mistakes and that our dispositions are themselves finite. He also interprets LW—again I think correctly—as denying that meaning addition by "+" is nothing but an irreducible mental event, experience, sensation, or feeling (see PI, §§557, 592, 675–76, 678). Thus in LW's view, meaning addition by "+" cannot be identified with either a dispositional or an experiential fact. So we cannot define, or even specify the necessary and sufficient conditions of, what it is to mean addition by reference to a series of counterfactuals or subjunctive conditionals, or by some sort of experiential statement.

The second part of LW's answer is that there is no need to provide such analyses, or truth conditions, in order to refute the skeptic's doubt. For we can identify games, edible food, selfish people, and instances of someone's following a rule, or meaning addition by the plus sign without having to overcome insurmountable difficulties. As LW observes, in some fields—for example, mathematics—we do not even have disputes "over the question whether a rule has been obeyed or not" (PI, §240).

A skeptic may object at this point that LW's account of "following a rule" deprives the expression of a definite sense. If having a definite, or determinate, sense means having statable nontrivial truth conditions that are jointly necessary and sufficient, then the phrase of course only will have an indefinite sense. But then so will many—indeed the vast majority of—declarative sentences in every natural language. So it would be well for philosophers to give up their demand that linguistic expressions have determinacy of sense, in the traditional sense explained. Interestingly enough, this is just what Kripke himself, like LW, seems to do in his own philosophical writings. Kripke, for example, doubts whether we can ever give necessary and sufficient conditions for reference, holding that such a philosophical analysis of reference is very likely to fail.[6] He quite sensibly does not conclude that this must leave reference "completely mysterious," but it seems that his "relative" SW—unlike LW and Kripke—cannot bring himself to give up this demand. SW insists from the start, and repeats the demand consistently, that a nonskeptical answer to the skeptic "must give an account of what fact it is (about my mental state) that *constitutes* my meaning plus, not quus" (p. 11, my emphasis; see also pp. 21, 22, 39, 54, where he again uses the word "constitutes"). This is really to demand that only a truth-conditions account of what it is to mean something by a word or to follow a rule will be an adequate account of it. When SW considers the response that meaning addition by "plus" is a state of a unique kind of its own, not reducible to anything else, he counters that this "leaves the nature of this postulated primitive state—the primitive state of 'meaning addition by "plus"'—completely mysterious" (p. 51).

Should we conclude that the sense of "following a rule" or "meaning something by a sign" is mysterious, or at least vague or unclear? And how are we to explain the sense of such expressions? LW replies that "we are dazzled by the ideal" (PI, §100). It does not follow that there is anything unclear in these expressions. We explain what it is to follow a rule, or to mean something by a sign, the way we do—by giving examples. Nor should we give in to the temptation to object that we should be able to do better than that—in particular, that we should be able to say more than that— for that presumes that the explanations of sense that we give are somehow not good enough. The great philosophical difficulty here, as elsewhere in philosophy, according to LW, "is to say no more than we know" (BB, p. 45). The discontent with our explanations rests on their not conforming to pre-conceived Humean notions of clarity and of explanation, in which complex ideas must ultimately be defined in terms of simple ones. This ideal continues to dazzle philosophers. We see, then, how profoundly mistaken it is to liken LW's reply to the skeptic to Hume's and to speak of his offering a "skeptical solution." As LW nicely sums it up: "The more narrowly we examine actual language, the sharper becomes the conflict between it and our requirement. (For the crystalline purity of logic was, of course, not a *result of investigations*: it was a requirement)" (PI, §107). It is also a requirement of our philosophical skeptic, SW, who seems to bear little family resemblance to LW.

Appendix, Notes, and Index

Appendix

Russell's Theory of Descriptions

Many respected philosophers agree in calling Russell's theory of descriptions his greatest philosophical discovery and a paradigm of philosophical analysis. He first expounded these ingenious ideas in his "On Denoting" (R, pp. 39–56), universally recognized as a masterpiece. Russell himself describes this as his "finest philosophical essay" (R, p. 39). Later explications of the theory by Russell can be found in *Principia Mathematica* (1910–13), *The Philosophy of Logical Atomism* (1918) (Lecture 5, "Descriptions and Incomplete Symbols"), and his *Introduction to Mathematical Philosophy* (1919) (Chapter 16, "Descriptions"). The last two versions are especially lucid, though they are less rich in content than "On Denoting."

There seem to be at least three considerations motivating Russell to develop his theory of descriptions. First, by 1905 he finds the theories of his predecessors Frege and Meinong no longer satisfactory; one of his aims is to refute them.[1] A second purpose of Russell's is to explain what sentences of a certain form mean—to develop a semantic system—by giving their truth conditions. Third and finally, he wants to do this in such a way that the puzzles he is concerned with will be resolved but without giving rise to any further puzzles or difficulties. It may be doubted whether he has succeeded in accomplishing either of these tasks—either adequately explaining what these sentences mean or developing a puzzle-free theory. He has succeeded in solving some of the puzzles, but unfortunately his theory gives rise to additional puzzles, as we shall see. Again, this does not detract from the achievement; for, as far as I know, no one has yet succeeded in giving an account of definite descriptions—phrases of the form "the such and such"—that is not subject to serious objections.

I shall discuss five puzzles or paradoxes Russell deals with, even though he only explicitly mentions three (R, p. 47).

Russell's Puzzles in "On Denoting"

The Paradox of Meaning

Consider a sentence that strikes us as perfectly meaningful, "The present king of France is bald." This sentence, however, has no referent—it "has certainly no denotation"—much less a unique one, since the definite description, "The present king of France" in 1989 does not refer to any existent individual. But then the sentence says nothing *about* anything. So it must be meaningless; it "ought to be nonsense." Russell counters that "it is not nonsense, since it is plainly false" (R, p. 46), and whatever is true or false must be meaningful. Even if you do not agree with Russell that the statement "is plainly false," you are still likely to agree with him that it is meaningful. Yet how can it be if it is meaningless, since it is not about something?

The Paradox of Existence

Consider positive and negative existential statements, statements that explicitly affirm the existence or nonexistence of something. There are puzzles connected with both kinds of statements. Take first negative existential statements, that is, those of the form "*a* does not exist," where *a* is a definite description—for example, "The golden mountain does not exist." What is it that does not exist? Answer: "The golden mountain," which seems to imply that it does exist or at least that it has some kind of reality. It appears that these statements are self-contradictory, hence false, since if *a* is meaningful, it must denote something—its denotation—which is its meaning. If so, we cannot meaningfully say that something does not exist without our statement being false. For we must be able to talk about *a* to say that it does not exist, in which case it will always be false to say that *a* does not exist. In short, all negative existence statements seem to be self-contradictory, hence false and factually empty. But we know that such statements sometimes convey genuine information about the way things are in the world. So we seem to face another paradox.

Let us consider now positive existence statements—something of the form "*a* exists." For reasons already given, it seems such statements must be tautologies or analytically true. But then they must be factually empty. It follows that no positive existence statement can convey any factual knowledge. Again we know, however, that sometimes they do, that they are not always analytically true or redundant.

Paradoxes Involving the Laws of Thought

There are three so-called laws of thought—the laws of contradiction, identity, and excluded middle—and they go back to the time of Aristotle. The law of contradiction, according to Aristotle, is the law that "the same attribute cannot at the same time belong and not belong to the same subject and in the same respect" (*Metaphysics* 1005 b19–20). Or, applying it to propositions: "*p* cannot be both true and false, at the same time and in the same respect," where *p* is any proposition. That is, not both *p* and not-*p*. The law of identity affirms that everything is identical with itself; that is, *a* = *a*, for any *a*. Finally, the law of excluded middle asserts that either a predicate is true of something—in which case we have something of the form *a* is F; or it does not—in which case, *a* is not F. We could call this the "either-it-is-or-it-isn't" principle. It also applies to propositions. That is, it says either *p* or not-*p*; there is no third alternative.

Now it seems that certain statements violate the law of excluded middle, or the law that says either "*a* is F" or "*a* is not F" must be true. The law seems to imply, Russell notes, that "either 'the present King of France is bald' or 'the present King of France is not bald' must be true" (R, p. 48). But if we look, first, at all the things that are bald, and then at all the things that are not bald, he says we will not find the present king of France among either group. It seems that the statement that he is bald is false and so is the statement that he is not bald. But then the so-called law of excluded middle is not a general truth of logic, contradicting what we said above. Russell's examples also seem to violate the law of contradiction. Consider, for example, "The present king of France is bald" and "The present king of France is not bald." These statements appear to contradict each other, in which case one must be true if the other is false. Yet Russell has already given us reason to think they are both false.

The Paradox of Identity

We all know that statements of identity—that is, statements of the form *a* = *b*, where "*a*" and "*b*" are different proper names or definite descriptions linked together by the "is" of identity—can be both true and informative. It is thus possible to convey information with the sentences "Scott was Sir Walter," "The morning star is the evening star," or "Marilyn Monroe was the woman who married Jim Dougherty, Joe DiMaggio, and Arthur Miller." Yet oddly enough, it seems that statements of this form, when true, can never be informative, since then they must be tautologies. As Russell says, "If '*c*' is a name, the proposition 'Scott is *c*' is either false or tautologous" (R, p. 245). It will be false if the two names name different things. But we know it is true; so we are driven to the conclusion that it is a tautology, even though we know it is not.

The Paradox Involving Oblique or Indirect Contexts

Did the First Gentleman of Europe (George IV) wonder about the law of identity? It seems to follow from the paradox of identity that the first gentleman of Europe must have wondered about the law of identity. Yet we know he did not. This paradox is closely related to the previous one. However, even without the paradox of identity, we seem to be able to prove that George IV must have wondered about the law of identity. Consequently, the present problem is independent and distinct from the previous one. The argument for saying this goes as follows. We know that (1) George IV wondered (wished to know) whether Scott was the author of *Waverley*. This is a historical fact. It is also a historical fact that (2) Scott was (or is) the author of *Waverley*. But (3) "If *a* is identical with *b*, whatever is true of the one is true of the other, and either may be substituted for the other in any proposition" (R, p. 47). So we conclude: (4) George IV wished to know whether Scott was Scott, even though we know that the First Gentleman of Europe never would have wondered about this, since he never had any interest in the law of identity.

Russell wants to resolve these puzzles. Like Wittgenstein, he also wants to show the fly the way out of the fly-bottle, although he wants philosophy to do other much more ambitious things as well (see Section 1.1). He does so by providing an analysis or interpretation of statements of the form "The such and such is so-and-so." His theory purports to tell us what they assert and imply (R, p. 44) and to give necessary and sufficient truth conditions for them. In his analysis of sentences involving definite descriptions the trouble-making phrase "the such and such" disappears. Russell assumes that the better a philosophical theory is, the more puzzles it will dissolve. He thinks he has successfully confronted all the above puzzles. It remains to be seen whether he has, and if so, how, and whether his theory has given rise to any new puzzles.

How Russell Dissolves His Puzzles

The Paradox of Meaning

The problem about meaning arose because the sentence we considered ("The present king of France is bald") lacked a unique referent; so it seemed to say nothing about anything, tempting us to conclude that it could not be meaningful, even though it obviously is. Russell's response to the

merely "substitution instances of the analytic equation $x = x$.[2]
Russell's analysis of statements of identity and his response to the
of identity has unacceptable consequences. Specifically, it results
breakdown in the rule of logic known as "universal instantiation
cation," (b) the rejection of the law of identity, or (c) the denial
s like (1) and (2) are substitution instances of the law of identity,
ugh we got (1) and (2) by substituting the exact same definite
n for both of the variables surrounding the equals sign. It seems
is zeal to avoid tautologies Russell goes too far—he transforms
true statements like (1) and (2) into statements that might not be
does this because he erroneously supposes that statements of
like (1) and (2) always assert or entail the unique existence of
ng.

may be doubted whether Russell has succeeded in giving us either
conditions or the meaning of the sentences he is analyzing. As
seen, for him, statements of the form "the such and such is so-
are elaborate, compound existential statements. They are only true
is a unique such and such, otherwise they are false. In fact, while
often correct, there are exceptions. For example, if we substitute
us" for "so-and-so" and "the Great Pumpkin" for "the such and
he resulting statement is true, but *only because* there isn't a such
h—namely, no Great Pumpkin—contradicting Russell's theory. It
lly implied that whatever is fictitious does not exist. Similarly, "The
Pumpkin is worshiped" may be true whether there is or is not a
Pumpkin—either way—once more constituting a counterexample to
's theory. This is because what is worshiped doesn't (logically) have
or not exist.[3] So Russell has neither provided us with the truth nor
sity conditions for statements of this form.
llows that it is doubtful whether he has succeeded in explaining what
saying or talking about when we make statements containing definite
tions, especially since he tries to explain their meaning in terms of
ruth conditions. Wittgenstein gives us additional reasons to doubt
ussell's theory captures the meaning of these statements. He does
directly by discussing a closely similar analysis of "My broom is in
rner." ("My only son" is an example of a denoting phrase for Russell
47].) Parodying Russell, Wittgenstein points out that you might say
broom is in the corner" is really a statement about the broomstick
e brush, since you could replace it by a statement giving the position
stick and the position of the brush. Moreover, you might argue that
econd statement is a further analyzed form of the first one, on the
ds that "if the broom is there, that surely means that the stick and

difficulty is to give us the truth and falsity conditions for such sentences.
Once we see what these are, we can no longer deny that the sentence is
meaningful, for any sentence that can be true (or false) must be meaningful.
According to Russell's theory of descriptions, the statement "The present
king of France is bald" is true if and only if three conditions obtain, otherwise it is false: (1) there is a present king of France, (2) there is not more
than one king of France, and (3) that individual is bald. Well, there isn't
a king of France now, nor was there one in Russell's time. Hence, Russell
would conclude the statement is false and therefore meaningful. First problem dissolved.

The Paradox of Existence

Here our problem concerns both positive and negative existential statements, that is, those that explicitly affirm the existence or nonexistence of
something. Let us consider first the positive ones—those of the form "*a*
exists," where "*a*" is a name or a definite description. It seems these statements must all be true if meaningful, for if they are meaningful, they must
be about something and have a unique referent. Yet we know that such
statements are sometimes false in spite of being meaningful. "The Great
Pumpkin exists," "The golden mountain exists" would be two examples.
Russell's theory shows us how this can be by giving us a semantical analysis
of the statements. The first asserts that (1) there is a Great Pumpkin and
(2) there is not more than one Great Pumpkin. Since (1) is false, the
statement is false (as well as meaningful). This dissolves the first half of
our paradox.

Let us turn now to the other half of the paradox, negative existential
statements. It seems these statements must all be meaningless or else false,
for if *a* does not exist, how can we talk about it?—there is no such thing
to talk about—so what we are saying must be meaningless and about nothing. Or, if it's meaningful, then it must be false, since there is such a thing
to talk about. But, again, we are convinced that some negative existential
statements are true as well as meaningful. For example, it is both true and
meaningful that the Great Pumpkin does not exist. Russell interprets negative existential statements to be simple negations of the positive ones.
Hence "The Great Pumpkin does not exist" would be interpreted as asserting that it is not the case that (1) there is a Great Pumpkin and (2) there
is not more than one Great Pumpkin. Since what it negates is false (see

the previous paragraph), what it asserts is true. This shows that negative existential statements can be both true and meaningful, which dissolves the second half of our paradox.

Paradoxes Involving the Laws of Thought

Here the puzzle is to explain how statements of the form "*a* is F" and "*a* is not F" can have opposite truth values if "*a*" fails to have a unique referent. As we have seen, there are reasons to think "The present king of France is bald" and "The present king of France is not bald" are both false. But this seems to violate the law of excluded middle as well as the law of contradiction. Shouldn't contradictory statements have opposite truth values? Yes, Russell replies—if they are truly contradictory. But "The present king of France is not bald" is ambiguous. It may or may not contradict "The present king of France is bald"; it all depends how it is interpreted. This can be brought out if we bear in mind that neither of these statements is truly of the subject-predicate form. Both are really disguised compound existential statements. Consider the positive one, "The present king of France is bald." It asserts that (1) there is a present king of France, (2) there is not more than one present king of France, and (3) that individual is bald. Call this *B*. It is not obvious that the negative statement "The present king of France is not bald" contradicts *B*, because it can be interpreted two different ways, depending on what is being negated. If what is negated is clause (3), then the statement is just like *B* except that the last clause says "that individual is *not* bald." The positive and negative statements will then be contraries, or statements that cannot both be true, though they can both be false. If what is negated, however, is *B*—the entire statement—then the negative statement is the contradictory of the positive one and the two statements will both have opposite truth value. These statements would then not violate the law of excluded middle or the law of contradiction.

The Paradox of Identity

Here our puzzle is to explain how true statements of identity—that is, statements of the form $a = b$, where "*a*" and "*b*" are different proper names or definite descriptions linked together by the "is" of identity—can be both true and informative. If true, shouldn't they be tautologies? If they are genuine proper names, Russell says yes, they will be tautologies, since

---

such names mean what they denote. But proper names and definite descriptions are Chapter 11). Indeed, grammatically prope nite descriptions. "Adam is the man with something like "The man who sinned in t without a navel." Analyzing this in accor descriptions, we quickly see that it is a con asserts that (1) there is a man who sinned in is not more than one such man, and (3) tha a navel. Clearly such a statement can be b need not be a tautology if true.

The Paradox Involving Oblique or Indirect (

It is a historical fact that George IV wondered of *Waverley*. But Scott was (or is) the author Should we conclude that George IV wondered that he wondered about the law of identity? Scott," if "Scott" were a genuine proper name cording to Russell (R, p. 245). We know, howe of Europe was not interested in the law of ide his lack of interest in this tautology? Well, the why "Scott was the author of *Waverley*" is not that George IV was merely wondering whether tential statement was true—namely, (1) that so (2) that not more than one person authored *W* individual was Scott. Such curiosity does not im gies. So this final paradox is also successfully dis

Some Puzzles and Difficulties in Russell's Theory

His theory has the consequence that (1) "The Em the Emperor of East Lansing," if true, is only conti may not be one and only one Emperor of East I moment East Lansing does not have an Emperor. his theory that (2) "The round square is the round since there cannot (logically) be such a thing. Yet a

brush must be there, and in a particular relation to one another; and this was as it were hidden in the sense of the first sentence, and is *expressed* in the analyzed sentence" (PI, §60).

Wittgenstein counters this argument in the following way. Suppose we were to ask someone who says that the broom is in the corner if he really means the broomstick is there, and so is the brush, and the broomstick is fixed in the brush. Wittgenstein contends that "he would probably say that he had not thought specially of the broomstick or specially of the brush at all. And that would be the *right* answer, for he meant to speak neither of the stick nor of the brush in particular" (PI, §60). The statement, then, is not about what the broom analyst says it is about. The speaker is talking about the broom, not about the parts it is made up of—the broomstick and the brush that is on it. Finally, Wittgenstein suggests the analysis does not really succeed in giving the meaning of the original statement, since we do not understand the analysis as well as we do what is being analyzed and they do not have the same use in the language. He brings this out by supposing that, "instead of saying 'Bring me the broom,' you said 'Bring me the broomstick and the brush that is fitted on to it'!" It would not be clear whether it was the broom that was wanted or something else. When you found out that it was the broom that was wanted, you would probably reproach the one who gave you the order, asking, "Why do you put it so oddly?" (PI, §60). Let us see next how similar objections apply to Russell's theory of descriptions.

First, compare what Russell says about "The father of Charles II was executed." He says this is really a statement about there existing an entity that begat Charles II, since you can replace it by a statement that says there was exactly one entity that begat Charles II and that entity was executed (R, p. 44). Moreover, Russell argues this second statement is a further analyzed form of the first one, because if the father of Charles II was executed, that means that there must have been one and only one entity that stood in a certain relation to Charles II—that is, it alone begat him—and that that entity was executed; and this was hidden in the sense of the first sentence, and is *expressed* in the analyzed sentence. Russell might say he is bringing out the underlying logic of sentences involving definite descriptions, which is obscured by their subject-predicate surface grammar. The parallels with the analysis of "The broom is in the corner" are striking. We shall see that Wittgenstein's criticisms of it seem to apply equally forcefully to Russell's analysis of definite descriptions.

Suppose we ask a historian—say Ranke—who writes that the father of Charles II was executed, whether he really means there was an entity that begat Charles II, only one such entity, and that that entity was executed.

He might say he had not thought specially of there being an entity that begat Charles II or specially of there being only one such entity. And, as Wittgenstein suggests, that seems to be the right answer, since he means to speak neither of the entity that begat Charles II, nor of there being only one entity that begat Charles II, when he made his statement. If so, it seems that the statement is not about what Russell says it is about after all. The historian was talking about the father of Charles II.

Finally, it seems Russell's analysis does not really succeed in giving the meaning of the original statement, since we do not understand the analysis as well as we do what is being analyzed, and the two do not have the same use in the language. We may even question whether the analysis in any way furthers our understanding of what it analyzes. Russell might reply that surely it does, since it states explicitly what is only implicit in the original statement. Wittgenstein might counter that even if this is true, it also obscures "an aspect of the matter" (PI, §63), just as the broom analysis did. This can be seen if we suppose that, instead of saying, "Get me the father of Charles II," you said, "Get me something that exists and that alone begat Charles II." It would not be clear whether it was the father of Charles II whom you wanted or somebody or something else. When you found out that it was the father of Charles II who was wanted, you would be likely to reproach the person who gave you the order by saying, as Wittgenstein suggests, "Why do you put it so oddly?" For this reason, along with the previously mentioned ones, it seems doubtful whether Russell has succeeded in rendering the meaning of statements containing definite descriptions.

Notes

Preface

1. Saul Wittgenstein is an imaginary character: Ludwig Wittgenstein as he strikes noted Princeton philosopher Saul Kripke.

Chapter 1. Wittgenstein's Conception of Philosophy

1. David Hume, *A Treatise of Human Nature,* ed. L. A. Selby-Bigge (London: Oxford University Press, 1958), p. xx.

2. See John Dewey's "Philosophy," in the *Dictionary of Philosophy and Psychology,* ed. James M. Baldwin (New York: Macmillan, 1928), vol. 2, pp. 290–96, and John Passmore's "Philosophy," in *The Encyclopedia of Philosophy,* ed. Paul Edwards (New York: Macmillan and Free Press, 1967), vol. 2, pp. 216–26.

3. R. H. M. Elwes, trans., *The Chief Works of Benedict de Spinoza: Theologico-Political Treatise* (New York: Dover Publications, 1951), vol. 1, chap. 14, p. 189.

4. Wittgenstein studied logic with Russell for five terms in the years 1912–13. At the time Russell and Moore were the two most eminent philosophy lecturers at Cambridge.

5. Gottlob Frege is a nineteenth-century German logician, admired by both Russell and Wittgenstein. He is one of the founders of modern logic. One of his most important books is *The Foundations of Arithmetic,* trans. J. L. Austin (New York: Philosophical Library, 1953).

6. Bertrand Russell, "On Denoting," *Mind* 14 (October 1905), pp. 479–93. This essay and his lectures on logical atomism of 1918 are both reprinted in *Logic and Knowledge: Essays 1901–1950,* ed. Robert C. Marsh (London: George Allen & Unwin, 1956), pp. 47, 178. R will be used as an abbreviation for the Marsh book.

7. G. E. Moore, "What is Philosophy?" lecture delivered in 1910, published in his *Some Main Problems of Philosophy* (New York: Macmillan, 1953), p. 14.

8. The technical distinction between "saying" and "showing" is a crucial one in his earlier philosophy. According to this philosophy, there are things that are not sayable—because they transcend the language, making utterance of them nonsensical—that are nevertheless showable. Whatever is showable, however, is never sayable.

9. From the "Big Typescript" (MS 213, 413), quoted by Anthony Kenny, in *The Legacy of Wittgenstein* (Oxford: Basil Blackwell, 1984), p. 42.

10. Many moderns may be unfamiliar with fly-bottles. A fly-bottle is simply a bottle used to trap flies. The fly goes into the bottom hole attracted by the smell of vinegar. It could find its way out if it only realized how it got in, but it doesn't.

11. See Richard Rorty's *Philosophy and the Mirror of Nature* (Princeton, N.J.: Princeton University Press, 1979), especially p. 13.

12. Kenny, *Legacy of Wittgenstein,* p. 43.

13. See, for example, Garth Hallett, *Wittgenstein's Definition of Meaning as Use* (New York: Fordham University Press, 1967).

14. William P. Alston, *Philosophy of Language* (Englewood Cliffs, N.J.: Prentice-Hall, 1964), p. 33n.

15. Gilbert Ryle, "Ordinary Language," in *Ordinary Language,* ed. V. C. Chappell (Englewood Cliffs: Prentice-Hall, 1964), pp. 24–40, see especially pp. 33–35.

16. J. O. Urmson, "Austin, John Langshaw," in *Encyclopedia of Philosophy,* vol. 1, p. 211.

17. O. K. Bouwsma, *Wittgenstein: Conversations 1949–1951,* ed. J. L. Craft and Ronald E. Hustwit (Indianapolis, Ind.: Hackett Publishing, 1986), p. 36.

18. That to have an opinion is a state of a person would seem to be an example of such a fact. See PI, §573.

19. "Deontologist" is a technical term used in ethics; "a priori," in epistemology; and "modus ponens," in logic. "Language-game" and "illocutionary act" belong to the special vocabularies of the later Wittgenstein and of J. L. Austin, respectively.

20. K. T. Fann, ed., *Ludwig Wittgenstein: The Man and His Philosophy* (New York: Dell, 1967), p. 316n.

21. Larry Wilde, *The Great Comedians Talk about Comedy* (New York: Citadel Press, 1968), p. 69.

22. Ibid., p. 100.

23. Walter Sorell, *Facets of Comedy* (New York: Grosset and Dunlap, 1972), p. 90.

24. Ibid., p. 22.

25. Norman Malcolm, *Ludwig Wittgenstein: A Memoir* (London: Oxford University Press, 1958), p. 29.

26. Richard Rorty, *Consequences of Pragmatism: Essays, 1972–1980* (Minneapolis: University of Minnesota Press, 1982), p. 34. See also *Philosophy and the Mirror of Nature,* p. 369.

27. Richard Rorty, "Keeping Philosophy Pure," paper presented at Michigan State University, May 31, 1973.

28. Fann, *Ludwig Wittgenstein,* p. 45.

29. This point is relevant to the paradox of analysis, which asserts that true analyses must be trivial, though we know that not all of them are. If they were all trivial, the observation "To say that a person is a bachelor is the same thing as to say that that person is an unmarried man of marriageable age" would be as uninteresting and uninformative to us as the trivial remark, "To say that a person is a bachelor is the same thing as to say that that person is a bachelor."

30. Willard van Orman Quine, "On What There Is," in *From a Logical Point of View* (Cambridge, Mass.: Harvard University Press, 1953), p. 4. Quine uses these words to describe his as well as other people's aesthetic sense.

31. The ontological argument for the existence of God is the attempt to prove God's existence simply from an examination of the concept of God. It goes, roughly, as follows. The concept of God is the concept of an all-perfect being. Existence is a perfection, a good predicate to have. Therefore this predicate applies truly to God, that is, God exists. The ontological argument for the nonexistence of the devil proceeds in a similar way. The concept of the devil is the concept of a being possessing no perfections. Existence is a perfection, or a good predicate to have. Therefore this predicate does not apply truly to the devil, that is, the devil does not exist. Hume, Kant, Frege, and Russell criticize and reject these arguments, pointing out that existence, while superficially a predicate, is not an ordinary predicate applicable to things like God and the devil. I must mention, however, that at least one Wittgensteinian is convinced by another, more complex version of the ontological arguments: Norman Malcolm. See his "Anselm's Ontological Arguments," in *The Existence of God*, ed. John Hick (New York: Macmillan, 1964), pp. 48–70).

32. See the *Apology*, in which Socrates says he never taught anyone anything.

Chapter 2. The Doctrine of Family Resemblance

1. George Santayana, *The Sense of Beauty: Being the Outline of Aesthetic Theory* (New York: Charles Scribner's Sons, 1896), pp. 10—11.

2. See Chapter 12 for an explanation of who this character is.

3. Richard Rorty, *Consequences of Pragmatism: Essays 1972–1980* (Minneapolis: University of Minnesota Press, 1982), p. xiv.

4. John Findlay may have been misled by this expression, for he asserts that "Wittgenstein's view of the meaning of general terms is just as rashly dogmatic as the Socratic view" ("The Logic of Mysticism," *Religious Studies* 2 [1967], p. 147). We shall see that, on the contrary, Wittgenstein's approach is quite undogmatic: he wants us to examine each case with an open mind, not assuming in advance what we shall find.

5. See Renford Bambrough, "Universals and Family Resemblances," in *Universals and Particulars: Readings in Ontology*, ed. Michael J. Loux (Garden City, N.Y.: Doubleday, 1970), pp. 109–27.

6. See D. F. Pears, "Universals," in *Universals and Particulars*, pp. 35–49. The strategy of the attempted dissolution is to show that all possible answers to the problem fail as explanations because either they are unclear or circular. So it is not a real problem. Real problems have answers, even though we may not know what they are.

7. K T. Fann, *Wittgenstein's Conception of Philosophy* (Berkeley: University of California Press, 1969), p. 47. The quotation comes from the beginning of William James's second lecture on the *Varieties of Religious Experience*.

8. G. H. von Wright, *Wittgenstein* (Minneapolis: University of Minnesota Press, 1982), p. 213.

9. Anthony Kenny, *The Legacy of Wittgenstein* (Oxford: Basil Blackwell, 1984), p. 59.

10. Robert J. Fogelin, *Wittgenstein* (London: Routledge & Kegan Paul, 1976), pp. 121–22.

11. K. T. Fann, ed. *Ludwig Wittgenstein: The Man and His Philosophy* (New York: Dell, 1967), p. 46. Wisdom really should have added the qualification that the alcohol be fit for drinking. For perfumes, hairsprays, and aftershave lotions all contain alcohol made unfit for drinking, and we would not call these things alcoholic drinks.

12. Fann, *Wittgenstein's Conception of Philosophy,* p. 62.

13. Fann, *Ludwig Wittgenstein,* p. 68.

Chapter 3. Wittgenstein's Freud

1. Garth Hallett, *A Companion to Wittgenstein's "Philosophical Investigations"* (Ithaca, N.Y.: Cornell University Press, 1977), p. 765.

2. I shall not be discussing Wittgenstein's impact on a whole school of "interpretative social science," including the philosopher of social science Peter Winch, the social and cultural anthropologist Clifford Geertz, and the historian and philosopher of science Thomas Kuhn. This literature is mostly peripheral to Wittgensteinian philosophy. It is also unlikely that Wittgenstein would approve of Winch's extended use of his phrase "forms of life." Wittgenstein introduces this term in the *Investigations,* uses it sparingly—only five times—and never the way Winch uses it. In Winch's *The Idea of a Social Science* (New York: Humanities Press, 1958), he extends its use to say that religion, art, history, the sciences, as well as certain life styles are forms of life. My concern here is not with the many purposes to which Wittgenstein's work has been employed. I stick to a social scientist who influenced Wittgenstein and was his contemporary, Freud.

3. Garth Hallett, *A Companion,* p. 765, says he knows of no evidence that Wittgenstein ever met Freud. However, Allan Janik and Stephen Toulmin, in *Wittgenstein's Vienna* (New York: Simon and Schuster, 1973), p. 172, report that his sister, "Margarete, the youngest of the three daughters . . . became a close friend of Sigmund Freud." According to Brian McGuinness, ed., *Wittgenstein and His Times* (Chicago: University of Chicago Press, 1982), p. 29, she was also analyzed by Freud. Apparently, Wittgenstein started reading Freud around 1919 (LC, p. 41). He seems to have read at least the following works: *Jokes and Their Relation to the Unconscious, The Interpretation of Dreams, The Psychopathology of Everyday Life,* and *Studies in Hysteria.* I suspect he also read *On Dreams,* for the reason given below, in note 17.

4. Frank Cioffi, "Wittgenstein's Freud," in *Studies in the Philosophy of Wittgenstein,* ed. Peter Winch (New York: Humanities Press, 1969), gives a nice account of this. See especially p. 193.

5. O. K. Bouwsma, *Wittgenstein: Conversations 1949–1951,* ed. J. L. Craft and Ronald E. Hustwit (Indianapolis, Ind.: Hackett Publishing, 1986), p. 59.

6. See "The Origin and Development of Psychoanalysis," by Sigmund Freud, printed in *Varieties of Personality Theory,* ed. Hendrik M. Ruitenbeek (New York: E. P. Dutton, 1964), pp. 27–28.

7. See, for example, Ilham Dilman, *Freud and the Mind* (Oxford: Basil Blackwell, 1984), p. 16, and Adolf Grünbaum, "Freud's Theory: The Perspective of a Philosopher of Science," 1982 Presidential Address delivered at the Eastern Meeting of the American Philosophical Association, 28 Dec. 1982, and published in the *Proceedings and Addresses of the American Philosophical Association* 57 (1983), p. 5.

8. Sigmund Freud, *Jokes and Their Relation to the Unconscious*, trans. James Strachey (New York: W. W. Norton, 1960), pp. 132, 97, 137–38, 135, 101.

9. John Rickman, the compiler of Sándor Ferenczi's *Further Contributions to the Theory and Technique of Psycho-Analysis*, trans. Jane I. Suttie (London: Hogarth Press, 1950), p. 197n, explains that "the term 'instance,' in German, '*Instanz*,' was originally a legal term, cf. 'court of first instance,' and is used in psycho-analysis, as in law, in the sense of one of a hierarchy of functions or authorities."

10. Thomas Bulfinch, *Mythology* (New York: Hamlyn Publishing, 1964), p. 9.

11. Erik H. Erikson, *Childhood and Society* (New York: W. W. Norton, 1963), p. 64.

12. See, for example, Barbara Von Eckardt, "The Scientific Status of Psychoanalysis," in *Introducing Psychoanalytic Theory,* Sander L. Gilman, ed. (New York: Brunner-Mazel, 1982), pp. 138–80; and Adolf Grünbaum, *The Foundations of Psychoanalysis: A Philosophical Critique* (Berkeley: University of California Press, 1984) as well as his 1982 Presidential Address, "Freud's Theory: The Perspective of a Philosopher of Science," referred to above. See also some of the earlier discussions about the logical status of psychoanalysis in Sydney Hook, ed., *Psychoanalysis, Scientific Method, and Philosophy* (New York: New York University Press, 1959) and in Herbert Feigl, ed., *Minnesota Studies in the Philosophy of Science,* vol. 1 (Minneapolis: University of Minnesota Press, 1956).

13. James Strachey, trans., *Standard Edition of the Complete Psychological Works of Sigmund Freud, Introductory Lectures on Psycho-Analysis* (London: Hogarth Press and the Institute of Psycho-Analysis, 1963), vol. 15, p. 74.

14. K. T. Fann, *Wittgenstein's Conception of Philosophy* (Berkeley: University of California Press, 1969), p. 87.

15. Rush Rhees, "Assessments of the Man and the Philosopher," reprinted in *Ludwig Wittgenstein: The Man and His Philosophy,* ed. K. T. Fann (New York: Dell, 1967), pp. 77–78.

16. Morris Lazerowitz (*The Language of Philosophy: Freud and Wittgenstein* [Boston: Reidel, 1977], p. 29) unfortunately fails to see this. He erroneously supposes that every mistaken mode of thought must be a neurotic mode of thought, ascribing to Wittgenstein the view that "philosophy . . . [was] a neurotic aberration which called for treatment." It calls for treatment, according to Wittgenstein, but not in his opinion because it is a "neurotic aberration." Malcolm reports that on at least two occasions Wittgenstein explicitly attacked the suggestion that he conceived of philosophy as a form of psychoanalysis (*Ludwig Wittgenstein: A Memoir* [London: Oxford University Press, 1958], pp. 56–57). Despite this, Anthony Kenny, in his most recent book on Wittgenstein (*The Legacy of Wittgenstein* [Ox-

ford: Basil Blackwell, 1984], p. 40) continues to speak of Wittgenstein as engaged in "a form of psychoanalytic therapy."

17. Strachey, *Sigmund Freud*, vol. 5, *On Dreams*, pp. 653, 672. The similarity of the wording here to the above quotation from the preface of the *Investigations* (p. ix) suggests that Wittgenstein also read Freud's *On Dreams*, which is a summary of *The Interpretation of Dreams*. Larry Hauser pointed this out to me.

18. Dilman, *Freud and the Mind*, p. 61.

19. Quoted by Anthony Kenny in his *Legacy of Wittgenstein*, p. 51. (From the "Big Typescript," MS 213, 406.)

20. M. O'C. Drury, "A Symposium," reprinted in Fann, *Ludwig Wittgenstein*, p. 69.

21. "Cartesian" refers to Descartes, the great French seventeenth-century mind-body dualist. He thinks the mind has direct, immediate, and certain knowledge of its own mental states—for example, its own present intentions—independently of knowing anything about the physical world. The mental and the physical are two separate worlds that only interact causally. Identity theorists, being materialists, reject this dualism. They believe we can understand our mental states simply by—and indeed only by—understanding the state of our brains, since they identify mental states with brain events or brain states. I shall discuss Cartesian dualism and the mind-brain identity theory in Chapters 5 and 7.

22. Dilman, *Freud and the Mind, p. 52.*

23. *Ibid., p. 98.*

24. *Sigmund Freud, quoted by Dilman, Freud and the Mind,* p. 128. (From the *Collected Papers*, pp. 253–54.)

25. McGuinness, *Wittgenstein and His Times*, pp. 42–43.

26. Philosophical behaviorism and the mind-body identity theory will be discussed in the next two chapters, Chapters 4 and 5.

Chapter 4. Behaviorism: Logical, Philosophical, Metaphysical

1. C. S. Chihara and J. A. Fodor, "Operationalism and Ordinary Language: A Critique of Wittgenstein," in *Wittgenstein: The Philosophical Investigations*, ed. George Pitcher (Garden City, N.Y.: Anchor Books, 1966), refer to Wittgenstein as a "logical behaviorist." Paul M. Churchland includes only Ryle and Wittgenstein in his list of suggested readings on philosophical behaviorism in *Matter and Consciousness* (Cambridge, Mass.: MIT Press, 1984). John W. Cook also tells us he is "prepared to argue that, despite his [Wittgenstein's] protestations to the contrary, he was a behaviorist" (*Religious Studies* 23 [1987], p. 217n).

2. J. B. Watson, *Behaviorism* (New York: W. W. Norton, 1970), p. 273.

3. B. F.Skinner seems to propose this as the correct account of liking Brahms in *About Behavior* (New York: Vintage Books, 1976), p. 54.

4. Wittgenstein's criteriological view will be discussed in Chapter 8. More will be said there about what he means by a criterion.

5. V. C. Chappell, ed., *The Philosophy of Mind* (New York: Dover, 1981), "Introduction," p. 9.

6. U. T. Place, "Is Consciousness a Brain Process?" in *The Philosophy of Mind,* pp. 101–109.

7. Scientific and methodological behaviorism are interchangeable terms.

8. Jerome A. Shaffer, *Philosophy of Mind* (Englewood Cliffs, N.J.: Prentice-Hall, 1968), p. 15.

9. Skinner, *About Behavior,* p. 59.

10. B. F. Skinner suggests such an account in *Beyond Freedom and Dignity* (New York: Alfred A. Knopf, 1971), p. 37.

11. Willard Van Orman Quine, "Two Dogmas of Empiricism," in *From a Logical Point of View* (Cambridge, Mass.: Harvard University Press, 1953), pp. 20–46.

12. The truth values of the "ordinary" if-then statement of logic are determined by the truth values of its component statements. So we can give a truth-table definition of this sort of "if . . . then. . . ." It turns out such statements are false only when the antecedent is true and the consequent false; in all other combinations of truth values they are true. Hence they are true whenever the antecedent is false. But obviously the falsity of the antecedent does not make all contrary-to-fact conditionals true, or they would all be true, and we know only some of them are true.

13. Norman Malcolm, "Behaviorism as a Philosophy of Psychology," in *Behaviorism and Phenomenology: Contrasting Bases for Modern Psychology,* ed. T. W. Wann (Chicago: University of Chicago Press, 1964), pp. 141–62.

14. Ludwig Wittgenstein, *Philosophical Psychology,* pp. 39, 40. Probably A. C. Jackson's unpublished notes.

15. G. E. M. Anscombe, "Wittgenstein's Philosophical Psychology," 1966 Summer Institute in Ethics and the Philosophy of Mind, unpublished lecture notes.

16. Shaffer, *Philosophy of Mind,* p. 20.

17. Norman Malcolm, "Wittgenstein on the Nature of Mind," Isenberg Memorial Lecture, Michigan State University, 11 October 1968. It has since appeared in *Thought and Knowledge* (Ithaca, N.Y.: Cornell University Press, 1977), pp. 142–43.

18. Paul Ziff, "About Behaviourism," *Analysis* (June 1958), pp. 132–34.

19. See Ronald Suter, "Paul Ziff on Behaviorism," *Michigan Academician* 3 (1970–71), pp. 19–23.

20. Churchland, *Matter and Consciousness,* p. 24.

21. Ibid., p. 70.

22. Gilbert Ryle, *The Concept of Mind* (London: Hutchinson's University Library, 1949), pp. 103–104.

23. See Arnold S. Kaufman, "Behaviorism" in *The Encyclopedia of Philosophy,* ed. Paul Edwards (New York: Macmillan and Free Press, 1967), vol. 1, p. 269.

24. See Chapter 8 for an account of the criteriological view.

25. See Friedrich Waismann's "Language Strata," in *Logic and Language,* 2d series, ed. Antony Flew (Oxford: Basil Blackwell, 1955), especially pp. 28–31. Like Wittgenstein Waismann was born in Vienna. He was an early follower of Wittgenstein. He moved to Cambridge to study with him.

26. See Chapter 2 for a discussion of Wittgenstein's doctrine of family resemblance.

27. See the Appendix for an explanation of Russell's theory of descriptions.

Chapter 5. The Mind-Brain Identity Theory

1. Not all philosophers draw this distinction, or draw it quite the way I am drawing it here. For example, David M. Rosenthal (*Materialism and the Mind-Body Problem* [Englewood Cliffs, N.J.: Prentice-Hall, 1971], pp. 8–9) uses the term *identity thesis* the way I use the term *identity theory*. V. C. Chappell (*The Philosophy of Mind* [New York: Dover, 1981], pp. 19–21), on the other hand, uses *identity theory* to cover both of the two things I wish to distinguish.

2. U. T. Place, "Is Consciousness a Brain Process?" in *The Philosophy of Mind*, ed. V. C. Chappell (New York: Dover, 1981), p. 101.

3. See the first page of Place's article, p. 101.

4. J. J. C. Smart, "Sensations and Brain Processes" in *The Philosophy of Mind*, pp. 160–72.

5. But what exactly is this distinction? Can you speak of pains and afterimages (the pictures you have in your mind of a scene that persists after you stop looking at the scene) as things that are describable without reference to behavior? This does not seem quite right. Wittgenstein suggests that the distinction may be between concepts that have an experience-content and those that do not. Speaking of meaning and intending, he says: "Meaning is as little an experience as intending. But what distinguishes them from experience? —They have no experience-content. For the contents (images for instance) which accompany and illustrate them are not the meaning or intending" (PI, p. 217).

6. Anthony Quinton, *The Nature of Things* (London: Routledge & Kegan Paul, 1973), p. 330.

7. Quinton, *Nature of Things*, p. 332.

8. Place, "Is Consciousness a Brain Process," pp. 104–105.

9. Smart, "Sensations and Brain Processes," p. 163.

10. Place, "Is Consciousness a Brain Process," p. 106.

11. Ibid.

12. Quinton, *Nature of Things*, p. 331.

13. Ibid.

14. As P. F. Strawson says, a person is "a type of entity such that *both* predicates ascribing states of consciousness *and* predicates ascribing corporeal characteristics, a physical situation, etc., are equally applicable to a single individual of that single type." From his article "Persons," included in *Individuals: An Essay in Descriptive Metaphysics* (Methuen, 1959), p. 102.

15. See his reply to objection 4 in Smart, "Sensations and Brain Processes," p. 168.

16. Norman Malcolm, *Problems of Mind: Descartes to Wittgenstein* (New York: Harper, 1971). The argument begins on p. 65.

17. Malcolm, *Problems of Mind*, p. 69.

18. Ibid., p. 70. Malcolm helps us to see why Smart's thesis cannot be true when it is made about sudden thoughts and bodily sensations. It does not matter for our purpose if the thesis is found to be false or meaningless, for if it is either, identity theory cannot be true.

19. Ibid.

20. Ibid., p. 71.

21. J. J. C. Smart, from *Philosophy and Scientific Realism* (New York: Humanities Press, 1963), p. 98, as quoted by Malcolm in *Problems of Mind*, p. 71.

22. Malcolm, *Problems of Mind*, p. 67.

23. Quinton, *Nature of Things*, p. 333.

24. Ibid., p. 335.

25. Ibid.

26. Ibid.

27. I shall argue more extensively for this point in Chapter 7, "Wittgenstein's Refutation of Cartesian Dualism," especially in Section 7.6, where I shall show that the qualitative/numerical distinction applies to material things like cars and pencils, but not to psychological things like headaches, thoughts, or emotions.

28. Quinton, *Nature of Things*, p. 335.

29. Malcolm, *Problems of Mind*, p. viii.

30. Jaegwon Kim, "On the Psycho-Physical Identity Theory," *American Philosophical Quarterly* 3 (1966), pp. 227–35.

31. J. J. C. Smart, "Brain Processes and Incorrigibility," in *The Mind/Brain Identity Theory*, ed. C. V. Borst (New York: St. Martin's, 1970), p. 107.

32. Ibid., p. 108.

33. Quinton, *Nature of Things*, p. 169.

34. Ibid.

35. Ibid., p. 347.

36. Ibid., p. 171.

37. Kurt Baier, "Smart on Sensations," in *The Mind/Brain Identity Theory*, p. 102.

38. C. V. Borst, "Editor's Introduction," in *The Mind/Brain Identity Theory*, p. 27.

39. Quinton, *Nature of Things*, p. 170.

40. More will be said on the notion of *conceptual ties* in the discussion of criteria in Chapter 8. See especially Sections 8.6–8.8.

41. More will be said about the difference between criterial evidence and non-criterial, or plain, evidence in Chapter 8.

42. Identity theory now begins to resemble a kind of fetishism.

43. A relation R is *transitive* if and only if whenever aRb and bRc, then aRc. For example, "is greater than" is transitive because if a is greater than b and b is greater than c, then a is greater than c.

44. This objection does not apply to identify theories which identify psychological things with brain states, since we could be in the same brain state even though we have different brains.

45. Quinton, *Nature of Things*, p. 337.

Chapter 6. Cartesian Dualism

1. See James B. Pratt's *Personal Realism* (New York: Macmillan, 1937) and Karl Popper's and John C. Eccles's *The Self and Its Brain: An Argument for Interactionism* (New York: Springer International, 1977).

2. *The Philosophical Works of Descartes,* trans. E. S. Haldane and G. R. Ross (New York: Dover, 1955), vol. 1, p. 325 (hereafter referred to as HR).

3. C. V. Borst, ed., *The Mind-Brain Identity Theory* (New York: St. Martin's, 1970). See Antony Flew's foreword, p. 5.

4. G. F. Maine, ed., *The Works of Oscar Wilde* (London: Collins, 1948), p. 56.

5. Note 31 in Chapter 1 gives a brief exposition of a simple version of the ontological argument much like Descartes's and points out one of several ways in which it is vulnerable to refutation.

6. Descartes writes to Mersenne (quoted by A. Boyce Gibson, *The Philosophy of Descartes* [London: Methuen, 1932], p. 204): "The feeling of pain exists only in the understanding [mind]; but I explain (mechanically) all the exterior motions which in us accompany these feelings, and which alone, to the exclusion of pain in the strict sense, take place in animals." In other words, without mind there can be no feeling, no pain.

7. La Mettrie is a French philosopher and physician. In his book *Man a Machine* (1747; La Salle: Open Court, 1912) he argues that man is no less a soulless mechanism than are other animals.

8. Lewis Carroll, *Through the Looking-Glass,* in *The Annotated Alice* (New York: Clarkson N. Potter, 1960), p. 341.

9. Robert Benchley's observation, *Inside Benchley* (New York: Harper & Brothers, 1942), pp. 182–83.

10. Example from Kubrick interview, *Playboy,* September 1968, p. 96.

11. E. S. Haldane, *Descartes: His Life and Times* (London: Murray, 1905), p. 378.

12. Alan Turing thinks we might have something approaching it by the year 2000. Or at least by then we might have a computer that could be successfully substituted for one of the players in his "imitation game." That is, you wouldn't be able to tell any more whether your questions were being answered by a computer or by a person at the other end of the teleprinter in the next room. See "Computing Machinery and Intelligence," by A. M. Turing, reprinted in *Minds and Machines,* ed. Alan Ross Anderson (Englewood Cliffs, N.J.: Prentice-Hall, 1964), pp. 4–30.

13. Arthur Clarke describes such a computer in his story *The City and the Stars* (New York: Harcourt, Brace and World, 1956). There we read about "the all-but-infinite intellect of the Central Computer. It was difficult not to think of the Central Computer as a living entity, localized in a single spot, though actually it was the sum total of all the machines in Diaspar" (p. 67).

14. *National Geographic* 132, no. 6 (December 1967), p. 877.

15. Gibson, *Philosophy of Descartes,* pp. 213–14, wonders why he "never pondered over [the] capacity of animals [to learn from experience]."

16. David Hume, *A Treatise of Human Nature,* ed. L. A. Selby-Bigge (London: Oxford University Press, 1958), p. 110.

17. G. E. M. Anscombe disagrees with Wittgenstein that there can be such a thing as a "natural expression of an intention." She thinks "the expression of [intention] is purely conventional [or, broadly understood] . . . 'linguistic.'" In her view, then, the brutes have intentions, but they are unable to express them. See her *Intention* (Oxford: Basil Blackwell, 1957), p. 5.

Chapter 7. Wittgenstein's Refutation of Cartesian Dualism

1. Lewis Carroll, "The Two Clocks," *The Complete Works of Lewis Carroll* (New York: Random House), pp. 1230–31.

2. W. T. Stace, *The Theory of Knowledge and Existence* (Oxford: Clarendon Press, 1932), p. 67.

3. Lewis Carroll, *Alice's Adventures in Wonderland,* in *The Annotated Alice* (New York: Clarkson N. Potter, 1960), pp. 37–38.

4. Frederick Jacobi, ed., *Tales of Grimm and Andersen* (New York: Random House, 1952), p. 174.

5. Stanley Cavell, *Must We Mean What We Say?: Modern Philosophical Essays in Morality, Religion, Drama, Music and Criticism* (New York: Charles Scribner's Sons, 1969), p. 244.

6. Stace, *Theory of Knowledge and Existence,* p. 67.

7. A. J. Ayer, *Philosophical Essays* (London: Macmillan, 1954), p. 195.

8. *The Collected Dialogues of Plato,* ed. Edith Hamilton and Huntington Cairns (Princeton, N.J.: Princeton University Press, 1961), *Theaetetus* 159d–e, 154a–b, 166d–e.

9. The principle of the indiscernibility of identicals is not to be confused with its converse—if (F) (Fx if and only if Fy), then $x = y$—namely, the principle of the identity of indiscernibles.

10. Don Locke, "The Privacy of Pain," *Analysis* (March 1964), p. 149.

11. You will recall that much was made of this point in the location objection to identity theory in Chapter 5.

12. Cavell, *Must We Mean What We Say?,* p. 244.

13. Thomas Reid, *An Inquiry into the Human Mind,* ed. Timothy J. Duggan (Chicago: University of Chicago Press, 1970), p. 206.

14. Donald Davidson, "Theories of Meaning and Learnable Languages," in *Proceedings of the 1964 International Congress for Logic, Methodology, and Philosophy of Science,* ed. Bar-Hillel (Amsterdam: North Holland, 1965), pp. 391–92.

Chapter 8. Characteristics of Criteria

1. A relation is irreflexive if and only if for no object a is aRa true. Thus "is lighter than" is an irreflexive relation since no object is lighter than itself.

2. A relation R is nonsymmetrical if and only if whenever aRb, it may or may

not be the case that *b*R*a*. Thus "loves" is a nonsymmetrical relation, since if *a* loves *b*, *b* may or may not love *a*. Love may be unrequited, but we know, fortunately, that it isn't always or necessarily unrequited.

3. Anthony Kenny, "Criterion," in *The Encyclopedia of Philosophy*, ed. Paul Edwards (New York: Macmillan and and Free Press, 1967), vol. 2, p. 259.

4. P. M. S. Hacker, *Insight and Illusion: Themes in the Philosophy of Wittgenstein*, rev. ed. (Oxford: Clarendon Press, 1986), p. 316. This is a greatly improved edition of *Insight and Illusion: Wittgenstein on Philosophy and the Metaphysics of Experience* (Oxford: Clarendon Press, 1972), a work Hacker wrote fifteen years earlier.

5. Hacker, *Insight and Illusion*, p. 315.

6. Kenny, "Criterion," p. 260.

7. Ibid.

8. J. M. Shorter, "Other Minds," in *Encyclopedia of Philosophy*, vol. 6, p. 9.

9. Ibid., p. 10.

10. Ibid., p. 9.

11. Norman Malcolm, "Wittgenstein's *Philosophical Investigations*" in *The Philosophy of Mind*, ed. V. C. Chappell (New York: Dover, 1981), p. 88.

12. P. F. Strawson, "Persons" in *The Philosophy of Mind*, p. 146.

13. Norman Malcolm, "Wittgenstein on the Nature of Mind," given as an Isenberg Memorial Lecture at Michigan State University, 11 Oct. 1968. It has since been published in *Thought and Knowledge* (Ithaca, N.Y.: Cornell University Press, 1977), p. 157.

14. The same charge could be leveled against functionalism, another reductionist view in philosophy of mind, which has not been discussed here. In his recent book *Representation and Reality* (Cambridge, Mass.: MIT Press, 1988), Hilary Putnam shows that we can neither reduce nor get rid of mental terms.

15. John Wisdom, "A Feature of Wittgenstein's Technique," reprinted in *Ludwig Wittgenstein: the Man and His Philosophy*, ed. K. T. Fann (New York: Dell, 1967), p. 361.

Chapter 9. Augustine on Time

1. This essay was originally published in the *Revue internationale de philosophie* 16 (1962), pp. 378–94. I am grateful to the editor for granting permission for its reproduction here, slightly altered.

2. Saint Augustine, *The Confessions* (New York: Modern Library, 1949), p. 247. All page references are to this text unless otherwise indicated.

3. In "St. Augustine's Account of Time and Wittgenstein's Criticisms," James McEvoy (*Review of Metaphysics* 38 [1984], p. 575) disputes this claim. He says "the account which Augustine gives of time is not subjective; it is personal and interior." Unfortunately, he fails to explain how a personal and interior account is not a variant of a subjective view. On the next page, McEvoy also makes a seemingly self-contradictory statement, namely, that "Augustine does not give a definition of time,

nor even perhaps an explanation of it . . . [though he does give us an]-account of time." Again, it is not clear what he might mean by this.

4. This suggestion of a possible twofold conception of time lurking in the background in Augustine's thought may account for Hugh M. Lacey's contention that "there are two strands to Augustine's philosophy of time, one subjectivist, one objectivist" ("Empiricism and Augustine's Problems about Time," *Review of Metaphysics* 22 [1968], p. 223). He accuses me and others (C. W. K. Mundle and R. M. Gale) of failing to recognize and treat the "objectivist strand." I don't discuss it simply because I find nothing clear enough there to be called an "objectivist view of time."

5. Lacey tries to show how Augustine's mental impressions might be measured. He thinks this could be done first by stipulating "that the memories of any two oscillations are equal in measure, and of measure 1 unit. Then in the normal recursive manner extend the metric to all the required metal impressions, e.g., a memory is of unit 2 if the process of which it is a memory coincides (in the memory) with two consecutive oscillations of the pendulum" (p. 227). But it is not at all clear how this is to be worked out or how it can be known to begin with that the memories of any two oscillations are equal in measure.

Chapter 10. Dissolving the Dream Argument

1. This chapter was originally published as "The Dream Argument" in the *American Philosophical Quarterly* 13 (1976), pp. 185–94. I am grateful to the editor for granting permission for its reproduction here, slightly revised.

2. *The Collected Dialogues of Plato,* ed. Edith Hamilton and Huntington Cairns (Princeton, N.J.: Princeton University Press, 1961), *Theaetetus* 158b–d.

3. Wing-tsit Chan, trans., *A Source Book in Chinese Philosophy* (Princeton, N.J.: Princeton University Press, 1963), p. 200. Subsequent page references to this work will be given in the main body of the text.

4. *The Philosophical Works of Descartes,* trans. E. S. Haldane and G. R. Ross (New York: Dover, 1955), vol. 1, p. 145. For Moore's argument, see his "Proof of an External World," *Proceedings of the British Academy* 25 (1939), reprinted in his *Philosophical Papers* (New York: Collier, 1962), pp. 126–48.

5. Descartes, *Philosophical Works,* vol. 1, p. 146.

6. David Hume, *A Treatise of Human Nature,* ed. L. A. Selby-Bigge (Oxford: Clarendon Press, 1958), bk. I, pt. I, sec. 1, p. 1.

7. Norman Malcolm, *Dreaming* (New York: Humanities Press, 1959), p. 108.

8. A. J. Ayer, "Professor Malcolm on Dreams," *Journal of Philosophy* 57 (1960), p. 533.

9. Isak Dinesen, *Seven Gothic Tales* (New York: Modern Library, 1961), pp. 402–403.

10. Woody Allen, *Getting Even* (New York: Warner, 1972), p. 68.

11. Douglas Odegard disagrees with this first horn of the dilemma. In his article "Berkeleian Idealism and the Dream Argument" (*Idealistic Studies* 11 [1981], p. 94), he asserts that it is not self-defeating to doubt that you are awake if you

doubt this just in the sense of saying that you may not be awake. Apparently you only undermine such a doubt if you refuse to say that you are awake. So to coherently doubt that you are awake just say you may not be awake while remaining willing to say that you are awake. But if you are willing to say that you are awake, presumably you believe you are, unless you are lying. Maybe that is why Odegard goes on to make the seemingly self-contradictory and irrational statement: "I can concede that I may not have any doubt about whether I am awake and still have such a doubt; and I can concede that any grounds which I offer for saying that I may be dreaming may not be solid and still accept such grounds." I fail to see how this helps Descartes or refutes the first horn of the dilemma.

12. In his article "Descartes' Children: The Skeptical Legacy of Cartesianism" (*New Scholasticism* 56 [1982], p. 363), Lawrence M. Hinman agrees with me on this second horn of the dilemma. He writes "[Possible reformulations of the dream argument] are all open to the following objection which Suter, following Wittgenstein, has presented. In order to *express* the doubt contained in the dream argument, one must know the meanings of the words which are employed in that expression; to know the meanings of those words is to know propositions of the type [being doubted]; from this it follows that the argument is self-defeating."

13. Curiously, Descartes agrees. He wants only philosophically justified doubt; this is essential to his methodology. Consequently, a proposition *p* is to be rejected only if a reason can be found that casts doubt on *p*. See his *Philosophical Works*, vol. 1, pp. 99, 100, 140, 145, 148; and vol. 2, p. 126. Unfortunately, Descartes does not seem fully to understand the implications of this view.

14. Carl Hempel writes in *Aspects of Scientific Explanation* (New York: Free Press, 1965), p. 102: "If under a given criterion of cognitive significance, a sentence N is non-significant, then so must be . . . any disjunction $N \lor S$, no matter whether S is significant under the given criterion or not."

15. Israel Scheffler, in *The Anatomy of Inquiry* (New York: Knopf, 1963), p. 134, says the "denials of significant sentences must themselves be significant." He writes: "Take any [true or false and hence] significant sentence and form its denial. This denial must, then, again be true or false—false if the original sentence was true, and true if the original sentence chosen was false. Thus, this denial must . . . be significant since all true or false sentences are significant."

16. On p. 129, Scheffler makes a stronger and more dubious claim from which premise 2 follows: "For every sentence S, S is true or false if, and only if, S is significant."

17. John Locke, *An Essay Concerning Human Understanding*, bk. 4, chap. 11, sec. 8.

18. Peter Strawson, "On Referring," reprinted in *Essays in Conceptual Analysis*, ed. Antony Flew (London: Macmillan, 1956), p. 29.

19. Ibid., pp. 30–31.

20. See A. J. Ayer's *The Problem of Knowledge* (Harmondsworth, Middlesex: Penguin, 1956), p. 35.

21. Michael Dummett, in his fine article on Frege in *The Encyclopedia of Phi-*

losophy, ed. Paul Edwards (New York: Macmillan and Free Press, 1967), vol. 3, p. 228, attributes to him the view that "the sense of a sentence [the thought expressed by a sentence] is built up out of the sense of its constituent words."

Chapter 11. Russell's Theory of Proper Names

1. Bertrand Russell, "The Philosophy of Logical Atomism," reprinted in *Logic and Knowledge: Essays 1901–1950,* ed. Robert C. Marsh (London: George Allen & Unwin, 1956), p. 178. R will be used as an abbreviation for this work.
2. See the Appendix for an explanation of Russell's theory of descriptions.
3. Bertrand Russell, "On Denoting," *Mind* 14 (October 1905), reprinted in R, p. 200.
4. See Appendix for an explanation of Russell's ingenious theory of descriptions and the puzzles it was meant to dissolve.
5. G. P. Baker and P. M. S. Hacker, *Wittgenstein Understanding and Meaning: An Analytical Commentary on the Philosophical Investigations* (Chicago: University of Chicago Press, 1980), vol. 1, p. 33. We have already seen in Chapter 9 how this conception of language affects Augustine's discussion of time.
6. H. O. Mounce, *Wittgenstein's Tractatus: An Introduction* (Chicago: University of Chicago Press, 1981) contends that the early Wittgenstein already appreciated this point. He says, "Wittgenstein would have said at the time of the *Tractatus* what he said later, namely, that the act of naming makes sense only because there is already a considerable amount of stagesetting in the language" (p. 33).
7. Lewis Carroll, *Through the Looking-Glass,* in *The Annotated Alice* (New York: Clarkson N. Potter, 1960), p. 269.
8. Anthony Kenny, *The Legacy of Wittgenstein* (Oxford: Basil Blackwell, 1984), p. 103.
9. It is also different. For example, unlike Russell, he never maintains that "this" and "that" are proper names, much less the only true ones. Further, contrary to the views of Jaakko and Merrill Hintikka expressed in *Investigating Wittgenstein* (Oxford: Basil Blackwell, 1986), chap. 3, the early Wittgenstein never identifies any of the objects of the *Tractatus* with sense-data. Unfortunately, it never tells us what they are.
10. Friedrich Waismann, "Verifiability," in *Logic and Language,* ed. A. G. N. Flew (New York: Doubleday, 1965), pp. 122–51.
11. Willard Van Orman Quine, "On What There Is," in *From a Logical Point of View* (Cambridge, Mass.: Harvard University Press, 1953), p. 8.
12. Peter Geach, *Reference and Generality* (Ithaca, N.Y.: Cornell University Press, 1969), p. 161.

Chapter 12. Saul Wittgenstein's Skeptical Paradox

1. Saul A. Kripke, *Wittgenstein on Rules and Private Language: An Elementary Exposition* (Cambridge, Mass.: Harvard University Press, 1982), p. 5. The first 113

pages of this book are an expansion of Kripke's talk, "Wittgenstein on Rules and Private Language," at the First International Wittgenstein Symposium at the University of Western Ontario in 1976. All page references are to this text unless otherwise indicated.

2. This is an expanded version of a paper given by invitation of the Second International Wittgenstein Symposium in Kirchberg/Wechsel, Austria, 29 Aug.– 4 Sept. 1977. It appeared in *Philosophy Research Archives* 12 (1986–87), pp. 183– 93, and is reprinted here, slightly expanded, with permission of the editor.

3. Colin McGinn points out that it does not. In his excellent book *Wittgenstein on Meaning: An Interpretation and Evaluation* (Oxford: Basil Blackwell, 1984), pp. 149–50, he faults Kripke for failing to recognize that these are two independent problems. An answer to the metaphysical problem does not guarantee an answer to the epistemological problem. Nor, conversely, does an answer to the epistemological problem guarantee an answer to the metaphysical problem.

4. McGinn, *Wittgenstein on Meaning*, p. 158.

5. D. W. Hamlyn, "Empiricism," in *The Encyclopedia of Philosophy*, ed. Paul Edwards (New York: Macmillan and Free Press, 1967), vol. 2, p. 504.

6. Saul Kripke, *Naming and Necessity* (Cambridge, Mass.: Harvard University Press, 1972), p. 94. Carol Slater drew this passage to my attention.

Appendix. Russell's Theory of Descriptions

1. There is reason to think that in this task he fails. For discussions of his attempted refutations of Frege and Meinong, see John R. Searle, "Russell's Objections to Frege's Theory of Sense and Reference," *Analysis* 18 (1957–58), pp. 137–43, and Ronald Suter, "Russell's 'Refutation' of Meinong in 'On Denoting,'" *Philosophy and Phenomenological Research* 27 (1967), pp. 512–16. Neither of these papers should be thought of as an attempt to disparage Russell's theory of descriptions, which remains one of the great philosophical achievements of our century.

2. Henry Leonard, "The Logic of Existence," *Philosophical Studies* (June 1956), p. 61.

3. For more on the topic of attributives that entail existence, nonexistence, and neither entail existence nor nonexistence, see Henry Leonard's 1964 Presidential address to the Western Division of the American Philosophical Association (reprinted in the *Proceedings and Addresses of the American Philosophical Association* 37, 1963–64). He recommends that it would be better to tie "questions of existence to *attributes*" rather than to subject-terms as Russell, Frege, and probably most other logicians do.

Index